Social Skills Assessment and Training with Children

AN EMPIRICALLY BASED HANDBOOK

APPLIED CLINICAL PSYCHOLOGY

Series Editors: Alan S. Bellack, *Medical College of Pennsylvania at EPPI, Philadelphia, Pennsylvania,* and Michel Hersen, *University of Pittsburgh, Pittsburgh, Pennsylvania*

HANDBOOK OF BEHAVIOR MODIFICATION WITH THE MENTALLY RETARDED
Edited by Johnny L. Matson and John R. McCartney

THE UTILIZATION OF CLASSROOM PEERS AS BEHAVIOR CHANGE AGENTS
Edited by Phillip S. Strain

FUTURE PERSPECTIVES IN BEHAVIOR THERAPY
Edited by Larry Michelson, Michel Hersen, and Samuel M. Turner

CLINICAL BEHAVIOR THERAPY WITH CHILDREN
Thomas Ollendick and Jerome A. Cerny

OVERCOMING DEFICITS OF AGING: A Behavioral Approach
Roger L. Patterson

TREATMENT ISSUES AND INNOVATIONS IN MENTAL RETARDATION
Edited by Johnny L. Matson and Frank Andrasik

REHABILITATION OF THE BRAIN-DAMAGED ADULT
Gerald Goldstein and Leslie Ruthven

SOCIAL SKILLS ASSESSMENT AND TRAINING WITH CHILDREN
An Empirically Based Handbook
Larry Michelson, Don P. Sugai, Randy P. Wood, and Alan E. Kazdin

In preparation

BEHAVIORAL ASSESSMENT AND REHABILITATION OF THE TRAUMATICALLY BRAIN DAMAGED
Edited by Barry A. Edelstein and Eugene T. Couture

COGNITIVE BEHAVIOR THERAPY WITH CHILDREN
Edited by Andrew W. Mevers and W. Edward Craighead

TREATING CHILD-ABUSIVE FAMILIES
Intervention Based on Skills Training Principles
Jeffrey A. Kelly

A Continuation Order Plan is available for this series. A continuation order will bring delivery of each new volume immediately upon publication. Volumes are billed only upon actual shipment. For further information please contact the publisher.

Social Skills Assessment and Training with Children

AN EMPIRICALLY BASED HANDBOOK

Larry Michelson
Western Psychiatric Institute and Clinic
University of Pittsburgh School of Medicine
Pittsburgh, Pennsylvania

Don P. Sugai
University of Massachusetts Medical Center
Worcester, Massachusetts

Randy P. Wood
Camarillo State Hospital
Camarillo, California, and
UCLA School of Medicine

and

Alan E. Kazdin
Western Psychiatric Institute and Clinic
University of Pittsburgh School of Medicine
Pittsburgh, Pennsylvania

PLENUM PRESS • NEW YORK AND LONDON

Library of Congress Cataloging in Publication Data

Main entry under title:

Social skills assessment and training with children.

(Applied clinical psychology)
Bibliography; p.
Includes indexes.
1. Child development. 2. Social skills. 3. Education of children. 4. Child psychology. I.
Michelson, Larry, 1952–   . II. Series.
HQ767.9.S664 1983   305.2'3   83-13679
ISBN 0-306-41234-9

©1983 Plenum Press, New York
A Division of Plenum Publishing Corporation
233 Spring Street, New York, N.Y. 10013

Printed in the United States of America

Ellin and Karen

To my parents, Anna and Gilbert, and my grandparents

In memoriam, to my mother, Sibyl Wood,
and my grandmother, Lora Franz

Nicole and Michelle

Preface

The purpose of this book is to provide readers with sufficient knowledge regarding social skills assessment and training with children so that they can implement and evaluate social skills programs on their own. Increased interest in promoting children's social skills has stemmed in part from advances in research that have shown the importance of childhood social competency for adjustment in both childhood and adulthood. There is a growing need for assessment and training methods that can be utilized by diverse groups of professionals and paraprofessionals. This book is intended for mental health workers, teachers, educators, clinicians, and child-care personnel. The book thoroughly reviews the literature to acquaint readers with relevant findings on social skills and to provide discussion regarding contemporary issues and assessment techniques. Subsequently, comprehensive procedures in the training of children's social skills are presented. Readers are also provided with 16 detailed training modules, each of which comprises a rationale, instructions, scripts, and homework assignments. These modules are designed to permit effective implementation of social skills training programs. Moreover, they provide a structured and programmatically designed format that builds in clinical flexibility for their use with individual children or groups of children.

These modules are followed by a clinical-issues section designed to address potential obstacles to effective training. Following these major sections, two appendixes have been included in the book. The first appendix is a step-by-step description of how to conduct an assessment. It provides test questions, behavioral rating systems, sociometric strategies, and related techniques, as well as instructions on how to use them. This section should prove useful to those readers who either have not performed assessments in the past or who have found it difficult to obtain these scales and scoring keys. The second appendix contains a comprehensive list of children's 16mm films, whose content is related to the development and/or facilitation of social competency, problem solving, and interpersonal relations.

Thus, the primary objective of this book is to help trainers carry out effective and systematic social skills programs. Previously, professionals interested in social skills training have found it difficult to obtain detailed and clinically relevant materials. In order to meet the demand for written information in this area, the authors have combined and integrated contemporary clinical applications and research findings design and an effective program for promoting children's prosocial behaviors.

The program that will be described has been empirically validated in several investigations (Michelson, Mannarino, Marchione, Stern, Figueroa, & Beck, 1983; Michelson & Wood, 1980; Sugai, 1979). These studies offer support for the potential usefulness of the social skills program with a variety of child populations. Although no social skills program can remediate every social skill deficit in every child, the authors believe that the present program is both relatively easy to implement and effective. However, readers are encouraged to make appropriate modifications in the program should any of the modules be either contraindicated or unnecessary for specific populations. Similarly, the training modules, although comprehensive in scope, may not accurately reflect the specific problem deficits experienced by every child. Thus, trainers need to make appropriate clinical and training decisions in order to maximize the potential benefit for each child. Whereas current research supports the techniques and strategies we describe, it is incumbent on all professionals to stay abreast of progress within this field and to incorporate more effective approaches when they are developed. In addition, not only are techniques important, but it is also vital for trainers to ensure that the content areas that are being taught are socially valid, topical, and supported by the child's environment of peers, parents, and adults. Moreover, the treatment strategies can and—it is hoped—will be used not just to remediate existing social skills deficits but to *prevent* future social dysfunctions and their many related negative side effects by dissemination of the program into the "affective-social" curricula of all schoolchildren. Ideally, this critical area of child development will be systematically taught in all schools as a standard and natural part of the educational process.

LARRY MICHELSON
DON P. SUGAI
RANDY P. WOOD
ALAN E. KAZDIN

Acknowledgments

A book such as this one requires a multitude of talents, the help of friends, and often hidden, but nevertheless vital, resources. We would first like to express our deepest appreciation to Karen Marchione, who conducted countless social skills training sessions, and because her intelligence, sensitivity, and clinical expertise helped refine this book's contents. Our gratitude is warmly extended to Sharon Foster, who provided a cogent, incisive, and detailed review of the draft, and whose feedback contributed greatly to the final form of the book. We would also like to extend much deserved thanks to Lollie Phillip, Nora Benedict, Lyle Mendive, Liz Wood, Danuta Bukatko, Anthony Mannarino, John Flynn, Mike Stern, Paul Martin, Michael Palmer, Edward Simco, and Michel Hersen. Many thanks are extended to our students, because their efforts and questions helped in the development of the volume. We are much obliged to Eliot Werner, Senior Editor of Plenum Publishing Corporation, for his support and encouragement. Appreciation is also extended to Academic Press and to the Association for Advancement of Behavior Therapy for permission to reprint materials. Finally, we would like to express our admiration and recognition of the many pioneers in our field, whose earlier efforts helped pave the proverbial road that we have just traversed.

Contents

Social Skills and Child Development

The development of social skills in children is receiving an enormous amount of clinical and research attention. Indeed, over 75% of all scientific articles in this area have appeared within the last decade (Michelson & Wood, 1980). The reasons for this sudden growth of interest in children's social skills can be traced to several factors. First, retrospective investigations have consistently found strong relationships between social competence in childhood and subsequent social, academic, and psychological functioning. Second, although academic institutions have been considered to be major socializing agents for children, few if any social skills training programs have been formally instituted. However, educators have begun to recognize the critical importance of social skills and interpersonal behaviors, which have been found to be requisite for successful life adaptation. Thus, there has been an increased demand for more systematic and effective strategies for the implementation of social skills training programs with children. Third, in schools, children evince a wide variety of unpleasant and maladaptive behaviors. These behaviors are not only aversive to adults in the child's environment but also have a negative effect on the development of rewarding peer relationships and academic performance. Recognition of these factors has led to the exploration of effective remedial and preventive strategies, among which social skills training is regarded as a viable and potent approach.

Unfortunately, only in recent years has there been any concerted effort to develop social skills training programs that would meet the needs of the children, parents, and schools. Despite the widespread recognition of this need, however, few if any comprehensive programs of training have been disseminated. This program, therefore, provides a unique and scientifically based step-by-step approach to the evaluation and development of children's social skills.

IMPORTANCE OF CHILDREN'S SOCIAL SKILLS

A child's interpersonal behavior plays a vital role in the acquisition of social, cultural, and economic reinforcers. Children who lack appropriate social behaviors experience social isolation, rejection, and overall diminished happiness. Social competency is of critical importance in both the present functioning and future development of the child. Social skills are not only important in regard to peer relations but also allow the child to assimilate social roles and norms. According to Hops (1976):

> The ability to initiate and maintain positive social interaction with others is considered by many to be an essential developmental achievement. Social interactions provide opportunities for children to learn and perform social skills that may critically influence their later social, emotional, and academic adjustment. (p. 1)

Thus, the primary objective of this chapter is to further delineate developmental, intellectual, and maturational correlates of social skills and to highlight the importance of social competence.

DEFINITIONS AND CONCEPTS OF SOCIAL SKILLS

To provide a basic understanding of the term *social skills*, various concepts and definitions of social behavior, assertiveness, and social competence must be considered. The complex nature of social skills has resulted in numerous definitions. Social skills are generally regarded as a set of complex interpersonal behaviors. Appropriate or "good" social skills lead to the greatest amount of personal and interpersonal satisfaction on both a short- and long-term basis. The term *skill* is utilized to indicate that social competence is not a global personality trait but rather a set of learned and acquired behaviors. For example, Rinn and Markle (1979) state:

> The phrase "social skills" is defined herein as a repertoire of verbal and nonverbal behaviors by which children affect the responses of other individuals (e.g., peers, parents, siblings, and teachers) in the interpersonal context. This repertoire acts as a mechanism through which children influence their environment by obtaining, removing, or avoiding desirable and undesirable outcomes in the social sphere. . . . The extent to which they are successful in obtaining desirable outcomes and avoiding or escaping undesirable ones without inflicting pain on others is the extent to which they are considered "socially skilled." (p. 108)

Libet and Lewinsohn (1973), have offered a more general definition of social skill as the ability to behave in ways that are rewarded and not to behave so that one is punished or ignored by others. Combs and Slaby (1977) define social skills as "the ability to interact with others in a given social context in specific ways that are societally acceptable or valued and at the same time personally beneficial, mutually beneficial, or beneficial primarily to others" (p. 162).

Utilizing a slightly different perspective that focuses primarily on the "qualitative outcome" of social behavior, Trower (1979) states, "the individual has goals or targets which he seeks in order to obtain rewards. Goal attainment is dependent on skilled behavior which involves a continuous cycle of monitoring and modifying performance in light of feedback. Failure in skill is defined as a breakdown or impairment at some point in the cycle . . . leading to negative outcomes." (p. 4).

However, these definitions are too general, broad in scope, or ambiguous for some researchers, who stress the situational specificity of social skills. Furthermore, some researchers have provided specific operational definitions of social skills to fit only the parameters of a particular setting, population, response, or social interaction (see Cartledge & Milburn, 1978; Lesbock & Salzberg, 1978; Michelson, DiLorenzo, Calpin, & Ollendick, 1982; Trower, Bryant, & Argyle, 1978; Wolpe, 1973).

Thus, defining social skills has become an assessment issue in its own right. Although a generally accepted definition of social skills remains to be devised, we present our own operational definition, of which the following components are regarded as being essential to an understanding of social skills.

1. Social skills are primarily acquired through learning (e.g., observation, modeling, rehearsal, and feedback).
2. Social skills comprise specific and discrete verbal and nonverbal behaviors.
3. Social skills entail both effective and appropriate initiations and responses.
4. Social skills maximize social reinforcement (e.g., positive responses from one's social environment).
5. Social skills are interactive by nature and entail both effective and appropriate responsiveness (e.g., reciprocity and timing of specific behaviors).
6. Social skill performance is influenced by the characteristics of the environment (i.e., situational specificity). That is, such factors as age, sex, and status of the recipient affect one's social performance.
7. Deficits and excesses in social performance can be specified and targeted for intervention.

In addition to these definitional components of social skills, the directionality of the deficits also need to be considered in conceptualizing social competency. This includes both social withdrawal and aggression.

It should be noted that although many writers distinguish among the terms *social skills, social competency,* and *assertiveness,* they will be used synonymously in this review and the following chapters. Similarly, terms such as *social withdrawal* and *passivity* will also be used generically.

SOCIAL WITHDRAWAL

Researchers have described the unassertive, socially withdrawn child as isolated, shy, passive, and lethargic. Passive behavior violates one's own rights by failing to express one's feelings, needs, and opinions. Passive responses can evoke feelings of inadequacy, depression, and incompetence. Over three decades ago, Salter (1949) noted that unassertive people tended to suffer from psychosomatic and psychophysiological disturbances.

Researchers suggest that unassertive children carry their social skill deficiencies into adulthood. In a longitudinal study examining the stability of childhood characteristics, Kagan and Moss (1962) found that "passive withdrawal from stressful situations, dependency on the family, lack of anger arousal, and involvement in intellectual mastery and social interaction anxiety were strongly related to analogous behavior dispositions during later school years" (p. 277). Social withdrawal in children may also represent a serious threat to both present and future functioning in that it has been associated in varying degrees with childhood psychopathology. Nonassertive children may permit others to violate their personal desires, feelings, and thoughts, which leads them to adopt an apologetic, self-effacing manner. The nonassertive child can also find social situations aversive due to anxiety related to interpersonal interaction.

Chittenden (1942) elaborated on the importance of assertiveness and social skills in children.

> The little child enters into his social group unequipped with the repertoire of responses he needs to enable him to engage in successful social interchange. His attempts to influence the behavior of others and his responses to their attempts to influence him are crude. He must learn, largely by trial and error and with more or less incidental help from experienced persons, which of these attempts and responses are likely to result in his acceptance by his associates and which will meet with their disapproval. Such a learning period, if marked with many failures and only chance successes, may result in the child's loss of interest in initiating social contacts accompanied by increased submission to other persons' attempts to influence him, or it may result in a more frequent use of force in the attempt to make himself successful. Neither of these possible results, if extreme, contributes toward the integration of the child and his social group. Consequently, the sooner that he builds up a fund of usable social knowledge and develops attitudes which indicate his increasing awareness of other individuals and their needs and desires, the sooner he will be in rapport with those individuals. (p. 1)

The relationship between social competence and peer interaction may have serious implications for the passive child. Because peer interaction is reciprocal, withdrawn children also elicit fewer positive social responses from others, resulting in a diminished level of social contact. Greenwood, Walker, Todd, and Hops (1977) demonstrated that peer interaction of 457 preschoolers was reciprocal at a rate of 0.97, showing a clear relationship between behaving and subsequently receiving positive social interaction. Additionally, Hartup, Glazer, and Charlesworth (1967) found popular children more socially rewarding to their peers than less popular ones. Thus, withdrawn children may experience less popularity than their socially skilled counterparts. The side effects of behaving in a socially withdrawn manner have been frequently documented. Popularity has been associated with academic achievement (Hartup, 1970), cognitive and emotional development, and social withdrawal in later years (Waldrop & Halverson, 1975). Gottman, Gonso, and Rasmussen (1975) reviewed several studies indicating a strong relationship between peer popularity and subsequent adult functioning. Unpopular children, as measured by sociometric techniques (see *Assessment Issues*, Chapter 2), are also disproportionately overrepresented among persons who have future contacts with psychiatric facilities (Cowen, Pederson, Babigian, Izzo, & Trost, 1973).

In summary, passive social behavior has been correlated with a variety of maladaptive processes. Developmental, interpersonal, and intellectual milestones may be thwarted and delayed, leading to even more pervasive dysfunctions. Similarly, children who manifest deficient social repertoires may be at risk for experiencing subsequent adult psychopathology.

SOCIAL AGGRESSION

At the other end of the social deficit spectrum are the children with behavioral excesses, typically said to be agressive, uncooperative, and demonstrative of acting out behavior. These children also fail to demonstrate the social skills necessary to perform effective and appropriate social interactions. Specifically, aggressive children behave in a manner that is unpleasant to others in the child's social environment. Quay (1972) and Patterson, Reid, Jones, and Conger (1975) identified many of the characteristics describing this dysfunction. These include verbal and physical assaultiveness, teasing, provoking, quarreling, fighting to settle conflicts, and violating or ignoring the rights of others.

Aggressive behavior leads to the violation of other's rights and feelings by the use of physical, psychological, or emotional force (Lange & Jakubowski, 1976). The aggressive child often uses tactics that are effective but rarely appropriate. They behave in ways which deprecate others or lead to humiliation, lowered self-esteem and defensiveness on the part of the recipient. Alberti and Emmons (1974) state:

> Aggressive behavior commonly results in a "put down" of the recipient. His rights have been denied, and he feels hurt, defensive and humiliated. His goals in the situation, of course, are not achieved. Although the aggressive person may achieve his goal, he may also generate hatred and frustration which he will later receive as vengeance. (p. 11)

This type of a social behavior may generate many negative side effects for the aggressive child. According to Patterson *et al.* (1975),

> the socialization process appears to be severely impeded for many aggressive children. Their behavioral adjustments are often immature and they do not seem to have learned the key social skills necessary for initiating and maintaining positive social relationships with others. Peer groups often reject, avoid, and/or punish aggressive children, thereby excluding them from positive learning experiences with others. Socially negative/aggressive children often have academic difficulties and may achieve at lower levels than their classmates. (p. 4)

Additionally, socially aggressive children tend to acquire academic skills at a reduced rate compared to nonaggressive children.

Aggression in social interaction tends to lead to counteraggression from one's peers as well as higher rates of social rejection from the environment. The message communicated to a recipient from an aggressive individual typically evokes feelings of worthlessness, anger, and frustration. The person who becomes aggressive may initially achieve particular ends but will eventually pay a price for violating others' rights and feelings. In the long run, the loss of friends, reduced interpersonal contact, and feelings of guilt can far outweigh the possible benefits of aggressiveness. Moreover, left untreated, aggressive children appear to make unsatisfactory adjustments as adults (Robbins, 1966). Aggressive children are not only less popular with their peers (Winder & Rau, 1962) but manifest a greater incidence of academic failure (Schindler, 1941), adult alcoholism, antisocial behavior, and psychiatric disturbances (Morris, 1956). (See Kohn, 1977; Kohn & Rosman, 1972a; and Lange & Jakubowski, 1976 for reviews and discussions of the importance of social skills.)

In summary, both the aggressive and passive child exhibit behavioral dysfunctions related to their inability to act effectively and appropriately within their social environment. The present and future happiness of these two types of children may greatly depend on whether their social skill deficits are remediated.

SOCIAL SKILLS AND ADAPTIVE FUNCTIONING

Research suggests that many socially incompetent children do not outgrow their interpersonal handicaps. Social skill deficits have been related to poor self-esteem (Percell, Berwick, & Beigel, 1974), external locus of control (Nowicki & Strickland, 1971), and depression (Lazarus, 1968; Wolpe, 1971, 1973). As social skill deficits appear to contribute to diminished positive social reinforcement, various investigators have considered the paucity of social reinforcement in interpersonal situations as an antecedent to depression (Frey, 1976; Lazarus, 1971; Lewinsohn, 1975; Wolpe, 1971). If a child's social repertoire is rarely reinforced, many important behaviors may subsequently be suppressed or extinguished. It is not surprising to find the research suggesting that unremediated behavioral deficiencies may be sustained or even magnified in adulthood.

Kohn and Rosman (1972) investigated the relationship between preschool social and emotional functioning and later academic performance and intellectual achievement. Assertive behaviors in preschool children were associated with school readiness and intellectual achievement in later years. The results "suggest that the child who is curious, alert, and assertive will learn more from his environment and the child who is passive, apathetic and withdrawn will, at the very least, learn less about his environment because of his diminished contact. . ." (p. 450). These findings are consistent with those from Kagan and Moss (1962), who noted that emotional independence from parents and teachers, assertiveness, and curiosity are reliable predictors of future intellectual achievement. Dorman (1973) also found assertion levels in young children to be related to intellectual functioning. The performance of an item analysis of the Stanford–Binet Intelligence Test revealed superior performance by socially skilled children on such areas as comprehension, verbal reasoning, and discrimination tests.

Social maladjustment in children has been associated with a variety of future problems including school maladjustment (Grounland & Anderson, 1963), dropping out of school (Ullmann, 1957), delinquency (Roff, Sells, & Golden, 1972), "bad conduct" discharges from the military (Roff, 1961), and adult mental health problems (Cowen et al., 1973; Roff, 1961). Conversely, social competency in childhood is related to superior academic achievement (Harper, 1976; Laughlin, 1954; Muma, 1965, 1968; Porterfield & Schlichting, 1961), and adequate interpersonal adjustment later in life (Barclay, 1966; Brown, 1954; Guinourd & Rychlak, 1962). According to Kohn (1977), preschool impairment of social skills was correlated with later emotional disturbance in the fourth grade. Social-emotional adjustment portended future psychological functioning.

Cowen *et al.* (1973) performed an 11- to 13-year follow-up of children who were identified as "vulnerable" to determine whether they had disproportionate rates of psychiatric disturbance as compared with control children. Retrospective analyses of the psychiatrically disturbed children's third-grade tests suggest that they were less popular and more negatively evaluated by their peers. The authors report that "given a comprehensive assessment battery including intellectual performance, teacher judgment, and self-report data, the ratings of the 8- to 9-year-old peers best predicted later psychiatric difficulty" (p. 455). These results suggest the significance of social competency and peer interaction in regard to future development.

Peer Relations

Peer acceptance and popularity appear to play an important role in childhood socialization. Social skills provide children with the vehicle through which they can give and receive positive social rewards, which, in turn, leads to increased social involvement, generating further positive interaction. The importance of social skills in acquiring peer acceptance has been well documented. Social skills have been associated with increased perceptions of friendliness, peer acceptance, and social participation (Marshall & McCandless, 1957). Conversely, peer rejection has been associated with aggression (Dunnington, 1957; Hartup *et al.*, 1967; Moore, 1967) and the display of negative social behavior (Kohn, 1977). Hartup *et al.* (1967) found that children's ability to act in a positive social manner was directly related to being accepted or well liked by one's peers.

Charlesworth and Hartup (1967) and Kohn (1977) report that peers who demonstrate greater positive prosocial behaviors receive these in turn, at higher rates themselves from their peers. Additionally, these children are rewarded by their peers for prosocial behavior, thereby creating a positive cycle of social interaction, peer acceptance, and social competency. Similarly, Gottman *et al.* (1975) investigated the relationship among peer relations, social skills, and popularity. The popular children were found to be superior in their ability to engage in and to elicit positive peer interaction, knowledge of certain social skills, and their referential communication skills (the ability to take the perspective of the listener). The child's ability to emit and elicit positive social behavior from his peers appears to be a crucial factor in his or her acceptance and popularity. Additionally, other factors identified as being related to social skills and peer relations include role taking (Reardon, Hersen, Bellack, & Foley, 1979), identifying and labeling emotions (Izard, 1971), and communicating accurately and appropriately (Asher & Parke, 1975).

In summary, popular children appear to socially reinforce their peers more often than do unpopular children and receive greater amounts of positive social responses in return from both peers and teachers. This positive cycle is perpetuated through adolescence and perhaps adulthood, creating a reciprocal interpersonal environment throughout life. Additionally, children who manifest positive social skills appear to perform better in academic, social, and emotional sectors. Conversely, socially deficient children generate, and thus receive, fewer positive social interactions from their social environment. This can have an immediate effect of creating isolation, aggression, frustration, and withdrawal. This phenomenon might lead to even further reduction in rates of elicited and emitted reinforcements during adolescence and adulthood and negatively affect the individual's ability to function adaptively in his or her social environment.

ACADEMIC ACHIEVEMENT

Social skills play an integral role in the complex fabric of interpersonal interaction. Because they are related to many aspects of functioning, it is not surprising that researchers have found significant relationships between social competency, creativity, academic achievement, and cognitive performance (Dorman, 1973; Feldhusen, Thurston, & Benning, 1973; Payne, Halpin, Ellett, & Dale, 1975). Kim, Anderson, and Bashaw (1968) found significant correlations between standardized measures of achievement and social behavior of children. Myers, Atwell, and Orbet (1968) conducted a longitudinal study in which third- and sixth-grade students were identified as either disruptive or behaving in socially appropriate ways. Achievement scores from these students were collected five years later. After controlling for intelligence, the authors found significant differences between the two groups, with the socially appropriate children excelling over the disruptive students.

Social skills not only affect peer relations but can also have notable effects on positive teacher attention and reinforcement toward the child. Several studies have experimentally demonstrated the effect of student social behavior on subsequent teacher–student interaction (Graubard, Rosenberg, & Miller, 1971; Klein, 1971; Noble & Nolan, 1974). In an excellent demonstration of this phenomenon, Noble and Nolan (1974) gave seven children instructions (outside the classroom) on how to make eye contact, request help, give compliments, and exhibit related social skills. The children significantly increased the amount of positive social reinforcement received from their teachers. Thus, children's social skills affect how they are perceived and responded to by their teachers as well as their peers, parents, and significant others (see Cartledge & Milburn, 1978; Greenwood, Walker, Todd, & Hops, 1977; Harper, 1976).

RELATED VARIABLES

Measures of social competency provide information as to the social behaviors in a person's repertoire, but they do not describe other variables that may influence the maintenance and severity of interpersonal skill deficits. Such variables as *locus of control* (the extent to which a person perceives that contingencies are controlled by themselves or others), *hopelessness* (negative expectancies of change in the future), and *irrationality* (entrenched beliefs that may or may not be rationally based) may provide additional prognostic information as to the possibilities of remediating existing deficits. For example, two children who are equally deficient in social skills may be very different in terms of their flexibility in learning new behaviors. One child may rely on others to control contingencies, may think that slight misfortunes are catastrophic, and may expect that the future will be worse, while another child may perceive that he has some control over his own contingencies, does not overreact to disappointment, and can see his current set of behaviors as a temporary state. The former child is more resistant to change, set in rigid belief systems, and pessimistic about the future. These factors may contribute to his problematic behavior patterns and also interfere to a greater degree with attempts to acquire adaptive behaviors.

Rotter (1966) described the internal versus external dimensions of locus of control in this way:

> If the person perceives that an event is contingent upon his own behavior, we have termed this a belief in internal control . . . when a reinforcement is perceived by the subject as following some action of his own but not being entirely contingent upon his action or is unrelated to his action and is beyond personal control, then this is a belief in external control. (p. 1)

Nowicki and Strickland (1971) adapted a locus of control measure for children and identified several behavioral correlates of internal and external responding. Internal locus of control has been shown to correlate with general measures of assertiveness, academic achievement, social involvement, delayed gratification, control of stress, and ability to take social action (Houston, 1971; Nowicki & Roundtree, 1971; Nowicki & Strickland, 1971; Rotter, 1966; Rotter & Mulry, 1965). In general, the greater a child's belief in internal control (e.g., how she/he behaves *does* influence her/his environment), the more assertive she/he is likely to be and the greater her/his chances of further developing a socially effective and appropriate repertoire.

External locus of control has also been shown to be related to the concepts of helplessness and hopelessness (Beck, Weissman, Lester, & Trexler, 1974; Hiroto, 1974; Procuik, Breen, & Lussier, 1976). These concepts are similar in that they are based on the perception by the individual that his or her behavior and its contingencies are independent. Failure to control one's interpersonal environment may lead to possible depression, social withdrawal, or extinction of adaptive social responses (Frey, 1976; Lazarus, 1976; Wolpe, 1971). Children who have developed unadaptive behavioral repertoires rather than assertive ones may become susceptible to helplessness and depression (Dweck, 1972; Seligman, 1975). Additionally, those who perceive their helpless state as "hopeless" may be less likely to change their behavior in an adaptive fashion. Having a dysfunctional expectation that events are uncontrollable is affected even more by the expectation of little change in the future (Beck *et al.*, 1974).

Another variable related to social competency, hopelessness, and the development of unadaptive behavior is the development of irrational beliefs (Dorworth, 1973). Ellis (1971) proposes that irrational beliefs are reciprocally involved with maladaptive behaviors. For example, a person who feels the need to "be loved by everyone" or that "slight misfortunes are disastrous" will behave in accordance with such irrational beliefs. More importantly, a child who has developed an irrational belief system may behave in a maladaptive fashion of either passive or aggressive responding. Children who have many irrational beliefs probably will be less assertive than children with more rational beliefs. Irrational belief systems may interfere with learning new and more appropriate behaviors and can increase resistance to change toward more adaptive responses (Dorworth, 1973).

Additional variables of interest include sex and IQ, and their relationship to social competency. Sex-role behaviors and types of nonassertiveness have been described by investigators as portraying females as passive and a distinct percentage of males as aggressive. The interaction of teachers with their students in terms of their distribution of approval for males and females has been shown to differ significantly (Meyer & Thompson, 1956). Indeed, a recent survey of elementary school teachers determined that the passive, acquiescent female was the best-liked type of student (Helton & Oakland, 1977).

Intelligence and social skills are also related. Children who learn and adapt quickly begin to develop effective interpersonal repertoires to achieve their goals. This may be reflected in academic (Crandall, Katkorsky, & Crandall, 1965; McGhee & Crandall, 1968) or in social performance (Thornton & Jacobs, 1972). The case may be, however, that the public school system may foster passivity which then competes with the development of assertiveness in intelligent children (Helton & Oakland, 1977).

The relationship of intelligence and assertiveness should come as no surprise. Intelligence probably aids in acquiring assertive skills; this in turn, allows for greater environmental interaction and learning opportunities, which are included in definitions of intelligence. The practical considerations of intelligence and assertiveness concern those children who are deficient in intelligence, assertiveness, or both. For example, will "growth" in intelligence be suppressed by lack of assertive skills? Further research is needed to clarify this issue, and perhaps it will underscore the positive benefits in an educational-academic sense of acquiring social skills.

The relationship between intelligence and locus of control has been investigated to a greater degree. IQ was determined as one of the main correlates of locus of control in a secondary school population (Nowicki & Roundtree, 1971). A scale for assessing children's beliefs that they, rather than others, are responsible for their intellectual-academic successes and failures demonstrated that IQ was related to perceived locus of control in elementary school populations (Crandall, Katkovsky, & Crandall, 1965). In general, the research suggests that individuals who perceive internal control over their behavior are more intelligent (Chance, 1965; Coleman, Campbell, Hobson, McPartland, Wood, Weinfeld, & York, 1966; McGhee & Crandall, 1968; Reimanis, 1970).

A recent, related area of research interest has been the debilitating effects of hopelessness on academic performance (e.g., Dweck, 1972; Dweck & Repucci, 1973; Seligman, Maier, & Solomon, 1967, 1969). Although no conclusive research has been reported, individuals who perceive their situation as hopeless appear less likely to attempt academic endeavors. In relating the implications of learned helplessness/hopelessness to education, Alba and Alvarez (1977) emphasize that experiences with controllability and uncontrollability over academic work, especially in the early grades, may be an important factor in future academic development. The possibility exists that these factors may influence or mediate acquisition and performance of social skills. However, due to the correlational nature of most of the studies, definitive cause–effect conclusions cannot be drawn. Indeed, these factors may represent components of a "larger cognitive-mediating process" which have not been defined thus far. In any case, due to the suggestive rather than conclusive nature of these findings, interventions for children directed at reducing "hopelessness" or "internal locus of control" would appear premature. Rather, as discussed in Chapter 3, it has been repeatedly demonstrated that training social skills leads to concurrent improvements on these other cognitive dimensions of functioning. However, research is needed to determine the interrelationships among assertiveness, locus of control, hopelessness, irrationality, sex, and IQ for children and their effect upon the development and maintenance of effective and appropriate social repertories.

Summary

A note of qualification regarding the research cited in this chapter is in order. These efforts are largely based upon correlational studies. They only suggest relationships and associations between social skills and future functioning; they do not prove them. Despite the causal ambiguity in many of the studies, they are, however, fairly suggestive, given their consistent results and their sheer numbers. Thus, the relationship between social competency and life adjustment appears to be both powerful and intricate. This cumulative body of knowledge, as viewed through an interdisciplinary perspective, supports the hypothesis that social skills in children are closely related to present and future social adaptation. Thus, there seems to be strong scientific rationale supporting the need for preventative and remedial social skills training for children.

Assessment of Social Skills

Assessment procedures that evaluate the effectiveness of training are important components of any social skills training program. Unfortunately, many social skills programs do not utilize an empirically based and comprehensive framework with which to assess their efficacy and, therefore, it is not known whether social behaviors were modified for the better. Furthermore, several evaluation strategies are deficient in identifying specific social skill deficits and excesses. Thus, several theoretical, methodological, and clinical issues pertaining to the assessment of children's social skills require further elaboration. The present chapter describes the functional purposes of assessment and provides a substantive review of assessment techniques and strategies along with their advantages and limitations.

Initial assessment can determine present knowledge of social skill components and measure the quality of actual social performance in children. The process of identifying and specifying problem social areas also allows for the subsequent evaluation of a child's progress during training. This information provides necessary feedback to trainers by "screening" and identifying specific children or specific social deficits or excesses. Children who have deficient social skills will usually score or be rated very low on the assessment instruments and measures. For an individual or a group of children, a specific social behavior (e.g., expressing complaints) may be the focus of assessment. Certain children may be determined to be problematic due to their poor performance in comparison with other children or their interference in the child's ability to interact successfully with the social environment. The specific behaviors of these children can then be "targeted" for training. Pre- and posttraining comparisons provide a measure of the effectiveness of the intervention and indicate which social skills have improved and where deficits remain.

ASSESSMENT ISSUES

ASSESSMENT MODALITIES

To measure social skills deficits and behavioral excesses, various types of assessment instruments and strategies have been developed (see Hops & Greenwood, 1980; Kent & Foster, 1979; Michelson, Foster, & Ritchey, 1981; Michelson & Wood, 1980a; Van Hasselt, Hersen, Bellack, & Whitehill, 1979). Primarily, three different modalities have been utilized for assessing social skills: behavioral observation, informant reports, and self-report measures. Behavioral observations usually involve actual observation of defined social behaviors in natural settings or simulated situations such as in role-play tests. Informant reports require social agents such as teachers, peers, and parents in the child's social environment to evaluate, describe, or rate social performance. Additionally, sociometric measures such as peer rankings and nominations are informant report techniques which indicate general social status. Self-report instruments such as questionnaires, scales, and paper-and-pencil inventories rely on each child's rating, evaluation, or description of his or her own social behavior. Methodological and practical issues related to each assessment modality will obviously influence the assessment strategy selected. Several general issues of primary importance in the selection and utilization of social skill assessment procedures are discussed in the following sections.

Social Validity

Assessment should reflect and be responsive to the child's social environment (Clark, Caldwell, & Christian, 1980; Wolf, 1978). An assessment device needs to identify clinically salient target behaviors that are considered important by the child's "reinforcement community," such as peers and adults. *Social validity*, in both assessment and training procedures, basically means that the behaviors which have been selected as "target behaviors" are genuinely important in the child's social environment. For example, if the behavior of "looking at the other person during a conversation (eye contact)" is important to the people that the child talks to, then it would be socially valid to include this as a target behavior in assessment and training.

Selecting a behavior that may not be important in a child's environment (e.g., shaking hands when greeting others) would result in assessment and training focusing on social skills which are of minimal, if any, relevance to the child's *real* social interactions. In fact, some social behaviors may be disliked by other children and might result in negative or aversive consequences if used. Thus, socially invalid assessment can lead to targeting relatively trivial behaviors. Therefore, in both the assessment and training of social skills, when determining the target behaviors to be remediated, consideration should be given to the *social importance, effectiveness*, and *functional utility* of the selected behaviors (Kazdin, 1977; Wolf, 1978).

Practicality

Each type of assessment strategy requires varying amounts of time, trained personnel, material, administration, scoring, and analysis. It is important to determine whether sufficient resources exist to complete a particular assessment strategy or combination of strategies successfully. Choosing an assessment strategy that is impractical generally results in technical problems, inaccurate or incomplete data, and overall reduction in the quality of program evaluation. Therefore, prior to incorporating an assessment strategy, careful analysis of the practical requirements is important to determine both feasibility and utility.

ASSESSMENT INFORMATION

Accurate interpretation of the assessment results depends upon which assessment techniques were used. Some assessment techniques primarily measure knowledge of social skills (e.g., self-report) while others measure actual performance of social skills (e.g., behavioral observation). Some measures tap only circumscribed skill areas, while others sample from a large range or domain of social behaviors. Limitations in the *amount* and *type* of information that an assessment technique can provide should be a major consideration in both selection and interpretation.

PSYCHOMETRIC QUALITIES

The accuracy and reliability of an assessment measure is usually described in terms of "psychometric qualities." Through statistical analysis of an assessment measure, information can be reported regarding such important psychometric qualities as external validity and reliability.

External validity represents how well the assessment instrument measures how the child would actually behave in the natural environment. High external validity is desired for an assessment instrument because it indicates that the information collected is accurate and honestly reflects how the child behaves most of the time. For example, if a child's scores on a self-report questionnaire indicated very good social skills in all areas but the child's usual behavior was actually very inappropriate, then the self-report questionnaire would be considered to have *low* external validity. One method of determining external validity is to correlate two different measures, such as self-report and teacher ratings. This procedure is termed *concurrent validity*. Concurrent validity can range from .00 (no concurrent validity) to 1.00 (perfect validity); most scores for social skills assessments fall between .30 (moderately low) to .80 (moderately high). In general, the higher the estimate of validity, the more accurate or "honest" the assessment measure.

Reliability can refer to how consistent the assessment results would be over repeated testings (test–retest reliability) and how consistently the components of the assessment device measure the same construct (internal consistency). Reliability, which is just as important as external validity, indicates whether an assessment measure can consistently give the same results. If a measure is not consistent, then it is not clear whether any changes in scores are really due to changes in the child's behavior or merely indicate a fluctuation due to the variability and unreliability of the assessment. Furthermore, if a scale does not meet minimal reliability criteria, it cannot be valid.

In summary, by taking into account psychometric properties, social validity, practicality and assessment information, the most appropriate technique(s) can be selected for a particular social skills training program. Attending to these issues will help avoid major pitfalls and should enhance the overall effectiveness of the training program. Proper consideration of these issues will help ensure that the assessment process will be functional and accurate. (For reviews of these issues see Anastasi, 1982.)

The following sections describe behavioral observation, informant report, and self-report techniques. Relevant research examples and issues—as well as advantages and limitations of each assessment technique—will be discussed briefly. A complete sample of each technique is presented in Appendix A, along with detailed administration, scoring, and interpretive information. Therefore, upon acquiring a working knowledge of the various assessment strategies in terms of the information that can be obtained and the limitations involved, specific techniques can be selected and utilized appropriately with the training program.

BEHAVIORAL OBSERVATION

Direct observation is one of the most commonly used methods of assessing social behavior. Two strategies utilized to measure interpersonal behavior among children include *naturalistic observation* and *analogue observation*.

NATURALISTIC OBSERVATION

The direct observation and rating of a child's social interactions in the natural environment is considered an ideal method of accurately assessing social skills (Eisler, 1976; Nay, 1977). Information obtained from naturalistic observation can be used to identify children who display socially inappropriate behavior and to assess the effects of training and treatment interventions.

Naturalistic observation is usually accomplished by having one or more observers record the frequency, duration, and/or quality of specified target behaviors. The target behaviors are "behaviorally defined" with a clear, easily observable description to allow reliable and accurate observation. For example, "eye contact" can be considered a component of "conversation with others" and could be behaviorally defined as "looking at the other person in the conversation for at least 60% of the time." With this behavioral definition, the frequency of eye contact across several conversations could be recorded by trained observers.

Observation procedures usually take place in settings such as classrooms and play areas. Observers try to place themselves unobtrusively in suitable positions where they will not interfere or unduly influence the interactions but will be able to accurately record the frequency and quality of the target behaviors. Participant observation is an alternative procedure in which the observer is part of the situation (e.g., teaching a class), interacts with the children, and records observations of social behavior.

Description of Measures. Observations of social behavior have been completed across various developmental age levels (Greenwood, Walker, Todd, & Hops, 1978; Meighan & Birr, 1979; O'Connor, 1969) and in various settings and activities (Allen, Chinsky, Larsen, Lockman, & Selinger, 1976; Bryan, 1974; Dorman, 1973). The situational specificity and the idiosyncratic characteristics of social behavior generally require researchers to develop original observation codes and formats in accordance with the target behaviors of interest and the parameters of the setting, activity, or stimuli involved (see Charlesworth & Hartup, 1967; Reid, 1978). Thus, existing observation codes show considerable variation, both in the behaviors observed and in levels of complexity of observational systems being used (Van Hasselt et al., 1979).

For example, studies of socially isolated children (see Allen, Hart, Buell, Harris, & Wolf, 1964; Buell, Stoddard, Harris, & Baer, 1968) have employed operational definitions of proximity to others, play with others, and interactions with peers or teachers. Additionally, Buell et al. (1968) utilized a time-sampling procedure with 10-second intervals and computed the percentage of intervals in which a target behavior was displayed. Strain, Shores, and Kerr (1976) and Strain (1977) employed an observational system to assess two-person interactions. The coding system included two general behavior classes, "motor-gestural" and "vocal-verbal" along with their positive and negative topographical features. Some of their behavioral definitions were "initiated" behaviors, which included responses emitted three seconds before or after another child's behavior, and "responded" behaviors, which included behaviors occurring within three seconds after another child's motor-gestural or vocal-verbal behavior.

Fairly elaborate coding systems have been developed for recording interactions between children and their peers, teachers, and parents. (see Durlak & Mannarino, 1977; Wahler, 1975). For example, one system for observations contained 19 response categories encompassing five general classes of behaviors: autistic, work, play, compliance–opposition, and social. This extensive observation was used primarily for assessing the classroom behavior of socially deficient children, but it may also be suitable for use in home or laboratory settings. (A sample of an observation system is presented in Sample A, the Social Skills Observation Checklist, of Appendix A. Complete information is provided regarding observation procedures, scoring, and interpretation of the results.)

Advantages and Limitations. There are numerous methodological issues concerning naturalistic observation methods, including expectancy bias among observers, observer reactivity (Romanczyk, Kent, Diament, & O'Leary, 1973), consensual "drift" (O'Leary & Kent, 1973), system complexity (Mash & McElwee, 1974), and knowledge of reliability assessment (Kent, Kanowitz, O'Leary, & Cheiken, 1977). An excellent review of these issues is presented by Foster and Ritchey (1979).

In Walls, Werner, Bacon, and Zane's (1977) comprehensive review of 118 behavioral checklists dealing with social skills and socialization, only 25 (21%) provided any information at all on reliability and/or validity of the instrument.

Cone's (1977) a detailed discussion regarding reliability and validity in behavioral assessment indicates the following problems with natural observation procedures: calculation, reactivity, and variables affecting the magnitude of observer agreement (see Johnson & Bolstad, 1973); distinguishing between observer agreement and observer accuracy (Gewirtz & Gewirtz, 1969); interpretations and remediation of low interobserver reliabilities, item (or situation) generality, and generalizability. (For reviews of the relevant assessment literature, see Foster & Ritchey, 1979; Kazdin, 1977; Kent & Foster, 1979; Michelson, Foster, & Ritchey, 1981; Michelson & Wood, 1980b.)

Practicality is an important variable when one is considering the use of naturalistic observation. The procedure requires training observers to achieve an acceptable level of interobserver reliability (agreement between observers), defining specific target behaviors, observation time periods for each subject, various materials such as checklists and stopwatches, and detailed scheduling of observers and subjects. If these requirements can be fulfilled, valuable information can be obtained for the identification of social skill deficits. This will also facilitate establishing a pretraining baseline and the evaluation of ongoing training.

Observation systems sometimes vary in the level of information they can provide. Since an emphasis is placed upon defining the target behaviors in very clear terms, some observation systems contain only simplistic behaviors that may not be very important or not be detailed enough to contain sufficient information. For example, it is easy to observe and reliably measure if a child "talks to another child," but what may be of importance is the content of the statement made to the other child. This is where most observation systems fear to tread, because it is often quite difficult to get observers to agree whether the statement made was a "compliment," a "sarcastic comment," or even just a neutral statement. Therefore, it is important to consider what level of information is needed and how accurate and reliable the observations must be if an appropriate observation system is to be selected.

Social validity should play an important part in evaluating any observation system to be utilized in assessing children's social skills. It is critical to ensure that the measured behaviors are important and meaningful in the child's social environment. A very detailed observation system with clear, precise behavioral definitions would be essentially useless if it only targeted such behaviors as "number of eye blinks," "left foot forward while speaking," and so on. Social interactions require complex observation systems to measure the socially important variables.

Assuming that the factors of practicality, type of information, and social validity can be adequately provided in an observation system, this method has a major advantage over other assessment procedures in that it usually has a high degree of external validity. The behaviors observed through naturalistic observation reflect quite accurately the usual social behavior of the child. If observations are made in many different settings and social situations and at different times throughout the day over a period of several days or weeks, an accurate measurement of the child's social skills and deficits can be made.

OBSERVATION IN CONTRIVED SITUATIONS

Role-play tests or simulated situations measure specific social responses in settings contrived to represent actual interpersonal problem situations. In behavioral role-play procedures, situations are generally presented to the subject by videotape, narrator, or live model. A prompt is then delivered by a confederate who asks for the subject's response. The child's response is later judged and rated on numerous verbal and nonverbal components to assess the level of social skill.

Assessment in simulated situations is particularly useful when the child has difficulty in situations that occur infrequently—that is, where little information concerning the child's social skill proficiency in those areas can be obtained by naturalistic observation. For example, if "responding to criticism from peers" was the target behavior and the situation occurred rarely, then naturalistic observation would take a long time, as the observers would have to wait until the child was in a situation where peers provided criticism. Role-play or contrived situations would automatically incorporate this component by having a peer/confederate deliver criticism to the child so that an observation of the responses could be made.

Observation in contrived situations allows every social skill content area to be evaluated in a standardized manner. All children are exposed to identical prompts and role-play partners, thus permitting comparisons of their responses.

Description of Measures. Ever since Rehm and Marston (1968) developed the original role-play test for use in outcome research, this assessment strategy has become an integral component in the analogue measurement of social skills. The basic format of role-play tests includes presenting the subject with a description of an interpersonal vignette wherein the subject is prompted to respond. For example:

> Narrator: You are watching your favorite television program when someone walks up to the TV and changes the channel. The person says: "I'm changing the channel, the show you are watching bores me."
> Child's response: _____

After the child responds to the prompt, he or she is presented with the next situation, and so on. A prompt is delivered by a confederate, who provides the antecedent for the subject's response. The subject's response is then recorded and rated on several verbal and nonverbal components. (A complete example of the procedures required to perform an assessment of children's social skills with a role play is presented in Sample B of Appendix A.)

Bornstein, Bellack, and Hersen (1977) developed the Behavioral Assertiveness Test for Children (BAT-C), modified from a similar test with adults (Eisler, Hersen, Miller, & Blanchard, 1975). The BAT-C is composed of scenes simulating typical interpersonal encounters of children. This and similar tests have been employed in numerous single-case and group studies to assess pretreatment levels of social skill as well as to evaluate therapeutic outcome (Beck, Forehand,

Wells, & Quante, 1978; Bornstein, Bellack, & Hersen, 1980; Ollendick & Hersen, 1980). (Scenes and target behavior definitions used in the BAT-C are presented in Sample B of Appendix A; Figures 5 and 6.)

Reardon, Hersen, Bellack, and Foley (1979) developed and evaluated the Behavioral Assertiveness Tests for Boys (BAT-B), which was designed to elicit both positive and negative assertive responses in young males. From an original pool of 50 scenes, 10 positive and 10 negative scenes were selected by teacher ratings to comprise the BAT-B. Examples of positive (Narrator 1) and negative (Narrator 2) scenes are described below:

> Narrator 1: You drew a picture in art class and the boy next to you says . . . .
> Prompt: Wow! That was really great!

> Narrator 2: Pretend that you are at home watching your favorite TV program with your friend. He gets up . . . .
> Prompt: Let's watch this instead.

The child's responses to each of the 20 scenes are rated on verbal and nonverbal components (see Eisler, Hersen, Miller, & Blanchard, 1973). These components include: (1) ratio of eye contact to duration of response, (2) smiles, (3) duration of reply, (4) number of words, (5) latency of response, (6) affect, (7) ratio of speech disturbances to duration of speech, (8) gestures, (9) compliance, (10) requests for new behavior, (11) regard, (12) spontaneous positive behavior, (13) appreciation, and (14) global rating of assertiveness.

Reardon *et al.* (1979) assessed 60 elementary school boys in Grades 3 through 8. Children were tested on role-taking ability, a self-report measure of assertiveness, and teachers' ratings. Results from this investigation indicated that high- and low-assertive children differed on a number of response dimensions related to both age level and type of scene (i.e., positive or negative). Assertive skill was associated with role-taking ability. Teachers tended to view the assertive boys as more sociable and interpersonally sensitive than unassertive subjects. Interestingly, there were no significant correlations between teachers' global ratings of assertiveness and self-report or role-play assessments.

Michelson, DiLorenzo, Calpin, and Ollendick (1982) investigated the situational determinants of the BAT-C with 30 psychiatrically disturbed inpatient children. The BAT-C was specifically revised for use with children in an inpatient setting and consisted of a total of 48 interpersonal scenes, half presented by a male adult partner and half by a female. The investigators wished to identify some of the salient behavioral components of assertion in four interpersonal situations: requests for new behavior, giving help, giving compliments, and accepting compliments. A second purpose of the study was to determine the effect of the sex of the person delivering the prompt on the BAT-C role-play scenes.

The results indicated that negative scenes elicited significantly different interpersonal behavior than did positive scenes. Responses of the children to negative scenes were characterized by increased eye contact, longer replies, and greater use of affective statements.

The children, however, did not differentially respond to positive and negative scenes on voice intonation or overall assertion as rated by adults. The results further indicated that the sex of the prompter played a significant role in child responses. Children spoke longer and with more appropriate voice intonation with male than with female prompters. They also received higher overall ratings on assertion with male than with female prompters. Higher assertive ratings in response to males were observed across both positive and negative scenes.

Another method of social skills assessment designed to obtain seminaturalistic data efficiently in a standardized manner is the contrived scenario. In a contrived scenario, a situation is set up without the child's knowledge (similar to a "candid camera" scene) and the child is exposed to certain stimuli (e.g., questions from confederates) that elicit social responses. The child's responses can be observed and rated to determine social skills deficits. •

Wood, Michelson, and Flynn (1978) developed a contrived interview, the Children's Behavorial Scenario (CBS), designed to elicit assertive or nonassertive responses. A trained adult confederate interviewed each child with questions, comments, compliments, and requests that represented various content areas of assertion. For example, a child was given an "unreasonable request," such as "I would like you to give up all your recess time for the next six months to pick up the paper around the school grounds." The child's response was unobtrusively observed and coded as assertive, aggressive, or passive. Also, aspects of the experimental room were designed to elicit assertive and nonassertive responses. For example, a small stack of books was placed on the only chair available for the child to sit on, and the child was monitored for appropriate requests to remove the books. Comparison of the CBS with a self-report measure of assertive behavior and teacher ratings showed statistically significant, though moderate, correlations among the three measures. (An example of the administration interview procedures, scripts, and response coding format involved in performing the CBS is provided in Sample C of Appendix A.)

Advantages and Limitations. Advantages of role-play tests include (1) flexibility in presenting a wide range of potentially relevant situations that cannot easily be replicated in the natural environment or clinical setting; (2) control over the places, persons, and environments presented to the child; and (3) accuracy in monitoring and measuring precise social skills components such as duration of eye contact, speech latency, speech duration, length of utterances, qualitative aspects of the response, and nonverbal dimensions of social skill.

Bellack (1979) cogently points out several limitations in the use of role-play tests. Included among these pitfalls are problems with adequate external validity due to the obvious differences between role-play tests and naturalistic social interactions.

> Role-play tests are highly structured, require facility at making quick, brief responses, and rely on the subject's ability to quickly take on roles in a series of diverse interactions. . . . Conversely, naturalistic interactions require only one role enactment in which the subject can gradually become enmeshed due to the extended nature of the interaction. These interactions are also less structured and place more emphasis on ability to maintain a conversation than on ability to make one or two discrete responses. (p. 91)

The contention that role-play tests are limited in these respects has gained support from recent findings with adults. Bellack, Hersen, and Lamparski (1979), and Bellack, Hersen, and Turner (1978) recently found little correspondence between a role-play test and a naturalistic interaction that used identical situations to prompt the same specific social skills components.

Other related questions concern whether role-play tests only sample "knowledge" of appropriate social responses and not responses the child actually employs on a day-to-day basis. These concerns imply that if a role-play test is used to assess the effects of social skills training, other measures of the child's behavior in the natural environment should also be included. Otherwise, training may be called "successful" even though it has merely taught children to "act" or "perform the role-play" rather than to change their behavioral repertoires (Beck et al., 1978).

There are other psychometric limitations (cf. Cone, 1977) to the use of role-play tests, including the absence of data concerning test–retest reliability; the lack of information regarding normative data (e.g., what is the normal response); the fact that situations developed for role-play tests have been devised more on the basis of face validity (e.g., what looks reasonable to the people constructing the role-play scenes) rather than on scientific principle; and the briefness of the interactional format of the role-play tests, which may be too restrictive, unrealistic, or anxiety provoking, thus reducing a child's chances of performing to the best of his or her ability.

Another limitation of role-play assessments revolves around the many variations that are available. Differing scenes, sex and age of prompters or "confederates," and the use of videotape versus live medium may influence the child's response, thus potentially biasing the information obtained through the procedure. The quality and quantity of scene elaboration and description (usually described by the narrator) can also vary substantially, raising similar concerns. Unfortunately, little systematic research has been completed to date to resolve these issues.

As with the other methods of assessing social skills in children, role-play tests should try to be as socially valid as possible. Most role-play tests seem to reflect the social environment by presenting situations involving adults and children which would likely occur in the daily routine. However, most researchers have not determined empirically that all the scenes on their role-play test were socially valid, so there is no guarantee that the scenes represent "slices of life" or that the scenes and the required responses address socially important areas of functioning for a child. Some role-play situations chosen for a test may be of a type that rarely occur in a particular child's life or may be measuring an aspect of social functioning that is relatively unimportant to all other members of the child's social environment. A better method of developing a role-play test has been to employ the "behavior-analytic model" (see Goldfried & D'Zurilla, 1969), which stresses social validity as a primary factor in designing the test. By this method, scenes, situations, and responses are selected according to whether they accurately reflect the social environment of the child and address important areas of social functioning for a particular child or group of children.

Further research efforts which include social validity in the development of role-play tests—along with improvements in the psychometric data regarding external validity and reliability—should enhance the ability of role-play tests to measure social skills accurately in children. However, at this point, there is sufficient evidence from research with adult and child populations to warrant caution in the interpretation of data from role-play assessments and to indicate that their use be supplemented with other measures of social skills.

A brief note is in order regarding caution in the use of the contrived interview technique (e.g., Children's Behavioral Scenario). In addition to facing many of the same problems noted above for role-play tests, contrived scenes involve ethical issues regarding research with children. Since this method requires deception of the child (e.g., via a "candid camera" scene), it must follow certain ethical guidelines such as ensuring that the experience of being involved in the deception not be harmful to the child (e.g., cause undue stress, anxiety, etc). Subsequently, "debriefing" sessions with the children to explain and discuss the deception and reduce any questions or concerns they may have about the experience; and the obtaining of approval from the parents/guardians specific to utilizing this type of assessment approach is strongly recommended.

INFORMANT REPORTS

Ratings and reports by peers, teachers, parents, and staff who are significant members of the child's social environment can provide useful information for assessing social skills. Information obtained from people who interact regularly with the child generally reflects their judgment of the appropriateness of the child's social behavior. These people, therefore, are in a position to indicate which social skills are deficient for particular situations. These judgments are useful in identifying socially incompetent and unpopular children and selecting them for social skills training. Additionally, as social agents (members of the child's social environment), they can provide socially valid feedback as to the effectiveness and generalization of training (Wolf, 1978). Informant report assessments primarily include teacher reports and ratings and sociometric (e.g., peer status) questionnaires. These reports and ratings can also be completed by other social agents, such as parents, neighbors, and peers.

TEACHER REPORTS AND RATINGS

Reports and ratings by teachers are often utilized in the initial screening and referral of problem children. Children who are judged as socially deficient on rating scales by teachers can be selected for further evaluation (such as naturalistic observation) in various settings. Although controversy exists as to the *external validity* and accuracy of teacher ratings, (e.g., without training, some teachers may be biased and provide inaccurate ratings of the child), such procedures may be both practical and socially valid because of the many opportunities that teachers have to observe children.

Description of Measures.   Teacher report and rating scales encompass a wide variety of standardized and nonstandardized measures which vary considerably in format and complexity. For example, several investigators have simply asked teachers to choose the most socially withdrawn children in their class (see Evers & Schwarz, 1973; O'Connor, 1969). In other studies, teachers were asked to rate children on 5- or 7-point Likert scales for each of several social skills categories (Chittenden, 1942; Gesten, 1976; Jones & Cobb, 1973; Rinn, Mahia, Markle, Barnhart, Owen, & Supernick, 1978). Many studies employed behavior checklists which required teachers to evaluate social behaviors of observed students (Cowen *et al.*, 1973; Feldhusen, Thurston, & Benning, 1970, 1973; Greenwood, Walker, & Hops, 1977; Walker, 1970).

One of the most widely used standardized measures of social functioning is the Walker Problem Behavior Inventory Checklist (WPBIC; Walker, 1970). The WPBIC can be completed in a short time and consists of a total score and five subtests: Acting Out, Withdrawal, Distractability, Disturbed Peer Relations, and Immaturity. Walker (1970) demonstrated that the WPBIC could discriminate between groups of identified behavior problem children and "normal" non-problem children. More definitive data regarding the *external validity* of the WPBIC have not been available, although comparison studies utilizing multiple assessment strategies, including the WPBIC, have indicated moderate correlations with observed behavior and sociometric ratings (Greenwood, Walker, Todd, & Hops, 1976).

Wood *et al.* (1978) developed the Teacher's Rating of Children's Assertive Behavior Scale (TRCABS), which required teachers to answer how the child would usually respond to another child or an adult in a variety of social situations (e.g., expressing complaints, compliments, etc). The authors found that both scores (one for responding to another child and one for responding to an adult) correlated moderately with a self-report measure of assertive behavior completed by the child (cf. Children's Assertive Behavior Scale, presented below in the section titled *Self-Report Measure*) and with a contrived behavioral interview (Children's Behavorial Scenario) carried out by an adult confederate. Although this rating scale was devised for use with teachers, it appears applicable to many other qualified informants in the child's social environment, such as parents, adult friends, and neighbors. (A modified version of the TRCABS entitled Informant Report of Youth's Behavior: Children's Assertive Behavior Scale is presented in Appendix A, Sample D, along with administration and scoring procedures.)

Another scale that has been widely used with parents and teachers and incorporates a number of social dimensions is the Peterson-Quay Behavior Problem Checklist (BPC; Quay & Peterson, 1967). The checklist consists of 55 items which the respondent rates as 0, 1, or 2, depending upon the degree to which each item constitutes a problem behavior of the child. Anchors are ambiguous, with 0 defined as "none," 1 as "mild," and 2 as "severe." While some of the items describe discrete, observable behaviors such as "fighting," others are nonoperationally defined trait labels such as "feelings of inferiority" and "lack of self-confidence." In spite of this, there is considerable evidence supporting the validity of the BPC. This scale has recently been revised to include 150 items (Quay & Peterson, 1979), and the revised measure covers areas not well developed in the previous version.

The Pittsburgh Adjustment Survey Scales (PASS) are teacher rating scales that were developed to evaluate social behavior of elementary school boys, ages 6 to 12 (Ross, Lacy, & Parton, 1965). The modified version of the PASS was used by Miller (1972); it included the 77 items from the Ross study plus 3 other items. Also included were 14 learning disability items and 2 anxiety items. This modified PASS was referred to as the Social Behavior Checklist (SBCL). The SBCL has been shown to be sensitive to the effects of training to improve self-control in second-grade boys (Camp, Blom, Herbert, & van Doornick, 1977) and thus could be an appropriate device for evaluating social skills training. The items also specify behavior more clearly than does the BPC and occasionally indicate specific antecedents or situational factors as well as responses. Whether the device is sensitive enough to monitor progress on an ongoing basis is an empirical question yet to be answered.

Most of the existing teacher rating scales are problem-oriented and therefore provide little information regarding the nature of children's social behavior. An exception to this is the Social Competence Scale (SCS; Kohn, 1977; Kohn & Rosman, 1972). There are two forms of the SCS, one for use in full-day preschool programs (73 items), the other for half-day and kindergarten programs (64 items). Items were designed to tap *adaptive* as well as problem behaviors and to describe specific, behaviorally anchored responses. Although originally designed for use with preschoolers, it may also be useful with older children: one research study found that scores on one of the two factors differentiated "liked from disliked" fourth, fifth, and sixth graders selected via a sociometric device (Foster & Ritchey, 1982).

Other teacher rating scales for assessing children's social behavior include the AML (Cowen, Dorr, Clarfield, Kreling, McWilliams, Pokracki, Pratt, Terrell, & Wilson, 1973); the Health Resources Inventory (Gesten, 1976); the Teacher Referral Form (Clarfield, 1974); and the 17-item teacher rating scale used by Cowen *et al.* (1973). These have been developed solely for use in the primary grades. Additional teacher inventories regarding children's social skills can be obtained from other sources: Greenwood, Walker, and Hops (1979); The Ohio State University Research Foundation (1979); Reardon *et al.* (1978); and Stephens (1978). Additional comprehensive compilations and references of scales measuring social competency among children and adolescents include *Measures of Social Skills* (Henrigues, 1977) and Rie and Friedman's (1978) *Survey of Behavior Rating Scales for Children*.

Advantages and Limitations.   Teacher reports and ratings have practical advantage over most assessment techniques in that they are easily administered. This facilitates mass screening to identify socially incompetent children, which can then be followed up by a more precise evaluation of these children's specific skill deficits. This practicality often outweighs some of the shortcomings of other informant reports.

Informant and teacher reports also have a built-in advantage regarding social validity because they represent ratings by members of the child's social environment. Informants are, in effect, "consumers" of the child's social skills and their reports of how they view the child's social behavior provide important information. Since one of the goals of social skills training is to improve the child's social functioning with such "informants," then the informants' judgments should be considered in determining whether a child has adequate social skills in all areas and whether the child's social skills have improved or not following training.

However, shortcomings of existing teacher report instruments are unfortunately numerous. First, inconsistent and variable ratings can occur when adults judge children's social behavior. For example, Reardon *et al.* (1979) suggest that the accuracy of teacher ratings depends upon the opportunities that the teacher has to observe the particular behaviors of interest. Other factors that can influence adult ratings are demand characteristics (e.g., trying to please the person asking all the questions), personal biases, expectancies, understanding of the behaviors to be rated, response set (e.g., reporting "all good" or "all bad" responses), and carelessness. However, many of these problems can be resolved through proper training of informants in rating children's social skills.

A related controversy regards the accuracy and functional utility of teacher ratings. For example, Greenwood *et al.* (1976) assert that teacher ratings are accurate measures of children's social behavior. In contrast, Rinn and Markle (1979) conclude that the usefulness of teacher ratings of children's social skills has not been demonstrated. For example, inexperienced teachers tend to over-rate maladjustment (Clarfield, 1974). Although at least one study (Stewart, 1949) indicates that teachers can, indeed, distinguish between school problems and "whole life" problems, their judgments do seem to be affected by variables such as the sex of the child (boys being more likely to be identified as maladjusted than girls), the sex of the teacher, age and grade level of the child, and socioeconomic status (Beilin, 1959).

Another limitation of informant reports is that many instruments contain a broad range of items that may not identify specific social deficits or excesses in specific situations. Additionally, these instruments may not be very sensitive to changes that result from training if the training programs focus on a very narrow range or specific group of social skill behaviors.

The above findings do not necessarily invalidate teachers' ratings of children's social adjustment. They do, however, point out that situational and interactor variables influence ratings of social competence. Behavior that teachers consider incompetent or maladjusted at one grade level may be socially effective at another grade level. To minimize the influence of extraneous factors, rating scales should be objective and clearly specify behaviors which are associated with social incompetence. Interpreters of the data should also remember that responses indicate only adult perceptions of the child's behavior—perceptions that may or may not correspond to the child's actual performance in social situations.

SOCIOMETRIC QUESTIONNAIRES AND RATINGS

Sociometric procedures generally involve the rating or ranking of social prestige, popularity, or competence by peers. For example, an entire classroom group of students may rate each other according to how well they are liked or disliked. Such information provides a method of selecting popular and unpopular children.

Description of the Measures. The peer nomination or partial ranking method is common sociometric procedure utilized in studies of children's peer relations. This method requires children to choose a predetermined number of peers for specific purposes, such as play or seating companions or best friends. A child's score consists of the number of nominations received. This technique has been used with both positive (e.g., "name three classmates you especially like") and negative (e.g., "name three classmates you don't like very much") criteria (see Hymel & Asher, 1977).

However, by providing a complete class list, nominations are less affected by memory (Asher, Singleton, Tinsley, & Hymel 1977). Another variation, the picture-board sociometric developed by Marshall and McCandless (1957), is suitable for children at the prereading level. Snapshots of peers are mounted on a poster, which is presented to each child. The child then points to his or her nomination in each category. Significant relationships have been found between "best friend" ratings and observed frequencies of peer interaction in "associative play" and "friendly approach." In addition, teacher ratings of friendship correlated significantly with the picture-board technique (Marshall & McCandless, 1957).

Improvements in reliability can be obtained through the use of the paired-comparison technique, in which the child makes choices for *all* classmates presented in a random order. Cohen *et al.* (1973) required that children nominate one or more peers for each of 20 roles, 10 positive and 10 negative, in a hypothetical class play. Cowen and de Van Tassel (1978) utilized pictures of all the classmates randomly paired with the subject's pictures to obtain rankings for all children and to avoid problems with forgetting and mistakes. The main drawback of this procedure is its length of administration time.

Another method for determining peer status utilized a rating scale rather than a ranking or peer nomination procedure. Each child is rated on a 3-, 5-, or 7-point scale by some or all of the peers in reference to specific questions or situations (e.g., "How much do you like this person"? "Is this child a leader in games"?) An instrument that combines the nomination and rating scale techniques is the Pupil Evaluation Inventory (Pekarik, Prinz, Liebert, Weintraub, & Neale, 1976). With this inventory, each child rates each classmate on 35 items. Classmates' names are listed horizontally and the rater places an "X" below the name of each child who meets the item description (e.g., "Is friendly"). (Sample E of Appendix A contains part of the Social Skills Sociometric Questionnaire along with administration and scoring procedures.) This instrument utilizes a three-point scale based on whether the child is not liked (1), not really liked or disliked (2), or liked (3). Each child is evaluated independently by the other children to determine how well they are liked or how much they are disliked within the group.

Advantages and Limitations.   Sociometric procedures, which have been utilized extensively in developmental and social psychology research, are a relatively new addition to behavioral assessment (Beck *et al.*, 1978; Drabman, Spitalnik, & Spitalnik, 1974). Sociometric assessment provides a measure of a child's social status from which children with low peer status may be identified and selected for further evaluation (Foster & Ritchey, 1979; Marshall & McCandless, 1957). Gottman (1977) and Gottman, Gonso, and Rasmussen (1975) suggest that a low rate of social interaction is not necessarily dysfunctional whereas *low social acceptance,* as measured by choice statements by peers, appears to be a more important factor. Sociometric measures have been shown to correlate moderately with various measures of social competence (Feldhusen *et al.*, 1970, 1973; Greenwood, Walker, Todd, & Hops, 1977), predict delinquency (Kohn, 1977; Roff & Hasazi, 1977), and problematic adult adjustment (Cowen *et al.*, 1973; Stengel, 1971).

A major advantage of sociometric measures is their inherent connection with social validity. Just as with "informant reports," described earlier, sociometric techniques collect judgments from important, perhaps *the* most important, members of the child's social environment: the peers with which the child must interact on a daily basis. These peers are also "consumers" of the child's social skills and their opinion of how well the child performs socially should be regarded. If a child is disliked by most peers, major social deficits may be indicated. In a similar fashion if, after social skills training, the child is liked more by most of the peers, the training's effectiveness would be given added support.

Note also that for any training effects to be maintained and to generalize to other settings, situations, or people, the trained behaviors must be reinforced. Since one of the primary sources of reinforcement for a child is the response of peers, it is important that the trained social behaviors be those that the peers will reinforce (e.g., through praise, smiles, or continued conversation instead of walking away). If the trained behaviors are not important to the child's peers, there will be little change in the sociometric rating and the trained behavior might fade away once the child returns to the usual social environment.

Limitations of sociometric techniques include a lack of demonstrated reliability with very young children (e.g., their ratings of whom they like or dislike can vary from day to day) and procedures that are impractical and cumbersome for day-to-day evaluation of peer status (e.g., ranking pictures of all classmates on a large board). Additionally, sociometric techniques do not usually provide information that defines the *specific* behavioral deficits and/or excesses that the child may exhibit. Little is known about *why* a particular child is liked or disliked, or which behaviors need to be changed and to what degree. When used to evaluate the effectiveness of training, sociometric measures tend to suffer from a lack of sensitivity due to lag time between the child's appropriate performance of the trained behaviors and changes in the judgements of peers regarding the child. A child may begin to exhibit the newly trained social skills, but peers may not change their opinion of the child immediately and may require time before adjusting their impression of the child.

SELF-REPORT MEASURES

Self-report measures can provide information regarding knowledge of social skills, social perception, and self-perception of interpersonal skills. In order to assess large numbers of children to determine levels of social functioning, it may be more efficient to employ self-report questionnaires or inventories than to assess subjects on a one-to-one basis. This assessment technique usually consists of having the child respond to a variety of social situations presented in a paper-and-pencil test. While self-report measures represent a convenient, quantifiable, and economical means of collecting data on how children perceive and report their social behavior, the subjectivity of self-report responses in conjunction with a lack of demonstrated external validity has resulted in their limited development and use.

Descriptions of Measures. Initial self-report inventories were usually modified versions of adult inventories which focus on assertive behavior, a subset of social skills. For example, the Rathus Assertiveness Scale (Rathus, 1973) was simplified and appropriate language modifications made for use with junior high school (Vaal & McCullogh, 1975) and elementary school students (D'Amico, 1976). However, reliability and external validity were not established and no further development or use of these instruments with children has been reported (Wood *et al.*, 1978).

Reardon *et al.* (1979) developed the Self-Report Assertiveness Test for Boys (SRAT-B) to measure assertive behavior in male children. Boys were asked to check response alternatives to several situations requiring positive or negative assertion which they might use in a real-life encounter. Reardon *et al.* (1979), however, found no evidence to support the external validity of this device.

Recently, Deluty (1979) reported on the development and evaluation of the Children's Action Tendency Scale (CATS), a self-report measure of aggression, assertion, and submissiveness. The scale is proposed to measure situation-specific interpersonal conflicts rather than assertive traits. Limitations of the scale include the absence of external validation, such as comparisons with behavioral observations, and a limited number of interpersonal situations. The scale has promise and should be considered for further clinical research prior to its dissemination.

Wood *et al.* (1978) developed the Children's Assertive Behavior Scale (CABS) to measure reported assertive and nonassertive behavior in children. Item categories consisted of assertive content areas dealing with a variety of situations and behaviors, such as giving and receiving compliments, complaints, empathy, request, refusal, and initiating, maintaining, and terminating conversations. Response categories for the 27 CABS items were varied along a continuum of passive–assertive–aggressive responses. For each item, five possible answers were presented in scrambled order; these included passive, very passive, assertive, aggressive, and very aggressive categories. Subjects selected the response which best represented their perceptions of their behavior for a specific situation. The scale generates separate passive (PACABS) and aggressive (AGCABS) scores. These two scores represent the severity and directionality of the child's nonassertive responses. This provides information as to whether the child is deficient in assertive responses due to passive or aggressive social behaviors.

Wood *et al.* (1978) and Michelson, Andrasik, Vucelic, and Coleman (1981) investigated the psychometric properties of the CABS. Wood *et al.* (1978) administered the CABS to 149 Florida fourth graders. The children's CABS scores were compared with behavioral observations and teachers' ratings on the TRCABS. Behavioral observations showed significant though moderate correlations with the CABS total score. Teachers' ratings showed significant though highly variable correlations, and test–retest reliability over a six-week period was moderately high (e.g., $r = .87$).

Michelson, Andrasik, and Coleman (1981) compared CABS responses with various types of peer, parent, and teacher ratings of social competence, popularity, and overall social skills. Children with unassertive versus assertive CABS scores were identified as different on peer, teacher, and parent ratings of social skills. Michelson and Wood (1980) found that the CABS was sensitive to treatment effects and could accurately differentiate children who had received social skills training from a control group. Moreover, teachers who were "blind" to treatment conditions, using the teacher's version of the CABS (TRCABS), rated children in the social skills training group to be more socially competent. Recently, Michelson and Wood (1982) reported extensive reliability and validity data on the CABS which indicates that the instrument appears to be reliable and valid. (An example of a self-report inventory of social behavior that can be completed by children is presented in Sample F of Appendix A. Administration and scoring procedures are provided for the Children's Assertive Behavior Scale along with a sample summary table of results for interpretation.)

Advantages and Limitations. Self-report assessment techniques have an advantage in the ease with which they can be administered to groups of children. They also provide information as to the content areas in which children show deficiencies in knowledge of social skills. Some instruments can further suggest the nature of the child's inappropriate responses (e.g., passive versus aggressive). This information can aid in developing and designing a training approach. For example, if a group of children or adolescents reported many inappropriate aggressive social skills, the training could be modified to emphasize more socially appropriate responding and replacement of aggressive responses. In addition, some self-report techniques are sensitive to social skill training interventions (e.g., pre- versus posttreatment differences) (cf. Michelson & Wood, 1980a) and can be useful in evaluating the effectiveness of training.

Previous studies examining self-report measures of social skills in children share a similar limitation. None of the inventories has been compared with naturalistic observations to determine whether what children say they do corresponds with what they actually do. A related disadvantage of the self-report inventory is that it relies heavily on the ability of the child to answer accurately and objectively concerning his or her own behavior. Children may answer in ways they think will please the examiner or may indicate how they wished they had behaved rather than how they actually behaved. Therefore, self-report inventories may not accurately reflect how the child actually performs in everyday life. They do provide some information of the child's knowledge of social skills and whether the child knows the correct responses. At this point, it is safest to assume that inventories may or may not reflect actual behavior and, at the least, are measures of the children's knowledge of correct social responses.

Misreading, misinterpreting, indifference, and external environmental factors can all undermine accurate assessment. Factors including the child's compliance, response set, recall, distortion, and anxiety also play a role in misleading measurement results. In addition, scoring procedures and summation techniques can influence test results. Regarding children specifically, these problems may be greatly magnified due to difficulties in reading and comprehension. Moreover, developmental factors may influence the accuracy with which children can observe and verbalize salient dimensions of their own behavior. Finally, written self-report instruments are obviously not suitable for the prereading child.

In summary, while self-report measures provide important information regarding content knowledge and social perception, they are subject to several limitations. Therefore, self-report techniques are best employed as part of a larger, more comprehensive evaluation battery. By employing self-report concurrently with other assessment techniques, information regarding the child's social competencies can be obtained across multiple dimensions, situations, and sources.

COMPREHENSIVE ASSESSMENT

Combinations of the various assessment strategies can be utilized in a comprehensive manner to effectively and efficiently measure social skills in children. As assessment techniques vary in reliability, validity, complexity, practicality, and information provided, multiple assessment takes into account the strengths and weaknesses of various measures relative to functions of the assessment process. These include the identification and selection of children with social skills deficits, problem definition, monitoring of progress, treatment outcome, and follow-up (Cone & Hawkins, 1977).

The primary purpose of screening is to identify children who evidence social skills deficits. At the screening level, assessment is general and attempts to evaluate all children. Two techniques particularly applicable for screening are informant reports and sociometric questionaires. These techniques can provide general information as to whether the child is socially unskilled or unpopular as judged by relevant agents in the social environment. Those children identified by the screening process can be assessed further to determine whether they should be selected for social skills training. The selection process can be added by the administration of self-report measures and extensive analysis of the results from both the informant reports and self-report instruments.

Identification of problematic social behaviors can be obtained from most assessment techniques except for sociometric questionaires. The commonly used technique at this level of assessment has been direct observation, either in naturalistic or simulated settings. Naturalistic observation can pinpoint specific problem behaviors and situations as they occur. Simulation observation can provide similar information though perhaps not as accurately, and allows for easy standardized comparisons among subjects. Although limited by the number and content of items, self-report and informant report measures can provide specific information about the nature of social behavior assets and deficits. In any event, the information obtained at this level of assessment should define target behaviors to be remediated. This information can then be utilized to design any training program that will best modify and shape the desired social skills.

To assess the effectiveness of any training program, it is essential to have a pretraining baseline for comparison with posttraining performance. Additionally, measures collected during treatment can be taken to provide ongoing information to indicate the intermediate effectiveness. Most of the assessment techniques are appropriate for pre- and posttraining evaluation measures although some are better than others. Sociometric questionnaires, for example, give an estimate of the change in judgment by the child's peers, but this may not be sensitive enough (due to lag time) to reflect training effects. It may, however, provide a good test of the social validity of treatment effects. Role-play tests may not always provide a good indication of a child's behavior change, especially when role-playing procedures are involved heavily in training. Thus, improved scores on the role-play tests may only indicate that the child has learned how to role-play better, not to behave differently in day-to-day social interactions. Likewise, self-report inventories have their own limitations in that they rely too heavily on the child's written report, which may not correspond with actual behavior. Following training, children may have increased their knowledge of social skill components without having necessarily improved their performance.

Informant reports have the practical advantage of being easier to administer to large groups, though they are also susceptible to biases and expectancies of the informants. Therefore, informant reports and naturalistic observation seem to have the best potential for yielding accurate and informative pre–post data, with supplementation by both self-report and sociometric measures.

ILLUSTRATION

Investigators at the Center at Oregon for Research in the Behaviorial Education of the Handicapped (CORBEH) have developed a comprehensive assessment package utilizing a multipurpose–multimethod approach to measure the social functioning of preschool children (Greenwood et al., 1976, 1977; Hops & Greenwood, 1980; Hops, Walker, & Greenwood, 1979; Walker & Hops, 1976).

This comprehensive assessment battery is entitled the *Social Assessment Manual for Preschool Level* (SAMPLE) and has primarily been used to assess "social withdrawal" in classroom settings.

Three types of assessment strategies were utilized in the SAMPLE package: (1) naturalistic observation of children's social interaction rate and peer contact; (2) teacher rankings of interactive frequency and ratings of social adeptness and popularity; and (3) peer picture sociometric nominations of acceptance and rejection. These assessment strategies were organized and implemented in four procedural stages. Initially, the classroom teacher ranked the interactive frequency of all pupils in the class. The probability of a child being identified as lowest in the class within five teacher rankings was approximately .77 (Greenwood *et al.*, 1976). Additionally, peer-picture sociometric nominations were obtained from all children to identify individuals with low acceptance or high rejection levels.

At the second stage, the five children ranked lowest by teachers were thoroughly evaluated by means of a more costly but more comprehensive observational procedure. Assessment at the second stage served to verify the accuracy of the teachers' judgments regarding the identified children's social behavior and to identify and define various parameters of social skill target behaviors (such as low rates of "initiation" and rates of "responsiveness to initiations by others").

The third stage, concerned with monitoring of progress during treatment, utilized naturalistic observations with normative comparisons. Scores derived from the observational data were compared to a normative data table obtained from extensive observations of preschool children. These comparisons enabled further screening of children identified as socially deficient; only children whose scores fell 1.5 standard deviations below appropriate age and sex norms were considered appropriate for treatment. Observational data for these youngsters also provided a pretreatment baseline. Continued observations during training provided individual monitoring of progress and treatment effectiveness.

The final stage was used to determine treatment outcome, making pre–post comparisons on all measurers. This step, in turn, could be utilized to identify additional target behaviors for further remediation. Follow-up evaluation also used the same approach. Treatment effectiveness and maintenance were comprehensively examined in terms of changes in rates of peer interaction and contact, acceptance and rejection by peers, and teachers' ratings of social competence and popularity.

This example of a comprehensive assessment strategy demonstrates how various assessment techniques can be combined effectively to measure children's social skills. By taking into account the advantages and limitations of each assessment technique, it is possible to design a complete battery of procedures which complement each other and provide initial screening information, define specific social assets and deficits, and evaluate ongoing and outcome results of training. However, the pragmatic aspects (e.g., time requirements, expenses, number of trained personnel involved, etc.) of utilizing this intensive approach need to be considered to ensure that the entire assessment strategy will be workable given the available resources.

CONCLUSIONS

After becoming familiar with each type of assessment and understanding the advantages and disadvantages of each, those involved in the social skills training project should decide which assessment technique to utilize. Two main factors to consider are the practicality of a technique and the types of information desired from the assessment. Some techniques may not be feasible because of limited resources. For example, the main type of information desired may focus only on the child's performance in natural settings (e.g., classroom, recess, lunch). The two types of assessment techniques which come closest to measuring social behaviors in these settings are naturalistic observation and informant report. Trainers may wish to observe children directly during the day but may lack time or personnel to record behaviors accurately. Therefore, trainers might choose informant reports and use available social agents such as teachers, peers, and staff members. If adequate resources are available, however, trainers should utilize concurrent multiple assessment techniques or comprehensive assessment strategies.

In considering the current status of assessing children's social skills, it is clear that no one approach has been shown to be *the* best method. Each has advantages accompanied by limitations which restrict its unqualified endorsement. This does not mean that there is no way to measure social skills accurately or that the entire assessment process should be avoided. The bottom line is that any of the assessment methods described can be very useful; the only way to go wrong is to not do any assessment at all. These assessment measures, even with their limitations, can greatly improve the screening and selection of socially deficient children, define and describe which social skills are needed, help design social skills training to meet these needs, and evaluate whether the training was effective.

(The reader is encouraged to utilize the information presented in this chapter and the materials referred to in Appendix A to develop an appropriate assessment strategy that can be implemented in conjunction with the social competency training program.)

3

Social Skills Training Methods

A variety of training procedures have been used to develop social skills in children. The common goal of the alternative methods is to train specific behaviors related to social interaction. The skills that are trained vary as a function of the characteristics of the child, including the child's specific problems, age, and social situations. Training has been applied to children with diverse target problems, including social isolation, lack of assertiveness, and aggressive behavior.

The techniques designed to develop social skills typically adhere to one of two general models. The first model views social skills problems as instances of skill *deficits*. The notion of deficits is based on the assumption that children do not have in their response repertoires the requisite skills to interact well with others.This view might explain a withdrawn child's behavior as a deficiency in skills for initiating peer interactions. An aggressive child might be described as lacking verbal persuasion skills for achieving what he or she wants. The goal of training would be to build the requisite skills to overcome problem social behavior.

The second model is based on the view that children may have the requisite skills but are experiencing competing emotional, affective, or cognitive states or processes that interfere with the expression of their abilities. Children may know the appropriate responses but are inhibited or thwarted in some way from performing them. The usual state considered to compete with manifestation of social skills is anxiety. This model might ascribe a child's avoidance of interaction with others to interpersonal anxiety. If the anxiety can be overcome through increased familiarity with the situation or systematic desensitization, these skills will presumably emerge. As another example, the behavior of overly aggressive children might be explained as a failure to empathize with their victims' affect.

The views that social skills problems are due to skill deficits or to interference of emotional or cognitive states are not necessarily incompatible. Both the absence of particular skills and the presence of competing emotional states may occur concurrently. Indeed, it is quite possible for deficits in behavior to precipitate social anxiety, which, in turn, can inhibit performance. Nonetheless, the skills deficit model has been adopted as the basis for generating treatment techniques. It is not entirely clear whether the benefits of social skills training derive exclusively or primarily from developing specific skills where deficits previously existed or from overcoming inhibitions. In adult treatment, direct skills training has been used to overcome anxiety and inhibitions, as in the case of phobias and obsessive-compulsive disorders (Emmelkamp, 1979; Rachman & Hodgson, 1980). Thus, development of specific response repertoires can overcome both inhibitions and specific response deficits.

This chapter considers several of the techniques commonly used to develop social skills in children. In addition to the material presented here, research related to the effectiveness of these strategies has been reviewed in several sources (e.g., Conger & Keane, 1981; Combs & Slaby, 1977; Michelson & Wood, 1978; Rinn & Markle, 1979; Van Hasselt *et al.*, 1979).

ALTERNATIVE TRAINING METHODS

Several different strategies have been used effectively to develop social skills. The techniques can be used individually or in combination. To clarify the procedures, applications of individual techniques will be discussed first. Then, ways of combining methods into social skills training packages are described.

MODELING

Definition and Illustrations. Modeling consists of exposing the child to live or film exemplars (models) who perform the requisite behaviors. The use of models is referred to as observational or vicarious learning, because the client learns by observing the model rather than by actually engaging in the responses directly or overtly (Bandura, 1969, 1973; Bandura & Waters, 1963; Rosenthal & Bandura, 1978). Several social skills training studies have relied upon modeling (Conger & Keane, 1981; Combs & Slaby, 1977).

The use of modeling can be illustrated by the study conducted by O'Connor (1969), who treated socially withdrawn preschool children. These children were exposed to a modeling film in which an initially withdrawn child engaged in social interactions. As a result, the withdrawn children markedly improved in their social behavior in class. Other children who were exposed to a control film that did not include modeling of social behavior did not improve.

In a similar demonstration, Keller and Carlson (1974) used film modeling to increase social behavior among socially isolated preschool children. These children were exposed to videotaped segments in which several socially appropriate behaviors such as displaying affection, smiling, and laughing were presented. The modeling film increased the children's social behavior during a free-play period. In contrast, children exposed to a control film in which social behaviors were not displayed did not improve.

Occasionally, live rather than film models have been used to develop social behavior. For example, Ross, Ross, and Evans (1971) provided a multifaceted treatment for a socially withdrawn six-year-old boy who exhibited extreme fear and avoidance of social situations. Several procedures were used which involved having one of the trainers engage in social interaction with the child's classmates, using symbolic models in pictures, stories, and movies of social interaction. Social interaction by two trainers was demonstrated and the participation of a trainer with the child in social interaction with peers was enlisted. Modeling with participation combined with other procedures effectively increased overall social interaction immediately after treatment and up to a two-month follow-up.

Important Considerations.   Many studies have shown the effectiveness of modeling in developing social behaviors. In addition, investigations have evaluated variables that contribute to modeling effects (see Rosenthal & Bandura, 1978). In general, modeling effects can be enhanced by providing persons with multiple models who perform the desired behaviors rather than with a single model. Also, a broad range of behaviors should be displayed by the model to develop a broad set of responses in the observer. Perceived similarity of the observer to the model is another variable that can influence modeling effects. When observers perceive themselves to be similar to the model, modeling effects are often greater than when they perceive themselves as dissimilar. The effects of modeling can be further augmented by providing opportunities for children to practice the behaviors they observe the model perform. Observing one or more models and then, immediately thereafter, rehearsing the observed behaviors produces greater improvement than does exposure to modeling alone. Both modeling and behavior rehearsal typically are included as parts of a larger social skills training package.

Positive Reinforcement

Definition and Illustrations.   Positive reinforcement refers to the process by which responses increase in frequency because they are followed by a reward or favorable event. The goal of social skills training is to increase the frequency of a variety of socially appropriate behaviors. If social behaviors are to increase, they must be followed by positively reinforcing consequences. These consequences may include social attention or approval, points or tokens that can be exchanged for other rewards, special privileges or activities, and so on.

A variety of reinforcement techniques have been used to increase social skills. When used by themselves, reinforcement techniques are usually applied in group situations such as a classroom setting, where teachers can provide consequences for interaction. For example, Pinkston, Reese, LeBlanc, and Baer (1973) used social reinforcement and extinction to develop appropriate social skills in a preschool child who displayed highly aggressive behavior and low rates of appropriate peer interaction. Aggressive behavior was treated first. Training consisted of not attending to the aggressive classroom behavior except to extract the child from his contact with others. The teacher attended to the child who was the victim of verbal or physical aggression and provided sympathetic attention to him or her. The aggressive child received attention later for nonaggressive behavior. This training regimen effectively reduced aggressive behavior, as demonstrated in several phases of a single-case experimental design in which attention was presented and withdrawn across phases. Subsequently, socially appropriate peer interaction was targeted directly, using positive reinforcement. The teacher provided the prompts to the peers to include the child in their interaction and provided direct reinforcement to the child for appropriate interaction. This procedure therefore increased appropriate peer interaction.

Some applications of reinforcement for social behavior have utilized peers as well as adults to help develop behavior. For example, Kirby and Toler (1970) increased the social interaction of a preschool child who rarely interacted with his peers. To prompt social interaction, the child was instructed to distribute candy to other children in class, which required asking children about their preferences. The teacher directly reinforced completion of this task with praise, money, and candy. The child engaged in increased interactions with peers during a free-play period in class after the reinforcement procedure had been completed. Teacher reinforcement for approaching other children, direct peer contact, and reinforcement generated from peers probably contributed to the increased frequency of interaction.

In a more direct utilization of peers, Strain, Shores, and Timm (1977) trained socially adept preschool children to improve the social behaviors of peers who infrequently engaged in positive interaction with others. Peer trainers were taught, through instructions and role playing, how to initiate interactions with the withdrawn children. After this training, the peer trainers were praised for helping their withdrawn classmates interact socially. The withdrawn children were not treated directly by adults. Peers who were trained and who received reinforcement for prompting interaction were quite successful in altering the social behaviors of the withdrawn students.

Important Considerations. As the above illustrations suggest, a variety of reinforcement techniques can be used to develop social skills. However, there are common requirements for the different procedures. First, when developing behaviors, it is important to provide reinforcement as soon as possible after the desired behavior is performed. If a child begins to interact with peers in class, it is critical to provide reinforcement immediately. A delay such as complimenting the child at the end of the day, may result in little or no effect on performance. As a general rule, then, *immediate reinforcement* is best.

Second, reinforcement should occur frequently, especially when the behaviors are just developing. The desired behaviors may occur relatively infrequently. To increase their frequency, the reinforcers should be provided for every or almost every instance of the behavior. Reinforcing the behavior each time it occurs is referred to as *continuous reinforcement*. If behavior is reinforced only once in a while, the procedure is called *intermittent reinforcement*. Behaviors develop at a faster rate when reinforcement is delivered continuously than when it is delivered intermittently. Once responding is at a high level, reinforcement can be delivered less frequently to maintain the behavior.

Two of the most important ingredients in an effective reinforcement program are *prompting* and *shaping*. Prompts refer to antecedent stimuli that help evoke the behavior. They include instructions, coaching, and modeling cues to help the child see what is to be done before the behavior is performed.

Prompts facilitate performance of the behavior. Once the behavior occurs, it can be reinforced. Eventually, the prompt can be removed without causing behavior to decrease in frequency. For example, to encourage social interaction in class, the teacher may instruct a child to play with peers on a particular task. The child's behavior can then be reinforced after he or she becomes involved in the task. As social interaction increases, the teacher's prompts are no longer needed. However, the initial use of the prompts speeds up the process of developing the behavior.

Shaping refers to reinforcing approximations of the final behaviors that are to be developed. Social skills training often aims toward the development of complex sequences of social behaviors, such as beginning a conversation, making requests of others, and standing up for one's rights. With severely withdrawn children, it may be difficult to reinforce the occurrence of these responses because they may never occur. Gradual steps toward these responses must be reinforced, so that the behaviors can gradually move in the direction of the final goal. For example, if a child plays near another child, it may be wise to reinforce this behavior, because it approximates social interaction. If the child looks at or says something to the other child, this too can be reinforced. Reinforcement for behaviors that increasingly approximate the final goal can be provided.

In using reinforcement strategies, careful consideration must be given to the precise behaviors that are to be rewarded. The success of training may depend on the responses that are targeted. For example, Walker, Greenwood, Hops, and Todd (1979) found that providing token reinforcement and praise to withdrawn children for such behaviors as starting a conversation or answering others actually suppressed overall interaction. In contrast, reinforcement of maintaining and continuing social interaction produced marked improvements in overall levels of interaction. At present, there are few comparisons that evaluate the impact of reinforcement on different types of responses and their implications for successful social skills training. The best recommendation at present is to provide reinforcing consequences for the individual responses that are deficient as well as to include reinforcing both the initiation and maintenance of social interaction.

COACHING AND PRACTICE

Definition and Illustrations. To evoke a desired behavior, a child can be coached or instructed on which behaviors to perform and how to perform them. Coaching may rely on several procedures aside from instructions. For example, the trainer may provide a model of the desired statements to explain how the child should speak to parents or teachers. The trainer may also provide feedback on how well the behaviors were performed by the child and what behaviors should be done differently. Coaching is therefore a multifaceted intervention, involving clear prompts for what to do, practice of the behavior, and feedback to reinforce correct elements of a response and to prompt improved performance.

Practice or rehearsal of the desired behaviors is a critical component of coaching; it is also sometimes utilized by itself. Practice consists of enacting the desired behavior or sequence of behaviors, such as role-playing the desired response. Through repeated practice of the desired response, the child learns how to perform new behaviors. The coaching sequence of instruction–practice–feedback, is repeated until performance matches the desired goal.

A few social skills training programs have utilized coaching and practice to enhance social skills. For example, Oden and Asher (1977) evaluated a social skills training program that emphasized instructions and practice. Children were instructed to utilize the behaviors in a play situation with a non-isolate peer. After practice, the interactions were reviewed with the trainer. Children who were coached showed increases in sociometric ratings relative to other conditions in which coaching was excluded. Although the gains were not evident on a behavioral measure, a one-year follow-up showed that the sociometric ratings continued to reflect treatment effects.

Ladd (1979) also used a training procedure that emphasized coaching to develop social behaviors among withdrawn third-grade children. Training was conducted with pairs of children, the subjects were coached on how to interact appropriately with others. Children who received the coaching improved relative to children who received only attention (placebo) or to untreated controls. Improvements in social interaction were reflected during free play and on a peer acceptance measure. Treatment effects were maintained up to four weeks of follow-up. Several other studies have examined the effectiveness of coaching in which children were given verbal instructions on how to perform, supplemented with opportunities to practice. Some programs have been successful, others have not (e.g., Gottman et al., 1975; Hymel & Asher, 1977).

Important Considerations. Coaching and practice can play an important role in developing social interaction. Although they are discussed here as relatively isolated procedures, they are usually used in conjunction with other strategies. For example, coaching can be enhanced by utilizing modeling as well as instructions. The child may grasp the required behaviors better by actually viewing the behavior as well as receiving instructional guides. Similarly, the feedback that follows practice provides a good opportunity to reinforce positive aspects of the child's performance.

Both coaching and practice emphasize aspects of training that need to be incorporated into social skills training programs. Coaching emphasizes the importance of clear and detailed guidelines for the child. Prompts of all sorts and direct modeling experiences can greatly speed the acquisition of the desired behaviors. Practice emphasizes the importance of actually performing the requisite behaviors. As noted earlier in the discussion of modeling, practice contributes uniquely to developing the desired behaviors. Hence, as part of training programs, children should have the opportunities to engage in the desired behaviors. However, practice alone will ordinarily prove insufficient without further coaching and feedback to shape the components of social behaviors.

TRAINING IN PROBLEM-SOLVING SKILLS

Problem-solving techniques are based on the view that deficient social skills result in part from inappropriate cognitive strategies that children apply in their interpersonal situations (see Urbain & Kendall, 1980). Procedures designed to develop cognitive strategies have been applied to a variety of age groups. In several years of programmatic research, Spivack, Shure, and their colleagues have developed procedures for training children to handle interpersonal situations (e.g., see Spivack, Platt, & Shure, 1976; Spivack & Shure, 1974). Their approach has been based upon demonstrated relationships between particular problem-solving skills (e.g., generating alternative solutions to social situations) and classroom adjustment. The training program focuses on developing the use of several problem-solving steps to help children generate alternative solutions to various interpersonal situations, to consider means and ends of social acts, and to examine the consequences of their behavior. Several studies have shown that training in problem-solving skills improves social adjustment (e.g., Spivack et al., 1976).

There are many variations of cognitive therapies designed to develop problem-solving skills in children (see Kendall & Hollon, 1979; Meichenbaum, 1977). In the usual program, children are trained to engage in a self-dialogue to identify the specific tasks that need to be performed in social situations. For example, in a typical variation of problem-solving training, children pose different questions or statements to themselves when confronted with a social situation. Typical of such statements are (1) What was I supposed to do? (2) I need to look at all my possibilities; (3) I have to concentrate or focus in on the alternatives; (4) I need to choose one; and (5) How well did I do? Each of the first four questions or statements requires the child to consider what has to be done before proceeding to the next step. This procedure includes some of the coaching and prompting elements discussed earlier, but the child self-administers the instructions. The final statement teaches the child to evaluate the effects of the final response that was selected. Hence, self-evaluation or self-reinforcement is a part of the procedure.

The utility of a problem-solving, cognitively based approach for developing appropriate social behavior was illustrated by Camp et al. (1977). The training program, referred to as "Think Aloud," was applied to boys who were identified as severely aggressive on the basis of their classroom behavior. Training included modeling of cognitive strategies such as approach behavior and problem-solving skills while children worked on various tasks such as copying designs and completing perceptual speed tasks. Training was extended to cover interpersonal situations that required use of problem-solving skills (e.g., identifying situations, anticipating alternative outcomes). After six weeks of training, boys who received training showed greater improvement in cognitive style than did untreated controls. On teacher checklist ratings of classroom performance, the treated group did not evidence a reduction in the rate of aggressive acts but did show significantly greater increases in prosocial behavior than did the untreated group.

Important Considerations.   One goal of training in problem-solving skills is to provide a strategy that can guide performance across a wide range of situations. Rather than teaching particular responses, the main focus is on developing a superordinate strategy. This is useful in part because training cannot fully anticipate all the specific behaviors the child will be required to perform, even though standard problem areas in interactions with parents, teachers, and peers can be included. The rationale for problem-solving training is to develop an approach that generates effective responses to new situations.

SOCIAL SKILLS TRAINING PACKAGES

Several programs have applied individual techniques such as those highlighted above to alter social behaviors. Many of the programs have been quite successful with relatively circumscribed treatments. However, a number of programs have applied multifaceted treatments or treatment "packages" in which the procedures noted above and others are combined (e.g., Hops *et al.*, 1979; Michelson & Mannarino, in press; Michelson & Wood, 1980b; Michelson, Mannarino, Marchione, Stern, Figueroa, & Beck, 1983). Combining alternative techniques is assumed to maximize the *impact, durability,* and *generality* of treatment effects. Also, as clinical populations with increasingly severe problems have been studied, the need for more intensive treatments has increased. Major ingredients frequently included in a social skills training package (illustrated in the training modules in the second part of this text) are described below, along with illustrations of their application. Social skills training packages vary but usually include the following components.

Instructions.   The initial step in social skills training is to convey information about the requisite behaviors. Instructions are provided to specify in concrete terms exactly what behaviors are required and how they should be performed. For example, a hypothetical situation may be presented to the child along with guidelines on how to act, what to say, and when to say it. An actual script or dialogue may be presented to the child to convey exactly what responses are required. When the behaviors are specified in detail, the child is more likely to be able to perform the response.

Instructions help break down the overall social response into separate components that can be identified (labeled) and trained. For example, instead of telling the child to go play with his or her friends, instructions would specify the behaviors that need to be performed, such as walking over to children who are already playing, asking them what they are doing, joining in by asking to take a turn, and so on. Although instructions are often an essential ingredient of social skills training, they are not, by themselves, likely to improve the behavior of children with serious social skills deficits.

Modeling.   While instructions may be useful as an initial step in describing the requisite behaviors, modeling provides direct examples of social skills. Typically, the trainer serves as the model, illustrating the exact behaviors that need to be performed. Live modeling provides greater flexibility than film models in illustrating or highlighting particular aspects of performance for the individual child. The advantage of modeling is that it depicts, in vivid detail, the complete social response and can convey more information than is possible through verbal means alone.

Rehearsal and Practice. After information and exemplars have conveyed the types of responses that the child should perform, the child must rehearse the appropriate skills. Depending on the type of social skills targeted, the severity of the child's deficits, and the age and abilities of the child, rehearsal may focus on a particularly concrete behavior, such as eye contact or posture, or on more complex responses, such as combining verbal and nonverbal behaviors in making an assertive response.

Feedback. Feedback consists of providing information about how well the response was performed. Detailed information can be provided to convey what aspect of the response was performed correctly, what could be improved, what might be done differently, and so on. After the child rehearses the response, the trainer and child discuss the performance. The feedback provided about the response is usually used as the basis for rehearsing the response again. Feedback may also be followed by modeling of the behavior by the trainer to demonstrate how the response could be improved. The child again rehearses the response and completes the sequence once more.

Social Reinforcement. Corrective feedback emphasizes aspects of the response that need to be changed or retained. Implicit in this information is an evaluation of how well the child has done, because the feedback includes a statement about the extent to which the response approximated the ultimate goal. Training effects can be enhanced by adding praise or social reinforcement to the feedback.

Reinforcement was discussed earlier as a technique often used on its own, especially in group situations such as the classroom, where teachers provide praise or other reinforcers to develop social behavior. In the context of a social skills training package, the trainer usually provides praise for the improved performance. Social reinforcement is especially useful for shaping successive approximations of the final response. Hence, early in training the child may be praised for performing a response which was far from perfect.

For example, the child may be requested to pretend he is approaching and asking a friend to play with him. The child may correctly walk over to the playmate (played by the trainer) and ask whether she wants to play. The child may actually walk up to the role-played peer and ask a question, in an almost inaudible voice, while staring at the floor. The trainer might then praise both the approach and the request. Rather than punishing poor eye contact and inappropriate intonation, the trainer would provide corrective feedback, rewarding what was done correctly and emphasizing what the child should concentrate on during the next practice segment.

Illustrations of the Combined Techniques. Instructions, modeling, rehearsal, feedback, and reinforcement represent an ongoing sequence of techniques used to develop particular skills. The sequence is not necessarily fixed during training, even though there is an obvious natural order of the steps. For example, a child may be trained to express complaints to his or her parents. Instructions and modeling by the trainer may convey how to perform in a particular situation. The child attempts the response and the trainer provides feedback. Feedback may be provided for a particular aspect of the response, which is followed by practice, additional feedback, reinforcement, and so on. At many different points, information and modeling are likely to be introduced by the trainer to convey the areas where changes in responding are needed. The child and trainer may exchange roles in the sequence, so that the child can see both the appropriate response on the part of the child and the likely reactions of other persons in the situation.

Social skills training packages involving the above ingredients have been applied successfully to a number of children with a variety of interpersonal problems. Bornstein *et al.* (1980) treated four highly aggressive psychiatric inpatient children. During training, the therapist began by presenting an interpersonal situation that could be role-played between the therapist and the patient. The patient responded as if he or she were in the situation. The therapist then provided feedback on performance and directions on how the response should be performed. After a discussion of the requisite response, the therapist modeled the response, then again told the child how to perform the target behavior. The child rehearsed the response again. Rehearsal and feedback continued in this fashion until the target behavior was achieved by the child. At this point, another interpersonal situation was introduced and training continued in the same way. Bornstein *et al.* (1980) found that several specific behaviors such as eye contact, requests of others, and overall assertiveness changed as a function of training.

Another illustration of a multifaceted social skills training package was provided by Michelson and Wood (1980a), who trained fourth-grade elementary school children in social skills. All training was conducted in an elementary school setting. The training program consisted of instructions, modeling, behavioral rehearsal, prepared scripts with assertive responses, reactions of others in the situation, and discussion. Multiple areas were covered, including providing compliments, making complaints, refusing others, requesting favors, asking why, requesting behavior changes from others, standing up for one's rights, and expressing empathy. The results revealed marked improvements after treatment relative to control subjects who participated in discussions unrelated to assertiveness.

Important Considerations.   Social skills training packages have been used extensively. Obviously, the package approach is designed to combine the advantages and to circumvent the limitations of any single technique. There are additional features that recommend the use of a multifaceted treatment package. The package provides an approach that uses antecedent events (instructions, models), direct performance of the desired responses (rehearsal, practice), and consequences (feedback, reinforcement). By encompassing these different facets of the training, impact on the child is likely to be optimal. In addition, the procedure lends itself well to individualization with particular children. As the child enacts the responses, the trainer can identify quickly and focus on those particular areas where additional prompting, practice, and feedback are needed. Thus, there is a corrective component inherent in the procedure that draws attention to the skill areas in need of concentrated attention.

Generalization Programming: Designing Classes to Maximize Effectiveness and Responsiveness

An important consideration for any social skills training program is how to increase effectiveness by ensuring that newly established social skills will be applied in appropriate situations outside the training setting. This is usually termed *generalization* (Beck, Forehand, Wells, & Quante, 1978; Rodgers-Warren & Baer, 1976). The rationale for emphasizing generalization is that "a functional behavioral change, to be effective, often must occur over time, other persons, and other settings, and the effects of the change sometimes should spread to a variety of selective behaviors" (Stokes & Baer, 1977). The following aspects illustrate the need for focus on generalization programming in all training, remediation, and prevention strategies.

Generalization does not naturally occur as the results of most educational training programs (Baer, Wolf, & Risley, 1968; Kazdin, 1980). For example, research has indicated that socially deficient children do not automatically acquire needed social skills through integration with regular students (Cooke & Appollini, 1976). It has also been shown that behaviorally disordered children are often ignored by their peers rather than becoming involved in interactions that facilitate the development of appropriate social behaviors (Strain & Timm, 1974).Thus, generalization is not usually a passive function where a skill, once taught, "magically" appears and continues to appear forever. Generalization requires an active role on the part of the trainer and must be programmed into the teaching situation. Unfortunately, the most common approach to generalization is "train and hope." In this approach, generalization is not specifically planned but is hoped for.

Procedures to Promote Generalization

Stokes and Baer (1977) described several techniques and methods for promoting generalization beyond the training setting, including maintenance over time and transfer across settings. These *generalization facilitators* are important to the success of any educational program designed to teach skills to be applied outside the classroom. Thus, it is important that as many as possible of the following facilitators be incorporated into social skill classes.

1. *Teach behaviors that will be supported by the natural environment.* This is one of the most dependable and functional facilitation techniques. Training is designed to ensure that the new repertoire of behaviors is supported and maintained by the natural contingencies currently operating in the youth's environment (see

Baer & Wolf, 1970). This is easily seen with social skills training, because most of the skills taught will usually be supported by parents, other teachers, and peers. For example, following the learning and practice of appropriate "compliment" responses, a youth will probably experience many positive consequences from others, and this will serve to maintain and strengthen this skill. The results of poor planning are seen in useless teaching efforts and unused skills if a particular social skill is not supported by the youth's environment (i.e., if the particular compliment taught is not acceptable to peers and friends).

2. *Teach a variety of responses.* Training one exemplar (one example or one response form) of a particular social skill will result in mastery of the specific examplar taught. To obtain generalization, however, multiple exemplars and responses should be included in training until sufficient responses are learned and generalization occurs to a variety of novel situations. Many diversified responses can be taught in social skills education through behavioral rehearsal (e.g., role-playing) interactions that include a wide variety of situations. Inclusion of many possible response interactions for one particular skill will increase the youth's ability to function appropriately with different persons in diverse situations. By teaching a variety of response forms for each social skill, the trainer is also being more responsive to cultural, religious, and ethnic backgrounds in that youths and their families can use whichever response form they prefer that is both effective and appropriate.

3. *"Train loosely" under varied conditions.* Rather than controlling all the dimensions of a training situation (which additionally limits the number of exemplars taught), a variety of stimuli should be included. Using varied conditions while teaching ("training loosely") can increase the generalizability of the skills being taught in that they will be associated with many stimuli instead of a specific few. For example, most social skills training is accomplished through the use of "scripts" that detail the specific situation and response for a particular social skill. To use the "train loosely" approach, students are encouraged to eventually initiate some of their *own* situations and responses (rather than having them supplied), thus ensuring that something more than one particular script is being learned.

4. *Train across multiple persons and settings common to the natural environment.* Generalization is facilitated by making the training situation as similar to the natural environment as possible. For example, inclusion of peers from the natural school, home, or neighborhood environment into a social skills class would provide relevant common stimuli for the student. Similarly, role playing might include many different combinations of partners (peer–adult, peer–peer, same sex–opposite sex, old–young, mixed race, high status–low status, stranger–friend, etc.) to approximate the real world. Through the use of common stimuli, students learn to respond to persons they will encounter outside the classroom. This increases generalization beyond what would be obtained if the students, for example, only role-played with the adult trainer as a partner.

5. *Fade training consequences to approximate natural contingencies.* Although an ever-growing body of research emphasizes the importance of immediate, frequent reinforcement contingencies in the acquisition of new skills, the generalization of these skills appears to rely on the *fading* of contingencies to approxi-

mate those operating in the natural environment. One fading technique is to move gradually from continuous reinforcement to intermittent schedules or delayed reinforcement (see Kazdin & Polster, 1973). As contingencies are faded, the student cannot easily discriminate between a training and a natural situation. Hence, students begin to perform similarly in all settings. This approach can be incorporated into a flexible school curriculum in the following manner. A social skills class may provide special privileges contingent on improvement in social skills. As the contingencies used in the class are faded (gradually withdrawn), they are applied at random times in *other* classes throughout the day. Under these conditions, the repertoires learned in the social skills training class will generalize to the other classes. Gradually, all contingencies will be faded so that the skills will be maintained by the natural social environment.

6. *Reinforce accurate self-reports of performance.* Verbal mediation, such as the reinforcement of self-reports of on-task performance, has been shown to increase a child's ability to engage in a task for longer periods of time without interruption (Israel & O'Leary, 1973; Jewett & Clark, 1979; Risley & Hart, 1976; Rodgers-Warren & Baer, 1976). These research findings suggest that reinforcement of accurate self-reports may increase the generalization of target behaviors. For example, giving *homework assignments* is a useful mediator in social skills training. After a skill is taught in class, students are instructed to perform this skill outside class. They later report their success and/or problems in applying the skill outside the training situation. When self-reports of performance are reinforced, additional efforts to utilize the trained skills outside class may increase. Both homework assignments and student self-reports on performance are considered mediators that may enhance transfer of learning to the natural environment.

7. *Train the ability to generalize by reinforcing new appropriate applications.* This method involves reinforcing generalization itself as if it were an explicit behavior. Role-play situations used in social skills training are usually specified by the trainer; however, students can also be reinforced for suggesting responses other than those specified in scripts or by the trainer. Such a procedure reinforces students for incorporating additional exemplars into the training situation, thus increasing generalization for many situations. Students are trained to generalize by exploring possible new responses that are potentially more effective and sensitive to their particular social environment.

8. *Use of peers.* Peers may be especially useful to help maintain behavior and to ensure its transfer across settings. Peers can be incorporated into training in different ways, such as using group reinforcement contingencies that foster interaction of all participants, letting peers initiate social interaction with target children, and using peer models. Peers have been used as the primary behavior change agents in classroom settings. For example, Strain *et al.* (1977) trained preschool children, using rehearsal and modeling, to interact with a withdrawn child and to continue their interactions even if these efforts were not reciprocated. At the beginning of each day, the teacher prompted the peers to try to get the withdrawn child to play. The withdrawn child increased in overall social responsiveness, and the gains generalized to initiation of responses to the peers.

The use of peers as part of programs to develop social behaviors has been reported in many investigations (Strain & Fox, 1981). In some cases, behaviors have been maintained or have generalized beyond the training situation. For example, Strain (1977) trained peers to initiate social interaction with behaviorally handicapped children in a special classroom setting. Social behavior generalized to the regular classroom for some of the subjects. However, in other studies the use of peers has not led to sustained training effects (e.g., Hops *et al.*, 1979). The methods of utilizing peers, durations of training, and target populations have varied considerably. Thus, the extent to which peer training can optimize maintenance and transfer remains to be elaborated.

9. *Other procedures.* Other approaches to the development of maintenance and transfer focus on the set or cognitive style of the child. Proponents of these approaches assume that if the child acquires generalized performance strategy, the desired behaviors will be transsituational. For example, the development of problem-solving skills may yield durable and broad intervention effects. The precise effects of problem-solving training as a contributor to maintenance and transfer have not been well studied. Preliminary evidence has been promising. In one program for preschoolers, training in problem-solving skills was associated with improved ratings of social adjustment up to two years after treatment (Spivack & Shure, 1974).

In summary, generalization is an essential feature of all socioeducational programs such as social skills training. Without generalization of newly established repertoires, new social skills will probably be employed *only* in the training setting, which is rarely the goal of a training program. Most importantly, generalization should be programmed into the training process rather than just "hoped for." Therefore, the generalization facilitators previously described should be planned as an integral part of the social skills training program, since their inclusion will maximize the effectiveness and responsiveness of the training.

RECOMMENDATIONS

As with training in social skills, the best strategy, given current information, is to adopt a multifaceted approach to maximize the likelihood that behaviors will continue after training. Some general recommendations culled from the current evidence can be used with the training modules presented later in the text. First, training should be conducted until the child consistently performs target skills at a high level. Length of treatment may be an important factor, especially when severe skill deficits are evident. A review of the social skills literature on children suggests that treatments that are in effect for longer periods of time tend to produce more durable changes than briefer programs. Many programs have reported only a single or few sessions (e.g., Strain & Timm, 1974; Strain *et al.*, 1977). Others that last for several weeks or longer tend to produce more durable changes (e.g., Baer & Wolf, 1970; Michelson & Wood, 1980b; Shure & Spivack, 1974).

Second, practice outside of the training sessions is likely to increase the durability and generality of treatment effects. If training is restricted to a particular setting, such as the classroom, or to individual treatment sessions, specific activities or "homework" assignments should be programmed as part of treatment. *In vivo* practice can ensure that behaviors will occur in the situations that are likely to be most problematic.

Finally, persons who can help support the child's newly acquired behaviors should be incorporated into the training program. Parents and teachers can be especially helpful because they have access to a variety of situations where the child's interpersonal skills may be problematic. Parents and teachers both are in a position to provide models, prompts, immediate feedback, and reinforcement for performance. It may also be useful to incorporate peers into training. Direct incentives can be provided to peers for interacting with or for providing support and reinforcement of the behavior of the target child. Group contingencies may also be useful to ensure that trained behaviors are reinforced outside of the training situation. In general, a broad range of persons and situations should be incorporated into training. To the extent that this is accomplished, maintenance and generalization training effects are likely to be increased.

Conclusions

Several procedures have been utilized to develop social skills in children. Individual techniques that have been utilized including modeling, positive reinforcement, coaching, practice, and problem-solving training. The techniques make important and interrelated contributions toward the development of appropriate social interaction. For that reason, combinations of the different techniques are frequently utilized as parts of a larger social skills training package. The sequence of procedures begins with providing appropriate cues to indicate the requisite behaviors. Modeling, coaching, and instructions are usually utilized for this purpose. The child then is required to practice the behaviors. After behaviors are performed, feedback, reinforcement, and further coaching are provided. The sequence continues with additional opportunities for practice until the child develops the desired level of performance. The social skills training package is continued in this fashion until a range of desired behaviors has been addressed.

Issues of obvious importance are the maintenance and transfer of social skills beyond the training situation. Although social skills may be supported by the natural consequences in the environment, such as increased positive responding from peers, these consequences may not occur frequently or consistently enough immediately after training to sustain performance. Hence, it is essential to include training procedures that will promote maintenance and transfer. As a general strategy, training needs to incorporate several different situations and persons and to develop a response repertoire that is not restricted to a narrow set of conditions. Whenever possible, peers, parents, and teachers should be incorporated into the training program. The child can be given assignments to practice responses outside of the training situation. Also, adults and peers should be enlisted to prompt and reinforce behaviors in a variety of settings.

Overview—Training Modules

The subsequent materials deal exclusively with the effective implementation of the social skills training program. Training methods have been specifically structured to address the needs and communication styles of children. Of course, children's individual social abilities and skill levels will vary. Therefore, numerous examples have been provided in the materials that follow to satisfy a wide variety of children's needs and abilities. Trainers are also encouraged to devise additional examples and practice scenarios that might be particularly relevant for problematic social situations or deficient skill areas that are not specifically covered in this volume.

Because the term *social skills* covers a broad range of behaviors, this chapter will divide social behavior into 16 groupings or "modules." Elements of each module share a common theme that is considered to be an important component of children's daily repertoire of social behaviors. These themes all pertain to the child's ability as an individual to behave in a socially competent manner. Related topic areas such as nonverbal behavior, decision making, and conflict resolution have also been included because of their obvious relevance to successful interpersonal interactions.

MODULE DEVELOPMENT

Over the past five years the authors have been actively involved in assessing and promoting social competence in children. As a result of our clinical and research interests, numerous studies employing the procedures described in Chapter 3 were performed. After we had conducted several training programs, it became progressively apparent that the most efficient and effective strategy for teaching social skills would be through systematic development and application of modules. The development of the modules was the result of extensive social validation among children, parents, teachers, child psychologists, educators, and child–clinicians. The social validation process consisted of normative surveys, questionnaires, assessment (behavioral observation as well as peer, child, parent, and teacher reports) and several large-scale investigations (e.g., Mannarino, Michelson, & Marchione, 1982; Marchione, Michelson, & Mannarino, 1983; Michelson & Mannarino, in press; Michelson, Marchione, Stein, Figeruoa, & Beck, 1983; Michelson & Wood, 1980 a,b; Michelson, Wood, & Flynn, 1978; Sugai, 1978).

The modules, as presented herein, reflect the latest refinements. They have been subjected to continuous improvement as additional experience and feedback was obtained from a variety of applied settings. As previously mentioned, these modules have been investigated systematically and have demonstrated significant effects across normal, at-risk, maladjusted, outpatient, and inpatient populations of children (see immediately preceding citations). Moreover, in a recent investigation (Michelson, Marchione, Stein, Figeruoa, & Beck, 1983) this social competency program was shown to be highly effective and superior to cognitive problem solving, no training, and Rogerian treatment up to a one-year follow-up assessment.

In general, social skills that were consistently identified as being vital to the overall social competency of children were developed into separate modules. A review of the social skills literature (see Chapter 1) also provided further data supporting the importance of the specific modules. Specifically, retrospective studies of adults experiencing a wide variety of interpersonal and psychological disorders suggest that they were deficient in prosocial and assertive skills. Therefore, as can be seen in each module, children are instructed on the importance of behaving assertively as well as recognizing and eliminating passive or aggressive social behaviors. As the reader will discover, a variety of social responses are presented in the modules, with emphasis on behaving assertively. What constitutes an assertive, passive, or aggressive response warrants a brief discussion. The three styles of relating and their descriptions include the following:

1. *Assertive behavior* is defined as a response that recognizes the needs, feelings, and rights of both the speaker and the listener, without violating the same, and trying to achieve a positive and *mutually* satisfying solution that enhances short- and long-term relationships. The speaker expresses himself or herself without putting the listeners down or allowing his or her own rights or feelings to be denied or violated. The tone of an assertive response is honest, positive, nonpunitive, fair, considerate, direct, nondefensive, sensitive, and constructive.

2. *Passive behavior* is defined as a response in which the person's rights, feelings, needs, or opinions are ignored, violated, or suppressed. The person allows the other person to take advantage of them, control them, and subjugate them. The person does not violate the other person's rights but instead allows his or her feelings and needs to be disregarded. The tone of a passive response is self-effacing, timid, shy, and withdrawn, reflecting low self-esteem, a "mousy," self-depreciating style, and a low self-concept.

3. *Aggressive behavior* is defined as a response in which the speaker violates, ignores, or restricts the feelings, opinions, needs, or rights of the listener. The

person takes advantage of the listener, tries to boss or control him or her, or blocks the open expression of the other's feelings. The tone of an aggressive response is bossy, demanding, self-centered, insensitive, and callous, showing disregard for others' feelings. It is haughty, manipulative, intimidating, negativistic, punishing, and pushy.

Therefore, when trainers implement the modules, it is important for them to encourage participants to become familiar with the differences between passive–assertive–aggressive social behaviors. To facilitate consistency across modules, trainer scripts are provided. These present the appropriate assertive response as well as both passive and aggressive responses, which the children are then asked to identify. Children in our previous studies greatly enjoyed identifying the aggressive (Monster), passive (Mouse), or assertive (Me) responses (see Palmer, 1977). However, to avoid negative practice, only assertive scenarios are illustrated for the children's scripts.

The modules were designed and *sequenced* in a progressively more complex manner. Thus, earlier modules focus on simple social skills, while later modules describe more complex skills which are built on the more fundamental ones. For a discussion of related and specific clinical issues, the reader is referred to Chapter 5.

The modules follow a standard format. Each is made up of three main sections: *Rationale, Procedures,* and *Class Discussion.* The first section, "Rationale," provides the trainer with a descriptive definition of the target behavior. This section also offers an explanation, integrating current theory and research where relevant, of why that behavior is of particular importance for children. This section is followed by a lecture for the children and a listing of both the benefits children may gain by acquiring the particular skills and the pitfalls they may encounter if they are deficient in those attributes. In the presentation of a new topic area to children, it is important that these benefits and pitfalls be emphasized. By doing so, the trainer is able to underscore the usefulness and practicality of learning or improving upon these behaviors. This will help the child to understand the importance of learning these skills and participating in the program.

The section entitled *Sample Lecture for Children* includes the actual "teaching" component of the module and provides the trainer with a sample introductory lecture on the topic as well as suggested questions to stimulate class involvement. This "lecture" is intended to serve as an example of how the topic can be introduced and classroom discussion encouraged. Trainers may wish to adapt or modify this script, or even devise one of their own to help meet the needs of the population with which they are working. The sample lecture can also be modified to accomodate either individual or group training formats.

In addition to the sample lecture, the *Procedures* section includes suggested scripts to be used by trainers in modeling target behaviors and practice scripts for the children. These scripts, when used in conjunction with the training techniques described in Chapter 3, can provide children with observational and experiential learning material. The trainers' scripts detail situations and dialogue illustrating the theme of the module. The trainer, working in conjunction with instructional aides or student volunteers (if available), models how a person might respond to the scripted situation in assertive, passive, and aggressive modes. In the absence of another adult, the trainer can model alone, "playing" or enacting both speaker and recipient, or the script can be modeled with one of the children. Following this modeling, the trainer explains why each performance was appropriate or inappropriate.

Trainers should emphasize the assertive response as the positive one. With younger children, trainers can utilize the concept of the Mouse (passive), the Monster (aggressive), and Me (assertive), as described by Palmer (1977). Likewise, "Agor the Aggressive," "Peewee the Passive," and "(child's name) the Assertive" can be used to label performances and increase the interest and enthusiasm of participants. Our clinical experience strongly suggests that children enjoy utilizing these labels, and they may enhance generalization. Next, a second script enacted by only a few students follows the same scenario. However, this time the class or group provides the feedback to fellow participants, guided by comments, prompts, and reinforcement from the trainer. When the trainer determines that the children can both perform and discriminate between appropriate and inappropriate responses, behavior rehearsal procedures are implemented for the entire class.

We recommend that scripts provided in the *Procedures* section be rehearsed directly. Each module includes general scripts that children can practice among themselves. Generally, scripts are designed for dyadic interaction, so that a large number of children can participate using a multiple small-group format with two to five participants in each group. Class or group members should be instructed to find a partner or be assigned one randomly and should choose one of the roles defined in the script. After the scenario has been rehearsed several times, the children should discuss why the particular behavior was appropriate. *Modules consist of appropriate responses only.* When this is completed, they should reverse their roles and rehearse the script several more times. Children may inadvertantly alter modules by use of inappropriate voice intonation or nonverbal gestures. In these situations, feedback from the trainer to the group can label the behavior (as passive or aggressive). Then the trainer reenacts the scenario in appropriate manner, following this modeling with an explanation. This is also followed by a discussion of the interaction. The trainer and any available assistants should observe the behavioral rehearsal phase and provide abundant positive feedback. This section is complete after all the practice scripts have been rehearsed and the trainer is confident that the children understand why and know how to behave in the specific social situation. To improve nonverbal communication skills, children may read the practice scripts for a particular skill and then practice the same assertive scenario without the use of scripts. This procedure approximates a "true" interaction by using eye contact, posturing, and improved spontaneity of verbal intonation.

The last section, *Class Discussion*, allows the class to regroup in order to discuss what they have been practicing. At this time, it is important for trainers to ask students about any difficulties that they might have encountered and to point out any problem areas that they have observed. This is followed by a general summary statement by the trainer that reiterates important aspects on topic areas, including definition, rationale, and benefits. Finally, suggested homework assignments are included at the end of each training module. As indicated, these homework assignments are optional; they are to be used at the discretion of the trainer. Trainers are encouraged to assign homework that might be of particular relevance to the population they are working with, as this would enhance the use of newly learned social skills outside the training session. Typically, assignments involve *in vivo* observation and practice of social behaviors and interactions covered in the training modules. Homework assignments are easy, nonthreatening, and generally require only a modest amount of time. When homework is assigned, trainers should review prescribed assignments and discuss them with students at the beginning of the subsequent training session. (Optional: A review of prior modules has been found useful at the beginning of each session prior to or following homework discussion. When time allows after discussion and homework assignment, children enjoy using this as an "imagination" period. The pairs that previously modeled a particular behavior through scripts are given the opportunity to enact a brief scenario from their own experiences that illustrates utilizing the assertive response. The children, as with previous modeling, provide reasons for appropriate responses. The children enjoy the opportunity to enact their new-found skills for the class or group; this also provides an opportunity to review and insure that the material has been assimilated from previous sessions.)

Training Format

To provide greater clarification, an outline of the training format is provided (see Table 1). Please note that specific training techniques are discussed in Chapter 3. Sample lectures and scripts are included in each module to convey the material using instruction, practice, feedback, modeling and reinforcement.

TABLE 1. An Outline of the Training Format

I. Rationale for trainer

II. Sample lecture for children
    A. Introduce topic
    B. Rationale
        1. Benefits
        2. Pitfalls

III. Modeling (with and without scripts)
    A. Between trainers
    B. Between trainer and children

Continued

TABLE 1 (*Continued*)

C. Between two children at the front of
   the class
   1. Feedback from trainer
   2. Reinforcement
   3. Feedback from class

D. Group discussion

IV. Behavioral rehearsal (with and without
    scripts—entire class)

   A. Role playing

   B. Role reversal

   C. Trainer's feedback

   D. Small-group discussion

V. Class discussion

   A. Feedback from trainer

   B. Summary and review

VI. Homework assignments

   A. Review of homework assignments
      (during next lesson period)

Social Skills Training Modules

MODULE 1: INTRODUCTION TO SOCIAL SKILLS

RATIONALE FOR TRAINER

When we speak of effective social skills, we are referring to repertoires of social behaviors that, when used in social interaction, tend to evoke positive reinforcement and generally result in positive outcomes. Acquisition of social skills prepares an individual for competent and effective participation in diverse aspects of human interaction. Thus, social skills training is, in essence, a program designed to teach and enhance communication and interpersonal skills, both implicit and explicit.

The term *social skills* denotes two basic, but nevertheless important concepts. First, *social* implies an interpersonal process. The nature of the interaction can range from the simple to the highly complex. However, as noted earlier (Chapter 1), social phenomena are generally quite intricate and are comprised of overt verbal and nonverbal responses, cognitive mediational processes. They require proper attention with regard to timing, exchange, and integration, if they are to be successful.

Second, the use of the word *skills* is both deliberate and necessary. Specifically, as social beings, we acquire the vast majority of our social repertoires through learning, typically in the form of modeling, rehearsal, instruction, corrective feedback, and so on. There are few, if any, identified genetically or physiologically "hard-wired" circuits for either specific or general social behaviors among humans. Therefore, the term skill is repeatedly used and emphasized as a means of arriving at a consensus that these vital yet fragile skills are indeed acquired via learning. Thus, the consistent use of the term *social skills* fosters the idea that these invaluable interpersonal competencies can and should be taught on a systematic basis using learning principles and techniques. It is not sufficient, as evidenced by the incidence and prevalence of childhood, adolescent, and adulthood-related problems, merely to rely on random forces to facilitate social competency. Indeed, the evidence supports the active use of social skills intervention programs as a potent means of facilitating childhood adaptation.

The importance of social skills training extends into two primary areas, both of which are related to the mental health of the individual: (1) *remediation* of existing deficits and (2) *prevention* of future deficits. Historically, programs teaching social behaviors were aimed at adults and tended to focus on existing social skills deficits (i.e., dating anxiety and socially related phobias) and selected aspects of psychiatric disorders (i.e., depression, alcoholism, and schizophrenia). More recently, investigators have demonstrated the utility of social skills training as a preventive model, with programs designed to encourage and expand on the natural, ongoing process of social maturation. The preventive approach prepares the youngster for the intricacies of human interaction by formalizing the development of successful social repertoires. The socially skilled child is better able to develop and thrive in today's complex social environment. Therefore, social skills training need not be thought of exclusively as a remedial program but can and should also be applied as a preventive strategy.

SAMPLE LECTURE ON SOCIAL SKILLS

Today, we are going to discuss what is known as "social skills." What this means is how we behave and what we say when we are with others. You all know that there are "good ways" and "bad ways" to talk to people. By learning social skills, you learn about the good, or appropriate, ways to do this. A boy or girl who has good social skills usually has more friends and better friendships than one who does not. If you have good social skills, you probably get along better with your teachers, your classmates, and members of your family than someone who does not have good social skills. It is important to learn these skills because they make you happier and result in fewer problems with others.

There are many different types of social skills that are good to know because there are many different situations where it is important to behave and talk appropriately (correctly). For instance, the way you talk to a friend on the playground is going to be different from the way you would talk to your teacher or your parents. You probably speak with your parents differently from the way you would speak to your teacher. The way that you speak to someone who is sad is probably going to be different from when someone is happy. Even when you are angry, you have to be careful about what you say, depending on who it is that you are talking to. So, it is important to know how to talk and behave in different situations with different people.

The word *social* means how we get along with others, including friends, brothers and sisters, parents, and teachers. The word *skill* means an ability or talent that you have learned or developed from practicing how to do something better and better. So, as you have probably guessed by now, social skills refers to how good we are at getting along with others. As you can imagine, there are a lot of different types of social skills. For example, there are very simple ones such as complimenting someone when you like something about them; then there are the more difficult ones like having to say "no" to a friend in a way that won't make them angry when he or she asks for a favor. Sometimes you want to settle a problem with a friend but you don't know what to do, that's a social skill, too. So, the purpose of speaking with you today is to talk about why social skills are important, find out what you think about them. Then, we will all take a turn practicing several social skills.

We will be meeting regularly to learn these skills to help you get along with others in a better way and you will hopefully find that this will make you feel happier about yourself and others will be happier with you too. Can anyone give me some examples of social skills? Well, social skills cover a variety of different areas. Some of the ones we will be discussing are: compliments, complaints, refusing unreasonable request, sharing feelings, standing up for your rights, requesting favors, requesting behavior change from others, conflict resolution, getting along with the opposite sex, dealing with adults, and related topics.

One of the basic ideas in social skills training is for you to learn how to tell the difference between passive, aggressive, and assertive social behavior. When someone acts passive, they don't express themselves. They behave like a mouse. They let other children boss them around, tell them what to do, and generally don't stand up for their rights. Their needs, opinions, or feelings are usually ignored, and other children may take advantage of them.

At the other extreme are children who, are aggressive or *monsters*. They are bossy and bully others. They pick on and put down other children. They only care about getting what *they* want, when *they* want it. They rarely care about how others feel and often get into trouble or fights. These children tend to take unfair advantage of others and usually have very few real friends.

So, it's pretty clear that both passive and aggressive social behaviors are not the best way to get along with others. They either lead to being hurt (mouses) or hurting others (monsters). I'm sure you know kids who behave like a mouse or monster, and it's fair to say that they are not usually happy people. Monsters have to be tough while mouses have to hide all the time. Today, I will introduce a new word and explain its importance. The word is *assertive*. *Assertiveness* refers to behaving not as a mouse, not as a monster—but as yourself. That is, to be assertive means to let others know how you feel and what you think in a way that doesn't offend them, but still lets you express yourself. You can recognize and respect their feelings, opinions, and desires so that you neither force yourself on others nor allow others to take advantage of you. It also, means standing up for your rights and always trying to be fair, just, and honest. To be assertive is not just a matter of "good manners." It is a way of acting toward others that lets them know your feelings and ideas without running over or ignoring theirs. Ideally, if *all* of us acted assertively, instead of like mouses or monsters, we would rarely, if ever fight, lose friends, or be afraid of being with others.

So, for the entire training program we will be using the terms "mouse," "monster," and "assertive." To help you become more assertive, we'll call assertive "me" from now on. Now, I'll be describing some social situations, and I would like all of you to listen carefully so we can try to tell the difference between the "mouse," "monster," and "me" social behaviors.

(*Optional:* At this point, the leader might indicate his or her social style using the three alternatives mentioned above. After which, the leader should then ask the children individually to undertake the same description. This encourages participation and maintains interest. In dealing with younger children, a touch of humor or drama to describe the "monster" or "mouse" during the initial discussion might also enhance interest.)

DISCUSSION QUESTIONS

1. Can anyone tell me what social skills are?
2. Why are social skills important?
3. Can you give me examples of situations where it is good to have social skills? Why?

OR

4. Can you give me examples of situations in which it is important to watch what you say and how you say it? Why?

Every time we speak to another person or group of people, it is important to keep in mind that what we say and *how* we say it can influence their reaction and what they will think of us. For example, if your friend's dog ran away and he or she was feeling bad, it probably would *not* be a good idea to say "Oh, cheer up! That mutt was dirty and ugly! He did you a favor by running away." Chances are, after saying that, you would have one less friend. Similarly, if your teacher announced that she has won a prize, you would not say, "Anyone can win that thing"; or "I think someone else deserved it more than you." As you can see, in both of these examples, someone said the wrong thing.

Knowing how to respond and say the right thing in these situations is called being socially skilled.

DISCUSSION QUESTIONS

1. How do you think the other person felt?
2. How might the other person react?
3. Can you give me several examples of things that would have been better to say? (At least 3)
4. Which one was the best thing to say? Why?

RATIONALE FOR CHILDREN

Benefits. When you have good social skills,
A. You develop a better understanding of others.
B. You understand yourself better.
C. You communicate better with others.
D. You make more friends and get to know the friends you already have better.
E. It is easier to join in on fun activities (e.g., clubs, games, etc.).
F. You can play a more important part in your family and be more involved in family decisions.
G. You may do better academically, have fewer problems with friends or peers, and show better adjustment later in life.
H. You may be better liked by teachers and classmates.
I. You may tend to be more popular, more likable, and a happier person.

Pitfalls. By having poor social skills,
A. You might not be able to communicate your needs or feelings to other people very well.
B. It might be more difficult to make new friends and to keep the friends you already have.
C. Others will find it difficult to understand you.
D. You could end up being left out of important or fun things that are happening (conversations, activities, etc.).
E. You may get lonely, lose friends, get into trouble with adults.

TRAINER'S SCRIPT

Now that you have an idea of what social skills are, I am going to show you a few more examples of some good and not-so-good social skills. Later, you can practice the good social skills on your own.

62

CHAPTER 5

The Importance of Social Skills

Situation 1. You suspect that a friend borrowed one of your books without asking first. You might say:

YOU: Excuse me, Tom/Betty, but did you borrow my math book? I can't find it anywhere.

FRIEND: Oh, yeah! I hope you don't mind. I just needed it for one problem.

YOU: Sure, it's OK for you to borrow it, but please ask me first. That way I won't think it's lost.

FRIEND: OK. I guess I was in a hurry.

(Assertive)—This is a good assertive response because
1. you avoid making your friend angry.
2. you will probably get your book back.
3. this will stop the same kind of problem from happening again because now your friend knows you want him/her to ask you before taking your book next time.

YOU: Gee, I sure wish I could find my math book. I hope nobody took it.

FRIEND: Oh, I borrowed it. I knew you wouldn't mind.

YOU: Whew! I thought I lost it.

FRIEND: Don't worry, I have it.

(Passive)—This was a passive and less desirable answer because
1. you didn't say what you really wanted to.
2. your friend may take advantage of you again in the future because he/she didn't understand that this behavior bothered you.
3. you may not get your book back.

YOU: All right! I caught you stealing my math book!

FRIEND: Are you serious? I was only borrowing it.

YOU: Sure you were (*sarcastically*): Thanks for asking!

FRIEND: Here, take your old book back!

(Aggressive)—This answer was aggressive because
1. you didn't say what you really wanted to.
2. your friend might be angry at you in the future and act the same way.
3. you might lose a friend because you verbally attacked and embarrassed him/her.

Situation 2. Your parents ask you to wash the dishes tonight.

YOU: I did them the last two nights. Isn't it (brother/sister's) turn?

PARENT: I guess you're right. I thought she/he did them last night.
YOU: No, I did—so can I go out (and play)?
PARENT: All right, go ahead.

> (Assertive)—This is appropriately assertive because
> 1. you explained your situation without arguing, whining, or being passive.
> 2. you were not disrespectful.

YOU: No! I'm not doing them tonight. You can make someone else do them!
PARENT: Don't you talk like that to me!
YOU: Well, it's not fair. You always make me do the dishes.
PARENT: Stop exaggerating and finish the dishes!

> (Aggressive)—This is an aggressive reply because
> 1. you failed to express your reason for not wanting to do the dishes.
> 2. you didn't give your parents a chance to explain their side of the story and you were disrespectful.
> 3. the response wasn't very effective because you had to do the dishes anyway.

Practice Scripts

Situation 1. A friend asks you to do a favor for him.

FRIEND: Would you mind helping me rake the yard after school?
YOU: Gee, I wish I could, but I've got to meet my mother later on.
OR
> I don't think I can, sorry.

Situation 2. A group of your friends are talking about last night's football game. You want to join them.

YOU: I saw that game, too! It was really great. Is anyone going to the game next week?

Situation 3. A store clerk gives you the wrong amount of change back.

YOU: Excuse me, but I think this is wrong. Don't I get back 20 cents?
CLERK: Well, let me check.

Situation 4. Your teacher tells you that you got the highest grade on your test.

YOU: Thanks, Mr. Smith. I did study pretty hard.
TEACHER: Well, it shows. Keep up the good work.

Situation 5. Some boys/girls at the playground tell you that you're too short to play basketball with them.

YOU: I have just as much right to play here as you do. Besides, you don't have to be tall to be good.
THEM: All right, let's see what you can do.

Situation 6. Somebody is smoking cigarettes next to you on the bus and it's making you cough.

YOU: Excuse me, would you mind not smoking? It's really bothering me.
SMOKER: Oh, I'm sorry. Sure, no problem.

Situation 7. Your brother looks unhappy and you want to know what the problem is.

YOU: Hi, is something bothering you? You look kind of sad.
BROTHER: Yeah, I didn't make the soccer team.
YOU: I'm sorry to hear that. Can you try again later?

SUGGESTED HOMEWORK ASSIGNMENTS

1. There are many times each day that you might use your social skills. Describe two of these. For each situation:
   a. Describe the situation.
   b. What was said?
   c. Were good social skills used? Why? Why not?
   d. How could you have said/done something better? Why?
2. Try to list as many situations as you can in which social skills play an important part. (You can use the examples from the lesson.)

Module 2: Compliments

Rationale for Trainer

Compliments make almost everyone feel good. There are two components of complimenting, *giving* and *receiving*. The ability to give positive and honest feedback to others has a number of benefits for both the giver and receiver. The importance of providing compliments in social relationships has been widely acknowledged in the literature. Children who can give honest compliments to their peers, parents, and teachers receive similar reinforcement in return. This cycle of giving and receiving social reinforcement helps to increase one's popularity, social involvement, and academic performance.

Sample Lecture on Compliments

Today we are going to discuss *giving* and *receiving* compliments. By *giving* compliments we mean saying something positive or nice to another person. Giving and receiving compliments makes most people feel good about themselves. Not only do *you* like to hear nice things about yourself—your friends, parents, and teachers also like to hear nice things about themselves. It is important to remember two key points when you give a compliment. First, you must be sincere; that is, you must *really* mean what you say. Second, you must use good timing. For instance, you wouldn't give a compliment in the middle of an argument.

Discussion Questions
1. Can anyone give me an example of a compliment?
2. Can anyone give me an example of when they gave someone else a compliment?
3. What happened? (How did that person feel? How did he or she react?)
4. How did you feel when you were complimented?

When you accept a compliment you feel good about yourself. Accepting a compliment is important for a number of reasons. When you accept a compliment, you are letting the other person know that you appreciate and like what he or she is saying. Not accepting a compliment makes the other people feel that you don't care about what they are saying or that you don't trust their opinions.

How do you feel when someone gives you a compliment? (Ask children to raise hands if it is true from them.)

1. Do you feel silly or embarrassed?
2. Do you feel happy?
3. Do you wonder what to say?
4. Do you give a compliment back?
5. Do you put yourself down?
6. Do you pretend you don't hear it?

RATIONALE FOR CHILDREN

Benefits.   When you give a compliment

A. you help other people feel good about themselves.
B. you let others know what you like about them.
C. you feel good because you can say something nice to another person.

By accepting compliments

A. you can make the giver feel that you appreciate what he or she is saying.
B. you know what others like about you.
C. you can feel good about yourself.

Pitfalls.   Not accepting compliments can lead to

A. your feeling bad about yourself.
B. your putting yourself down.
C. making givers feel bad because you have put down their opinions and feelings, so they may not want to compliment you again.

Not giving compliments

A. can lead to your not saying nice things you might really want to say.
B. doesn't let other people know what you like about them.
C. may lead others to feel you don't like them.
D. reduces the chance that others will want to compliment you.

TRAINER'S SCRIPT: GIVING COMPLIMENTS

As you probably know, giving and receiving compliments is not always easy. Because it is so important, it would be a good thing to learn to do. What we'll do today is to practice giving and receiving compliments. First, I'll show you some examples; then you will have a chance to practice on your own.

Situation 1.   Someone has completed a project which you think is very good.

YOU: I really liked your project.
OTHER: Thanks, I worked hard on it.
YOU: I thought it was really interesting.
OTHER: I enjoyed working on it; it was fun. Thanks.

(Assertive)—This statement was assertive because
1. you've told the person about your positive feelings in a pleasant, honest way.
2. you were believable—you didn't say it in an exaggerated manner.

YOU: Is that your project?
OTHER: Yes, that's mine.
YOU: Oh.

(Passive)—This statement was passive because
1. you didn't say how you felt about the project.
2. you didn't let the other person know that you were appreciative of their work.

Situation 2.   You see a person you really like.

YOU: I think you're a really nice person
OR
  I like doing things with you.
OTHER: Thanks.

(Assertive)—This statement was assertive because
1. you made your feelings known in a pleasant, simple manner.
2. you probably made the other person feel good because you let them know that you liked them.

YOU: You're really the greatest person in the world!
OTHER: Oh. C'mon. Don't be silly.

(Aggressive)—This statement was aggressive because

1. you exaggerated the compliment, which makes it hard to believe you.
2. the other person may feel that you are making fun of him/her.

TRAINER'S SCRIPT: RECEIVING COMPLIMENTS

Situation 3.   Someone has commented on a project that you made.

OTHER: Hey, I really like your project.
YOU: Thanks, I worked hard on it

OR

  I'm glad you like it.
  (Assertive)—This response was assertive because
  1. you have accepted the compliment in a nice way.
  2. you let the person giving the compliment know that you appreciated what they said.

OTHER: Hey, I really like your project.
YOU: It wasn't so hot.
OTHER: I thought it was pretty good.
YOU: No, not really.

  (Passive)—This response was passive because
  1. you have made the other person feel silly for being nice.
  2. you have questioned the other person's judgment about your project.

OTHER: Hey, I really like your project.
YOU: Yeah, it was the best!
OTHER: I thought it was interesting.
YOU: You better believe it was, cause I did it!

  (Aggressive)—This was aggressive because
  1. your response doesn't acknowledge the other person's compliment.
  2. you seem to be conceited.

Situation 4.   Someone says the following to you.

OTHER: I think you're really nice.

YOU: Thanks.

OR

That was nice of you to say.

(Assertive)—This response was assertive because
1. you have accepted the compliment in a nice manner and made the other person feel good, too.

OTHER: I think you're really nice.
YOU: (Blushing, acting embarrassed, make no comment.)

OR

Ah, C'mon.

(Passive)—This response was passive because
1. you didn't respond to their compliment.
2. you might make the other person feel silly because you didn't appreciate what they said.

OTHER: I think you're really nice.
YOU: Yeh, I am the best, I can't be beat!

(Aggressive)—This response was aggressive because
1. you have overreacted to their compliment.
2. you have made it hard for the other person to offer other kinds of positive statements.
3. it seems like you are bragging, and this may turn off the other person.

PRACTICE SCRIPTS

The following scripts present situations that demonstrate giving and receiving of compliments.

Situation 1. You see a friend at a party and he/she looks really good. You want to let him/her know that you like the way he/she is dressed.

YOU: You really look nice.
OTHER: Thank you.

Situation 2. After spending the afternoon with a new classmate, you want to tell him how you feel.

YOU: I'm glad we played together. It was fun. I think you're really a nice person.

OTHER: That's nice of you to say. Thanks.
                            OR
        Makes me feel good to hear that. Thanks.

Situation 3.   A friend of yours helps you find some money that you lost.

YOU: I think what you did was really great! Thanks for your help.
OTHER: You're welcome.
                            OR
        Nice of you to say so.

Situation 4.   You have helped an older person carry some groceries up the stairs to his apartment.

OTHER: It was nice of you to help me with these groceries. Thank you.
YOU: You're welcome; I was happy to help.

Situation 5.   After a hard game of tennis, your friend compliments you.

OTHER: You played a great game.
YOU: Thanks, I really worked hard for that last point.

Situation 6.   Your friend studies hard and receives the highest grade on the math test.

YOU: You did a really good job on the test.
OTHER: Thank you.

Situation 7.   In gym class, one of the students runs over a mile.

YOU: You're a good runner.
OTHER: Thank you. I practice every day.
YOU: Well, you sure did a good job.

Situation 8.   While walking home from school, your friend helps a younger boy who stumbled and fell.

YOU: It was nice of you to help that little kid.
OTHER: Thanks. He's o.k. He just scraped his knee.
YOU: He's lucky that you were around.

Situation 9.   Someone shoves a child during recess. You tell him/her to stop.

friend: You did a good job of defending that kid.
YOU: Thanks. I don't like to see anyone being pushed around.

Suggested Homework Assignments

1. Give a sincere compliment to one member of your family every day.
2. Give at least one sincere compliment to each of your teachers.
3. Give at least one sincere compliment to a friend.
4. When you receive a compliment, notice how you feel (proud, embarrassed, etc.) and what you do. How did you make the other person feel?

Module 3: Complaints

Often, people who complain are thought of as rude, abrasive, or insensitive. However, making complaints is an important social skill that requires tact and timing and that should have a positive purpose. Some mental health experts have suggested that making complaints serves as a controlled means of preventing displays of frustration and anger. Children who are able to use complaints constructively have the ability to verbalize their concerns and to rectify aversive conditions in their environments. The rewards for using complaints can be twofold. First, making complaints serves to eliminate or reduce irritation and distress, thus contributing to the child's general sense of well-being. Second, children who have organized and verbalized complaints are more objective and open-minded when they receive complaints from others. By analyzing the content of a complaint that someone is making to us, we learn about things we are doing that affect others adversely. An appropriate response to a complaint will often improve the nature of the immediate interaction and will give us information on how we might behave differently in future interactions.

Sample Lecture on Complaints

Making a Complaint.   Today we are going to talk about complaints, why they are necessary, and how they can sometimes be good to make. A complaint is a statement about someone or something that you don't like. However, the best and fastest way to correct a problem, or whatever it is that bothers you, is to let the person or people responsible know that you are unhappy. This is how we use a complaint. It is important to remember, though, that when a person complains to you, it is probably because he or she wants to make things better with you. You should use a complaint only to make things better, never as a way of hurting others or making them feel bad.

Discussion Questions

1. Can anyone give me an example of a complaint?
2. Do *you* have anything that you would like to complain about?

3. How do you feel after you have made a complaint?
4. What happened after you complained? (How did the other person react? did the situation change?)

When Others Complain to You.   Learning how to react to somebody else's complaint is just as important as learning how to make complaints. It is not very easy to listen to other people tell you about things you do or say that they don't like or that causes them to feel hurt. Sometimes, listening to other people's complaints can save a friendship or maybe even start a new one. This does not mean that you have to believe every word they are telling you, but it does show them that you respect them enough to listen to what they have to say. You can learn a lot about yourself, as well as the person who is complaining, by listening to and thinking about what that person has to say.

DISCUSSION QUESTIONS

1. Has anyone complained to you about something you have said or done?
2. How did you feel? Did you feel (ask children to raise their hands if it is true for them)
   a. Angry or mad
   b. Embarrassed or silly
   c. Sad or unhappy
   d. Like fighting
   e. Thankful
3. Could the person who complained to you have done so in a better way? How?

You see, most complaints can really be made in a nice way, so that people probably won't get mad at you because you have hurt their feelings. It is much easier to listen to complaints if they are made correctly, because then our feelings are not hurt.

DISCUSSION QUESTIONS

1. Does anyone here know somebody who complains a lot?
2. What do you think about a person who complains "all the time"?
3. What does that tell you about how to use complaints?

Complaints can be good if they are used only when necessary. If they are used too often, people will think you are a "complainer" and will not pay attention to you. So when you have a complaint, it is important to make sure that it is really necessary. If your complaint is necessary and important, you will probably get a better response from the person with whom you are speaking.

RATIONALE FOR CHILDREN

Benefits. By making a positive, constructive complaint, you

A. help to reduce sources of irritation and dislike between you and others.
B. can improve your relationships with others.
C. let others know that you care enough about them to share your feelings.
D. can sometimes help to make things better or safer for you and others (i.e., complaining about poor service).

By listening to others complain, you

A. let them know that you are interested in what they have to say.
B. can learn about the problems that might be hurting your social life (i.e., your weak points).

Pitfalls. Not making a complaint when it is appropriate to do so can lead to

A. feeling frustrated with yourself.
B. getting unnecessarily angry with the other person.
C. increased problems between yourself and others.

Not listening or paying attention to other's complaints

A. might result in other people avoiding you.
B. can make them angry or frustrated with you for not caring.
C. might not help you to learn what it is that you do that bothers other people.

TRAINER'S SCRIPT

Now that we've shown how and when to use complaints to make bad situations better, it is important to practice both making and listening to complaints. First, I'll show you some examples of how to make and receive complaints and then you'll have a chance to practice on your own.

GIVING COMPLAINTS

Situation 1.   Your friend returns a book he/she borrowed, and the pages are wrinkled from something being spilled on them.

YOU: These pages are all wrinkled! They weren't like this when I loaned you the book. What happened?
FRIEND: My little brother spilled milk on the book when I was reading it. I'm sorry. Maybe I should get you a new one.
YOU: Well okay, and then I'll give you this one.

(Assertive)—This response was assertive because
1. you have expressed your disappointment about your book being ruined.
2. you gave the other person a chance to explain.
3. you let the other person know that you weren't happy and the next time they will probably take better care of your book.

YOU: My book doesn't look quite the same.
FRIEND: What do you mean?
YOU: Oh, nothing in particular.
FRIEND: It's the same book that you loaned me last week.

(Passive)—This response was passive because
1. you didn't say what you meant so your friend doesn't understand.
2. you didn't give the other person a chance to explain so you may be left with angry, frustrated feelings.
3. the incident will probably happen again because you didn't let the other person know that you didn't like the condition of your book.

YOU: You ruined my book!
FRIEND: No, I didn't! It was like that before.
YOU: You liar, it was perfect when I loaned it to you.
FRIEND: You're crazy. Don't blame me for your old book.

(Aggressive)—This response was aggressive because
1. you accused the other person and didn't give him/her a chance to explain.
2. you made your friend feel bad and angry at you.
3. you didn't really explain what was wrong with the book or suggest a way of repairing the damage.
4. you are left feeling frustrated and angry.

Situation 2. Someone has said something that hurts your feelings.

YOU: You know (name), I feel pretty bad about what you said about me yesterday. Please don't say it again.
OTHER: Gee, I'm sorry. I didn't think it would bother you that much.

(Assertive)—This response was assertive because
1. you made it clear how you feel.
2. you've given the other person a chance to "patch" up the problem.
3. the other person may avoid hurting your feelings in the future.

YOU: Hey (name), you didn't really mean what you said the other day, did you?
OTHER: Well, I guess not. (not convincing)

(Passive)—This response was passive because
1. you didn't say what you really meant.
2. you're forcing the other person to answer rather than giving him a chance to explain.
3. the other person does not understand how you feel and, therefore, might make the same mistake again.

YOU: You know (name), that was mean thing you said yesterday. I'm really mad. You're a jerk!
OTHER: Oh, yeah? Well, I meant every word of it!

(Aggressive)—This response is aggressive because
1. you probably made the other person angry by attacking the person instead of the problem.
2. you did not give the other person a chance to explain.
3. the other person does not understand how you feel; therefore, he/she might make the same mistake again.

PRACTICE SCRIPTS

Situation 1. Some children sitting behind you are making it hard for you to hear the teacher.

YOU: I can't hear the teacher. Could you please not talk so loud?
OTHER: Sorry. I'll try to be a little more quiet.

Situation 2. You see a friend making fun of one of your classmates.

YOU: I don't think you should tease (name). He's starting to feel bad.
OTHER: I didn't realize it even bothered him. I guess you're right.

Situation 3. You are late for a movie because one of your friends arrived late.

OTHER: (Name), I just wanted to let you know that when you are late we all have to wait to get started.
YOU: I'm sorry. I'll try to be on time from now on.

OR

I didn't know that it caused that much trouble.
I'm sorry.

Situation 4. You overhear a friend saving some bad things about another girl.

OTHER: You know (name), if you didn't say such nasty things about other people, they would invite you to play with them more often.
YOU: Really? I didn't know that I was doing that. I'll be more careful about what I say.

Situation 5. Sometimes it's important to complain about things that are done to you but that the other person may not be aware of. In this situation, it is important to avoid being harsh.
  The cashier at the grocery store gives you an incorrect amount of change.

YOU: Excuse me, Mr. Smith, I don't think you gave me the right amount of change. Would you please recheck this?
MR. SMITH: Oh, yes. Let's see, you're right. I owe you 35 cents.

Situation 6. Someone has made you angry because of something he just said.

YOU: You know (name), when you say that, it makes me mad because it's not very fair.
OTHER: I'm sorry it bothers you, but I'm not sure of what I said that makes you mad.

Situation 7. You are playing tennis in gym and your partner keeps hitting the ball high and out of the court.

YOU: I don't like to chase the ball all the time. Would you like me to show you a better way to hit it?

PARTNER: I guess I could use some help. I can't seem to hit the ball right.

Situation 8.   Your friend returns three albums that he/she borrowed and one is scratched.

YOU: (Name), my record was scratched when you returned it yesterday.

FRIEND: Are you sure? It played okay for me.

YOU: Yes, it's a pretty big scratch. I think you should replace it.

Situation 9.   You walk into class and see your friend writing in your notebook.

YOU: I don't like it when you borrow my things and don't ask first.

FRIEND: I only borrowed it for a few minutes.

YOU: Next time just ask me first. You know I'd loan you paper any time you want. I just want to know first.

Situation 10.   You and a classmate are given an assignment to work on a project. He isn't doing any work.

YOU: You know, we're suppose to make this project together and you're not doing your part.

CLASSMATE: What do you want me to do?

YOU: Well, if you could finish this part that would be fair.

SUGGESTED HOMEWORK ASSIGNMENTS

1. Write down at least two things that bother you and that you should have complained about.
2. Watch your friends or family to see how they use complaints. Are they used in a way that avoids making the other person angry?
3. While watching television, write down some situations that people are complaining or should be complaining about. What would you have said? How would you have answered? How would you have answered the complaint?

Module 4: Refusal or Saying No

Saying no is not always easy to do. Sometimes a person might feel that it is not possible to refuse a friend or relative. The ability to refuse another's requests in a tactful and nonpunitive fashion requires much skill. The person who consistently gives in to other people's requests, regardless of whether they are appropriate or not, is sometimes regarded as a "mouse," a "pushover." By saying no, when appropriate, a person expresses how he/she feels regarding a request or invitation. Researchers have found that individuals who lack the ability to refuse requests often feel disappointed, frustrated, and resentful.

Children who learn to refuse requests appropriately gain more control over their own social interactions. Exercising the right to refuse a request can also help children understand better the importance of their contribution in acknowledging a request. Thus, the social reinforcement gained by the youngster in honoring a request is bolstered by the self-reinforcement that can result from the proper refusal of a request. Furthermore, along with the successful acquisition of this social skill can come the realization and understanding that *being* refused need not be felt as hurtful or demeaning.

Sample Lecture on Refusal

Today we are going to discuss what *refusal* is and how to use it correctly. To *refuse* is to be able to say no in a nice way when somebody asks you to do something. I'm sure that there have been times when each of you has been asked to do something that you didn't want to do or that you knew you shouldn't do. For instance, one day you could be watching your favorite show on television, one you have been waiting all week for. Just then, your best friend comes by and asks you to walk him to the store. What would you do?

Well, you could say "Get lost, I'm busy" and probably lose your friend; you could go with him and end up feeling angry about missing your show; or you could say no, but in such a way that you wouldn't hurt your friend's feelings. Can anyone here tell me how you could do that?

POSSIBLE RESPONSES

"Why don't you watch this show with me and then we can go."
"Gee, I'm sorry, but I can't go now. I could go a little later on, though."
"I'm sorry, I really can't right now."
"I want to finish watching this program; then I'll be glad to go."

There are ways of saying no that are less likely to hurt the other person's feelings. That is why it is important to learn how to make a refusal correctly. It really means finding a nice and polite way to say no, such as "I'd rather not do that."

DISCUSSION QUESTIONS

1. Can anyone give me an example of a time when they had to or should have made a refusal (said no)?
2. What happened
   a. When you said no politely?
   b. When you got mad at the person and said no?
   c. When you said yes when you wanted to say no?
3. How did you feel or how do you think you would feel after saying no or refusing properly?

Now let's look at what happens to the person who is asking you for a favor. Pretend that you are the one who wants somebody to walk to the store with you, but your friend wants to watch the television show. How would you feel if she did not know how to refuse in a nice polite way and just said "no," or "get lost"? You would probably feel hurt or mad. What if your friend told you that she wanted to watch the show first and then go with you? Well, you might feel a little disappointed, but at least you would know why your friend said no and that she thought enough of you to go with you after the show.

When saying no, you must choose both the right words so you can say it in a nice way and also the right time to speak up. If your parents or teachers ask or tell you to do something, you must be careful not to be disrespectful. It is not right to say no just to act smart or because you are mad.

RATIONALE FOR CHILDREN

Benefits.   By making a refusal or saying no

A. you let others know where you stand and how you feel.

B. you can help to prevent people from taking advantage of you.
C. you feel good because you do not have to do something you don't want to do.
D. you are less likely to be asked a second time to do something that you don't want to do something that is wrong.

Pitfalls.   By not refusing or by not learning how to say no

A. you might end up doing something you do not like, which could make you feel angry, frustrated, or unhappy.
B. you could end up doing something that may get you into trouble (like going out and playing when you should be studying, or cutting classes when friends ask you to skip school).
C. you could be giving other people (children) the wrong impression about the kind of person you are or the kinds of things you like to do.

Trainer's Script

As you will see, making a refusal is not always easy, even though it is important to do. Because it is a good thing to be able to do, we are going to practice different ways of saying no. First I'll give you a few examples of refusing requests and then you will have a chance to practice on your own.

Situation 1.   A boy or girl from your class sees you at the front of a long line at the movies.

OTHER: Hey, how about letting me cut in here? Then we can sit together.
YOU: No, I don't think so. It wouldn't be fair to these other people.
OTHER: Aw, c'mon! They won't care.
YOU: No, I don't think it would be right. But, listen! If it's not too crowded, I'll try and hold a seat for you, OK?

(Assertive)—This is an assertive response because
1. you have made your point so that the other person understands why you have refused.
2. you've suggested another way for your friend to sit with you without violating the rights of the other people waiting in line.

OTHER: Hi! Hey, how about letting me cut in here? Then we can sit together.
YOU: Gee, I don't know.

OTHER: Aw, c'mon! Who's gonna care?
YOU: Well, I guess so.

> (Passive)—This is a passive response because
> 1. you didn't express how you really felt and, you've done some-
>   thing that you know is not right.
> 2. you've probably made other people in the line angry with you.
> 3. people might think that you are a "pushover."

OTHER: Hi! Hey how about letting me cut in here? Then we can sit
together.
YOU: Are you kidding? I've been waiting for an hour.
OTHER: Aw, C'mon! What's the big deal?
YOU: Get lost!

> (Aggressive)—This is an aggressive response because
> 1. you've made your point but probably lost a friend or even made
>   an enemy in the process.
> 2. you didn't explain the reason you were making a refusal.

Situation 2. A friend wants to borrow your skates for tonight.

OTHER: Would it be all right if I borrowed your skates tonight?
YOU: I'm sorry (name), I don't really like to lend them out.

> (Assertive)—This is an assertive response because
> 1. you answered honestly.
> 2. you explained why you are refusing them.

OTHER: Would it be all right if I borrowed your skates tonight?
YOU: Well, I might want to use them later, but I guess it's OK.

> (Passive)—This is a passive response because
> 1. you're not being honest with your friend, and you're doing some-
>   thing you don't want to do.
> 2. you may end up being angry with your friend for borrowing your
>   skates.
> 3. Now you won't have the skates for tonight.

OTHER: Would it be all right if I borrowed your skates tonight?
YOU: Go buy your own! No one ever borrows my skates!

> (Aggressive)—This is an aggressive response because
> 1. you are being rude.
> 2. you may have hurt your friendship.

3. you didn't explain your reason for the refusal.

PRACTICE SCRIPTS

Situation 1. A classmate wants to borrow some money from you.

OTHER: Can you lend me a dollar?
YOU: No, I don't like to lend my money, it always causes problems.

Situation 2. A friend wants to borrow your bicycle.

OTHER: Could you lend me your bike?
YOU: No, I really don't like to lend it out.

Situation 3. A friend, who is also in your class, is having problems with his math.

OTHER: C'mon (name), do my math homework for me.
YOU: No, I don't want to. It's not right. We'll probably both get into trouble.

Situation 4. You are watching your favorite television program when someone walks in.

OTHER: May I change the channel?
YOU: Please don't! I'm watching my favorite show.
OTHER: If you're my friend, you'll let me watch my show.
YOU: No, I want to watch this show; it's only fair, since I was here first.

Situation 5. You've shared some of your candy with a friend.

OTHER: Can I have some more of your candy?
YOU: No. I really want to save the rest of it for later.

Situation 6. A classmate has been assigned to pick up litter on the playground and would like your help.

OTHER: Would you mind helping me pick up trash during recess?
YOU: No. I'm sorry but I'd rather not.

Situation 7. A friend wants to play and visit with you after school.

OTHER: I want to come over and play with you this afternoon.
YOU: I'm sorry. I have a lot of homework. Maybe some other time.

Situation 8.   You are busy working on an assignment when your teacher says to you:

TEACHER: Excuse me (name). How about taking these books to the library for me?

YOU: I'm sorry, but I'm really trying to finish this assignment on time. Would it be okay for someone else do it this time?

Situation 9.   Your parents are having some of their friends from work over for a party. Before the guests arrive, your mother says:

PARENT: I want you to introduce yourself to everyone at the party tonight.

YOU: Gee, Mom, I'd like to but I'm too embarrassed. Maybe you could introduce me to just your closest friends.

Situation 10.   Your friends are on their way to the local store. One of them says:

OTHER: Come on, the candy is out on the shelves. We'll see how much we can take without paying for it.

YOU: No, I don't want to get into trouble.

OTHER: Chicken!

YOU: It's not right! I'm not a chicken; I'm smart.

SUGGESTED HOMEWORK ASSIGNMENTS

1. Every day we are forced into situations where we have to say yes or no to someone's request. Write down three examples that happened to you, how you responded, and whether you answered the way you really wanted to.
2. While watching a favorite television show, write down examples of situations in which a person did not make a refusal that should have been made. Why should the person have refused? How would things have worked out if the person had done so?

Module 5: Requesting Favors

Rationale for Trainer

We frequently find ourselves in situations where we request favors of others. Whether asking directions from a stranger or requesting telephone assistance from an operator, we are, in fact, requesting a favor. In many cases, simple common sense keeps us keenly aware that a minor change in the way that we phrase a request can have a dramatic effect on the way it is perceived. Thus, with even a little social savvy, we can increase the chances that others will respond positively to our requests. By enhancing these skills through learning and understanding the strategies of human interaction, we can become quite adept in the art of making requests. Needless to say, the rewards to be gained from acquiring such a skill can be immeasurable.

For children, the importance of developing skills in requesting favors becomes even more important by virtue of their dependence on others (e.g., parents, teachers, etc.). Children who are able to organize and verbalize their desires and needs clearly and appropriately are those to whom others will most readily and positively respond. This seemingly obvious though largely underplayed skill has typically been addressed as a courtesy or a formality of etiquette for children. Yet its contribution to the successful social interaction of the child, the adolescent, and the adult underscores its significance.

Sample Lecture on Requesting Favors

Today, we are going to talk about *requesting favors,* or how to ask someone to do something for you. I'm sure that all of you have asked someone else for a favor. For instance, when your pencil point breaks during a test. You might turn to your schoolmate and ask him or her whether you might borrow a pencil. That is asking for a favor. Many things happen to you every day that make it important for you to know how to ask for help, to borrow something, or to ask for information.

However, there are "right" and "wrong" ways to ask someone for a favor. You are probably aware of this even though you don't think about it each time you ask for a favor. Let's pretend that you want to ask a friend to help you with some of your homework. How would you ask him or her for help? Would it be better to say, "Hey, you have to help me with my math." Or, do you think it would be better to say, "You know (name), I would really appreciate it if you could help me with some of my math homework." Of course, the second request was the better of the two. First of all, it was a polite way of asking for a favor and didn't just rudely demand help. Second, when you ask in this manner, your friend knows exactly what you want and how important the favor is to you.

DISCUSSION QUESTIONS

1. Can anyone give me an example of a common everyday request?
2. Can you give me at least two different ways in which you might make the request (ask the favor)?
3. Which do you think is the best way to ask? Why?
4. How do you feel when someone asks you for a favor in a rude way, or when people are pushy?

When you make your request in a pleasant, thoughtful way, you really have a better chance of getting what you want.Now that we know how important it is to make a request properly, there is one other thing that you should keep in mind. No matter whom you ask or what favor you are requesting, the other person always has the right to say no. We hope that, if this is the case, they will say no in a nice way that doesn't embarrass you or make you angry. *Remember, it is the other person's right to refuse the favor, just as it is your right to ask the favor.*

DISCUSSION QUESTIONS

1. Have you ever asked anyone for a favor and been turned down?
2. How did you feel?
3. What did you do then?

There are some things you can do if someone refuses your request. What you should *not* do is be mean or sarcastic (tease the person). What you *can* do is make sure that your request has been understood by making yourself a little more clear. If you think you have done this and the answer is still no, you would do much better to leave that person alone and either ask someone else, or drop the issue for a little while. One thing you might consider doing is explaining the importance of your favor and that you will be happy to return the favor in the future. If you continue to ask when someone has said no, the person may become angry and not want to talk to you for a while. Perhaps, it was just a bad time to ask and another time might be better. It is important for you to think about all of these things when you make a request.

RATIONALE FOR CHILDREN

Benefits.   By making a request in a nice way

A. you can make others aware of your needs in a pleasant and nonthreatening manner.
B. people might do more favors for you without thinking that you are a nag or a pest.

Pitfalls.   By not making a request

A. you do not let others know about your desires and needs.
B. you can end up feeling frustrated because you still need or want something.

By making a request in the wrong way

A. you can make someone angry and uncomfortable.
B. you increase the risk that the other person will refuse you.
C. people might think of you as disrespectful or discourteous.
D. you might hurt your chances of having *any* of your requests honored.

TRAINER'S SCRIPT

Situation 1.   You have just realized that you forgot to bring your lunch money to school. You are going to have to borrow some from a friend.

YOU: Hey (name), I forgot my lunch money for today. Could you please lend me 35 cents and I'll pay you back tomorrow?
FRIEND: I don't know. I was planning on saving my extra money for this weekend.
YOU: Oh, I'll give it back to you tomorrow morning, so you'll still have it for the weekend.
FRIEND: Sure. Remember to return it tomorrow.
YOU: Thanks a lot!

(Assertive)—This answer is an assertive because
1. you have asked in a way that is pleasant and doesn't put your friend on the spot.
2. you'll probably get the lunch money you need.

YOU: (Name), I forgot my lunch money. I wonder what I should do.

FRIEND: Well, I'm not sure.
YOU: I only need 35 cents.
FRIEND: Sorry, I really can't.

> (Passive)—This is a passive statement because
> 1. you failed to give your friend all the information needed to make a decision in your favor.
> 2. you might have to skip lunch since you did not express your needs.

YOU: Give me 35 cents for lunch until tomorrow.
OTHER: I don't know. I was planning on saving my money for this weekend.
YOU: Oh, c'mon! Don't be so cheap!
OTHER: No, I really can't. Sorry.
YOU: Well, thanks a lot! Some friend.

> (Aggressive)—This is an aggressive statement because
> 1. you were too pushy and probably made your friend angry.
> 2. you didn't get the lunch money because you spoke in a rude manner.

Situation 2.   You didn't bring your basketball to the court and would like to borrow one from a friend.

YOU: Could I play with that ball when you're done?
OTHER: Sure! Here you go.
YOU: Thanks.

> (Assertive)—This is an assertive statement because
> 1. you were polite and pleasant, which probably helped you get what you requested.

YOU: I don't have anything to play with.
OTHER: Sorry, I can't help you.

> (Passive)—This is a passive statement because
> 1. you did not clearly state what you wanted.
> 2. you may have to ask a second time.

YOU: Hey, give me the ball!
OTHER: No! I'm going to keep it. It's mine!

> (Aggressive)—This is an aggressive statement because
> 1. you were rude.

2. you probably made the other person angry.

YOU: Could I play with that ball when you're done?
OTHER: No, I'm taking it home.
YOU: I forgot mine and we won't be able to play if you don't lend me your ball.
OTHER: I'm sorry, but I have to take it home.
YOU: Well, I guess I'll have to find something else to do.

(Assertive)—This is an assertive statement because
1. you explained in a nice way why you needed the favor.
2. you accepted the refusal and decided on another alternative.
3. the other person may be more likely to let you use the ball next time because you were assertive and not aggressive.

PRACTICE SCRIPTS

Situation 1. You are with some friends at a drive-in and would like to get a snack. You just noticed that you didn't bring any money.

YOU: Would you do me a favor and buy me an ice cream cone? I'll pay you tomorrow.
OTHER: Sure.
YOU: Thanks a lot; I sure was hungry.

Situation 2. You want to ask a classmate for some help with a difficult homework assignment.

YOU: Could you help me with my homework after school?
OTHER: OK.
YOU: Thanks! It's nice of you to help.

Situation 3. You just found out that a friend has a book that you have been looking for.

YOU: I'd like to borrow your book for a few days. Would that be all right with you?
OTHER: Sure, just try to take good care of it.
YOU: I will; thanks.

Situation 4. You would like to invite a friend over for dinner. You are asking your mother for permission.

YOU: Mom, may I invite Eileen to dinner?

MOTHER: Certainly; just let me know a few days before so I can prepare a
  bigger meal.

YOU: Gee! Thanks a lot.

Situation 5. You need some help fixing your bicycle and want to ask
a friend to help you.

YOU: I need some help fixing my bicycle after school. Could you give me
  a hand.

OTHER: I'm not doing anything right after school; why don't we work on
  it then?

YOU: Sounds great! Thanks.

Situation 6. You don't understand the homework assignment that
your teacher gave you. You walk up to her after class and say:

YOU: Ms. Jones, I really don't understand the homework assignment.
  Could you please go over it again with me?

TEACHER: I'd be happy to. It's good that you asked.

YOU: Thank you.

Situation 7. You are calling the theater to get some information
about today's schedule.

YOU: Hello, could you tell me what's playing on the second feature?

OTHER: Sure, it's *The Incredible Space War*.

YOU: Oh, thanks, By the way, could you tell what time the show
  finishes?

OTHER: About 10:30.

YOU: OK. Thank you.

Situation 8. You are at the movies and have lost your wallet. You
want to report this to the manager.

YOU: Excuse, me, but could you help me find the manager?

OTHER: The manager is the person with the red coat by the candy
  counter.

YOU: Thank you.

SUGGESTED HOMEWORK ASSIGNMENTS

1. Every day you make requests and ask for favors. Try to remember
   what requests you have made and what the results were.

2. Using the requests that you remembered for question 1
    a. take the requests that someone said no to and see if you can change them so that they sound better. How would the person now answer you?
    b. take the requests that others said yes to and see whether you can list what was good about the way you said them.
3. Write down requests that other people have made of you. Did they make them correctly? How could they have been better?

Module 6: Asking Why

One of the more common errors that we make in our daily interactions with others is the failure to ask why. When we ask why, we are essentially requesting additional information about a situation, a statement, or an interaction. This information can help to clear up ambiguities, misconceptions, and misunderstandings that could result in unpleasant or embarrassing situations. By asking why, we obtain new information that can often influence our decisions and the course of action we choose.

For children as with adults, asking why serves as a means of gathering additional information about an issue. However, for the youngster, the importance of developing the ability to ask why appropriately becomes even more significant. The question not only enhances decision making but also serves as a valuable instrument for learning in general. Answers to "why" questions fill information gaps. Thinking about cause and effect helps to develop reasoning skills and plays an important role in the development of decision making and other cognitive abilities. Thus, what might be routine for the adult is an important learning mechanism for the child—socially, emotionally, and educationally.

SAMPLE LECTURE ON ASKING WHY

Today we are going to the discuss importance of asking why and present examples of how to do it. People usually ask why when they are not sure about something and when they want more information. We also ask why when we are curious about people's reasons for asking or doing something, or don't understand those reasons or decisions. Thus, asking why is a valuable skill to learn.

DISCUSSION QUESTIONS

1. Can anyone give me an example of a situation where we ask why?
2. Why do we ask why?

95

Asking why is something we do very often. In school, we ask our teachers and schoolmates; at home, we ask our parents, brothers, sisters, and friends. However, there is a right and wrong way to ask why. For example, your best friend tells you, "I don't think I'll be able to go to the show tonight." You might say, "What? You can't do that!" Or you could say, "Oh, that's too bad, I was really counting on your going. Why can't you go?" Although both are ways in which you can respond to your friend, only the second way really asks the question "why" and gives your friend a fair chance to explain what the problem could be. It is possible that after this explanation, things can still be worked out. For instance, maybe your friend had some extra chores or work that you could help with. It is important to remember that asking why can be done in many different ways. It is often better to add the reason you are asking for the information so people can understand that you are not being disrespectful or acting "smart."

So you see, asking why is good because it helps you to get important information. With this information, you can make better decisions about what to do and what to say.

RATIONALE FOR CHILDREN

Benefits.   Asking why can help you
A. understand the reason for the request when you are asked to do something.
B. in making a decision about what to do.
C. understand exactly what is expected of you.
D. learn something new.
E. understand better what is being said.
F. let the other person know that you are listening and interested.

Pitfalls.   By not asking why
A. you could end up doing something that you do not like to do.
B. you might miss out on something that is important to know.
C. people will think that you understand what they are saying when you really don't.
D. you might end up doing the wrong thing.

TRAINER'S SCRIPT

What we are going to do today is practice how to ask why. First, I'll give you some examples of asking why; then you will have a chance to practice on your own.

Asking why is important in getting more information and should not be used in a "smart" or sarcastic manner. This will only make people angry and less likely to explain their requests or statements.

Situation 1.   Your family is sitting at the dinner table having dessert.

PARENT: I don't want you or your sister to go out to play this evening.
YOU: May I ask why? I wanted to go out and play a little.
PARENT: I thought we all could go to the show tonight.

(Assertive)—This is an assertive response because
1. you made your point about going out to play in a polite and appropriate way without making your parents angry.
2. you explained the reason for asking why.

PARENT: I don't want you and your sister to go out to play this evening.
YOU: Oh, OK.
PARENT: I thought we might all go out to the show later.

(Passive)—This is a passive response because
1. you've accepted your parents' request and didn't ask for the information that you wanted.
2. you didn't explain the reason why you needed the information.

PARENT: I want you and your sister to stay in the house this evening.
YOU: Oh, Dad! Not tonight! What's the big deal about going out to play?
PARENT: Well, OK, if that's the way you want it. We were all going to the show later on, but you can stay at home and study.

(Aggressive)—This is an aggressive response because
1. you were disrespectful and contrary in your response to your parents.
2. you failed to ask for additional information and to give your reason for needing the information.
3. you failed to explain your point.

Situation 2.   You've said something that has upset your friend, Jim, and he has walked away. A second friend says:

FRIEND: I don't think you should have said that to Jim.
YOU: Why do you feel that way?

(Assertive)—This is an assertive response because
1. you have expressed an interest in what the other person is saying.

2. you will better understand how the other person is feeling.

FRIEND: I don't think you should have said that to Jim.
YOU: Oh?

(Passive)—This is a passive response because
1. you really don't know why the other person feels that way because you didn't ask.
2. the other person might not think that you care because you didn't ask why or explain how you felt.

FRIEND: I don't think you should have said that to Jim.
YOU: Oh, really? So what's your problem?

(Aggressive)—This is an aggressive response because
1. you are being rude and not considerate of the other person's feelings.
2. you have probably angered both Jim and your friend.
3. you didn't learn from the situation.

PRACTICE SCRIPTS

Situation 1. A friend of yours wants your help. You would like to know what it is that you are being asked to do.

OTHER: How about coming over after school and helping me with some things?
YOU: What kind of things are you talking about?
OTHER: Oh, just some work on my bicycle that I need help with.

Situation 2. Your brother is looking for some help with a chore. Since you already have plans made, you would like to know whether the request is a important one.

OTHER: Are you free later on? I think I'll need some help.
YOU: What is it that you need help with?
OTHER: I was going to clean the garage out and I'll need some help.
YOU: Sorry, but I'd rather not.
                                  OR
    OK, I'll be glad to help you.

Situation 3. You've been accused of something but are not sure of what. You want more information.

OTHER: You're always making a big deal out of little things.
YOU: I'm not sure of what you are saying. What do you mean?

Situation 4. You are in a store and a salesperson comes over to you.

SALESPERSON: You are not supposed to be in the store, you will have to
  leave.
YOU: Why? I just want to buy something.
SALESPERSON: You have to be with an adult. That is our rule.

Situation 5. You are at a restaurant and the check appears to be too
high.

YOU: Sir! I think there is a mistake. Would you please explain these
  charges?
WAITER: Certainly. This is for the extra cheese on the sandwich.
YOU: Oh, I didn't realize that was extra. Thanks.

Situation 6. Your parents say the following to you.

PARENT: From now on your bedtime will be 9 o'clock on weekends.
YOU: Why did you pick 9? It seems sort of early.
PARENT: We want to make sure that you get enough sleep so that you
  wake up early enough for school.
YOU: Can we try my bedtime at 10 and see if that works out?
PARENT: All right. Let's try 9:30 for a while and see how it works out.

Situation 7. Someone asks to borrow your expensive new jacket.

OTHER: Can I borrow that nice new jacket of yours?
YOU: Why do you want to borrow it?
OTHER: I was going to a camp picnic and the jacket would look really
  nice.
YOU: I'm sorry, but that jacket is only for special occasions. I wouldn't
  want it to get dirty.

Situation 8. Your brother/sister wants you to carry his/her books
home from school.

BROTHER: Could you carry these home for me?
YOU: Why do you need me to carry them?
BROTHER: I have to take my costume home for the play and I won't be
  able to carry both at one time.

Suggested Homework Assignments

1. Write down the next time someone asks you to do something. Figure out at least three different ways to ask why. Then answer:
   a. How would the other person have felt/responded with each of the three ways?
   b. What kinds of information could you have received each way?
   c. Which would have been the best way to ask why?
2. The next time you watch TV, keep a record of:
   a. How many times the question "why" or something like it comes up. (Give at least 5 examples.)
   b. The times people should have asked why and didn't. Why didn't they? (Give at least 2 examples.)
   c. Times when asking why was not appropriate or not done correctly. (Give at least 2 examples.)

Module 7: Requesting Behavior Change

Rationale for Trainer

Sometimes it becomes important to let other people know that their behavior disturbs or bothers us. This is not always an easy thing to do, as people sometimes feel threatened and react defensively. However, at other times the individual is not aware that he or she is doing something that is bothersome. In this situation, a tactfully made comment or request can be welcome information. In most cases, the act of requesting behavior change of another person can be mutually beneficial. The person who makes the request may be able to change an uncomfortable situation, and the person of whom change is requested receives necessary feedback.

Studies of the content of dyadic interaction have established that when people communicate with each other, they constantly monitor each other's reactions and adjust their own behavior accordingly. A skillfully made request for behavior change can serve as a more immediate way of facilitating this process. It is important to emphasize that tactless and impulsive attempts to do this can easily result in making the other person feel intimidated, angry, and defensive.

For children, especially those with immature social styles, learning how to request behavior change appropriately becomes even more significant. In peer interactions as well as child–adult interactions, skill in requesting behavior change allows the child to have greater impact on the social environment while reducing the risk of being antagonistic or disruptive. Thus, the child can assume a more active role in developing and restructuring the social environment.

Sample Lecture on Requesting Behavior Change

Today we are going to talk about how to ask somebody to stop or change what they are doing. Sometimes people do things that bother or irritate us, though they may not know that they are doing that. When this happens, things can get pretty uncomfortable. It's not easy to tell people that what they are doing bothers you, especially if the person involved is an adult or a good friend. Chances are that if you don't do it right, the person will get mad at you. At the same time, if you don't say anything at all, you might end up getting angry. So it is important to say

101

something, and it is even *more* important to say it in a nice, respectful, and thoughtful way. What we will be talking about is how to do just that.

Let's pretend that you and your best friend are studying in the library together for an important test. Your friend begins to hum a song, not realizing that this is bothering you. What can you do?

DISCUSSION QUESTIONS

1. What kinds of things do you think could happen if you decided not to say anything?
2. What could happen if you said something?
3. How could you say something so that you would not upset your friend?

As you see, there are a lot of ways that you could react to your friend. But if you wanted to keep your friend, you would probably want to say something like: "Hey, Karen, it's hard for me to study when you're humming. Would you mind not humming, or humming a little more quietly? Thanks." By talking to your friend about the humming, you are asking that she change that behavior because it bothers you. The good thing about doing it like this is that you are saying it in a nice way that lets your friend know that you are not angry. It also shows your friend that you are being courteous and thoughtful. Just imagine what might have happened if you said, "Hey Karen, knock if off!" or "C'mon Karen, stop being a pest. Cut the humming, huh?" *Remember you want the other person to change a behavior. You don't want to put the other person down.*

RATIONALE FOR CHILDREN

Benefits. By requesting in a nice way that a person change his or her behavior
   A. you let the person know that something he or she is doing makes you feel uncomfortable or even angry.
   B. you can make the person aware of something he or she is doing that they may not be aware of.
   C. you can let the person know that you care enough to tell him or her about the problem behavior.

Pitfalls. By not requesting behavior change from another person in the right way
   A. you could end up becoming more angry or frustrated about what the person is doing.

B. you can anger or lose a friend because you might have threatened or been rude to her or him.
C. you are not helping the person to understand that something he or she is doing bothers you.

TRAINER'S SCRIPT

You can see how important it is to request behavior change when necessary and to do it in a thoughtful, respectful way. I'm going to give you a few more examples of how to ask people to stop or change what they are doing. After that, we will all practice requesting behavior change from others.

Situation 1. A person sitting in front of you at the movies is talking so loud that you are having trouble hearing the show.

YOU: Excuse me, but I'm having a little trouble hearing the movie. Would you mind not talking so loud?
OTHER: Oh, I didn't realize I was that loud. Sorry about that.
YOU: Thanks.
OR
Thank you.

(Assertive)—This is an assertive response because
1. you told the person the behavior you wanted her or him to change.
2. you have succeeded in getting the other person to be more quiet without putting her or him down.
3. you were pleasant but told the person politely what you wanted.

YOU: (Speaking out loud but not to the person talking) Gee, it sure would be nice to hear the movie!
OTHER: (May not be aware that you are talking of him; makes no response.)
OR
Are you talking to me?
YOU: Well, kind of.
OTHER: All right; why didn't you say so!

(Passive)—This is a passive response because
1. you did not ask the other person directly.
2. the person could have misunderstood you or failed to hear your request that he change his behavior.

YOU: You're making me miss the show. Would you mind shutting up?
OTHER: You don't have to be so nasty about it; I didn't know anybody could hear me.

> (Aggressive)—This is an aggressive response because
> 1. you made your point, but in a rude manner.
> 2. you might end up in an argument or even a fight.

Situation 2. Your parents still call you by a nickname that they used when you were younger, and you don't like it anymore.

YOU: Dad, I wish you wouldn't call me by that name anymore. It really embarrasses me in front of my friends.
PARENT: I'm sorry, I didn't know that it bothered you. It really is just a habit.
YOU: Well, it's okay at home. It's just when we go places I don't like.
PARENT: I'll be more careful next time.

> (Assertive)—This is an assertive response because
> 1. your father has a better understanding of your feelings.
> 2. you handled this problem in a mature, direct manner and explained which behavior was bothering you.

YOU: (You grumble to yourself because your parents have just called you by your nickname in front of some friends.)
PARENT: What's the matter? Are you upset about something?
YOU: Oh no. I was just thinking about something.
PARENT: Oh, okay.

> (Passive)—This is a passive response because
> 1. you did not ask your parents to change a behavior that bothers you very much.
> 2. you will probably become more angry the next time.
> 3. they will probably keep using your nickname.

YOU: You know, Mom, with that stupid name you make a fool of me when we go out. Could you stop it? I can't stand being out with you!
PARENT: What's the matter? I don't know what you're talking about. I treat you the way I always have.
YOU: Well, I hate the name "Babyface"!!
PARENT: You don't have to be so rude. I didn't know that "Babyface" bothered you. You'd better learn some manners.

> (Aggressive)—This is an aggressive response because

1. you have made your mother angry with you.
2. you have not made your feelings clear.

Practice Scripts

Situation 1. You are studying for a test. Your brother has some friends over who became noisy.

YOU: Say, would you people mind turning down the music a little? I'm trying to study! It's too noisy for me to work.
OTHER: Sure. We didn't know you were studying.
YOU: Thanks.

Situation 2. A classmate is cutting into line in the cafeteria and you don't feel that this is right.

YOU: Would you please stop cutting into line? It isn't fair to the rest of us.
OTHER: OK. I didn't think anybody cared.
YOU: Thanks. Listen—tomorrow, why don't you get in line with me?

Situation 3. A friend is making fun of you and you don't like it.

YOU: I'd like it if you would stop teasing and making fun of me. I thought we were friends.
FRIEND: We *are* friends! I was just being funny. I'll try to stop.
YOU: Thanks.

Situation 4. You and your friends are walking to school together. You are carrying a lot of books, which is making you walk more slowly.

YOU: Hey, would you guys mind slowing down just a little? These books are pretty heavy.
FRIEND: Sorry, we'll all walk a little slower.
YOU: Thanks.

Situation 5. You are trying to tell a story and your friend keeps interrupting.

YOU: I'm trying to tell the rest of the story, could you wait until I'm finished and then we'll listen to your story.
FRIEND: But I just wanted to add a few comments.
YOU: Well, I would like it better if you waited until I finished.
FRIEND: Okay.

Situation 6. You and your friend are playing at the playground.

YOU: You know (name), you've had the ball a long time. Let everybody
  · have a turn.
FRIEND: I thought I was! Here you can have it for awhile.
YOU: I just thought I'd tell you before somebody does get mad.
FRIEND: Okay.

Situation 7. Your friends are playing a game that you want to join.
They aren't letting other kids join in.

YOU: I wish you would let me play, too. Everyone should have a chance
  to play.
OTHER: OK. We can all take turns.
YOU: Great! Thanks.

Situation 8. You are trying to draw and one of the kids keeps shak-
ing the table.
  YOU: Would you please stop shaking the table. I can't draw when the
table moves.
  OTHER: I'm not moving the table.
  YOU: Yes you are, everytime you lean forward the table moves.
  OTHER: Alright, lets find a way to make the table less wobbly.

SUGGESTED HOMEWORK ASSIGNMENTS

1. Think about at least one thing that someone has been doing or
   saying that bothers you. Answer the following questions.
   a. Why haven't you said something yet?
   b. Can you list three different ways to make your complaint?
   c. How would the person react to each way? Why?
   d. Which is the best way? Why?
   e. Can you think of a better way to say it?
2. Take the problem that you talked about in assignment 1 and what
   you would say to the person (Item 1d or 1e) and practice saying
   this until you feel comfortable with it.
   a. Find the person who is involved and request the desired be-
      havior change.
   b. Later on, write down what you said and how the person
      responded.
   c. Could you have done or said something better? If so, what?
      Why is this better?

MODULE 8: STANDING UP FOR YOUR RIGHTS

RATIONALE FOR TRAINER

Often, when we hear people talk about assertiveness, they are talking about standing up for one's rights. Although assertiveness involves a much broader range of behaviors and situations, it does seem that, in standing up for one's rights, one's ability to be assertive is clearly put to the test. *Specifically, standing up for your rights refers to the act of asserting yourself in situations where others have purposely or accidentally infringed upon or violated your rights.* By this, we mean to include not only those constitutional/legal rights that we are all guaranteed but also those rights that are an inherent part of social interactions. For the sake of simplicity, we might refer to these as the rights established and protected by the rules of etiquette and mutual respect in social interaction.

Learning to stand up for your rights is really a three-step procedure. First, an individual must become aware of and understand his or her rights. This point is a developmental issue, as acquisition of this understanding depends upon intellectual as well as social development. Second, one must be able to understand when one's rights have, in fact, been violated. As with the first step, the child's level of social maturation serves as a measure of the ability to tell when this occurs. Third, once an individual understands what his or her rights are and when they are being threatened, it becomes important to learn how to communicate to others that they are trespassing on one's personal rights. The skill with which an individual is able to do this is another aspect of the ability to stand up for one's rights appropriately.

This module focuses on developing skills in the area of communicating to others that they are infringing on your rights. Clearer definition of what those rights are serves as a secondary emphasis. For children, the need for skill in this area is of great importance. As children mature, their rights and responsibilities increase. Thus, learning how to protect and "stand up" for these rights becomes an integral feature of social skills development.

SAMPLE LECTURE ON STANDING UP FOR YOUR RIGHTS

Today we are going to discuss why and how you should stand up for your rights. By standing up for your rights, we mean letting other people know when they are not treating you fairly or when they are doing something to you that you don't like. Sometimes this could mean just telling people how much they can expect of you and at other times it could mean having to put your foot down and set limits. Of course, this might be a little difficult to do, but you have to remember that what you are really doing is protecting yourself.

What if, one day at school, some children wanted to test you to see how much bullying you would take? Suppose they came up to you during recess and told you that you couldn't use one side of the playground. What would you do? Well, you know that you have a *right* to use the whole playground and you also know that they *don't* have a right to boss you around. This is one example of when standing up for your rights is important.

DISCUSSION QUESTIONS

1. Why is it important, in this situation, to stand up for your rights?
2. What would happen if you didn't?
3. What would you say to these children in this situation?

This is a pretty tough situation, but it would probably get worse if you didn't stand up for yourself. Perhaps you might say something like: "This playground belongs to all of us and we all have to share it. You really can't tell me that I can't use a part of it; that's not fair. If you try to stop me (or bother me again), I'm going to talk to the monitor." They might tease you or even get mad at you, but at least you would have told them that you're not going to let yourself get pushed around.

That was kind of an extreme case in which it was necessary to stand up for your rights. There will be times when the others don't even know that what they are doing is going against your rights. A simple situation like getting a warm soda in a restaurant is another example. In this case, you are paying for a good, cold soda and it is your right to get what you pay for. If you don't assert yourself or stand up for your rights, not only will you be taken advantage of, but it might happen to someone else or maybe even to you again in the future. So, it is important to assert yourself to stand up for your rights.

DISCUSSION QUESTIONS

1. Can anyone give me an example of a situation where you should stand up for your rights?
2. What are your *rights* in this case?
3. What could happen if you didn't say or do something?
4. What would be the best thing to say in this situation? Why?

RATIONALE FOR CHILDREN

It is important to recognize that standing up for one's rights includes a number of skill categories that have been discussed previously. For additional information on "benefits" and "pitfalls," please refer to the modules on complaints, saying no, asking why, and requesting behavior change.

Benefits. Standing up for your rights lets others know
A. that you think they have violated your rights or taken advantage of you.
B. that you feel you have been dealt with or treated unfairly.
C. that you *will* stand up for yourself if it is necessary.
D. what your "boundaries" are; that is, how you want to be treated and what you will *not* put up with.
E. that you "stood up" for yourself so that you can feel confident and proud.

Pitfalls. By not standing up for your rights

A. you allow and possibly encourage others to take advantage of you.
B. you may lose out on things that are rightly yours.
C. you may be treated unfairly by others and lose their respect.
D. you let others take advantage of you and treat you unfairly, which can make you lose your self-confidence and self-respect.

TRAINER'S SCRIPT

As you have probably noticed, there are a lot of different situations when it would be good for you to stand up for your rights. What we are going to do next is go over a few more examples that I will demonstrate for you. When we are done with that, we will all have a chance to practice how to stand up for our rights.

Situation 1. You and a friend are playing a board game. Your friend says to you:

FRIEND: You can't do that! I don't think you can move that way.
YOU: I think I can, I read all the rules carefully.
FRIEND: But, *I* never played that way.
YOU: Well, the rules say that I can move that way. I can get the rules if you would like to see for yourself.

(Assertive)—This is an assertive response because
1. you have made your point in an informative way.
2. you made your point without getting your friend upset.
3. you made a suggestion to resolve the problem by offering to check the rules.

FRIEND: You can't do that! I don't think you can move that way.
YOU: Are you sure? Gee, I thought that I read you could.
FRIEND: Yeah? But, *I* never played that way.
YOU: Well, I guess we can play your way.

(Passive)—This is a passive response because
1. even though you think that you are right, you have not stood your ground.
2. you might get a little angry with your friend for understanding.
3. you might get angry at yourself for not standing up for what you believe.

FRIEND: You can't do that! I don't think you can move that way.
YOU: Oh, yeah! You want to bet? I thought you knew how to play this game.
FRIEND: Yeah? But, *I* never played that way.
YOU: Tough! You're playing my way now, the right way.

(Aggressive)—This is an aggressive response because
1. you might be right, but you may upset your friend by being bossy about your point.
2. your friend will be less willing to play with you again.

Situation 2.   You are in a store looking for a gift for a friend. One of the store clerks comes up to you.

CLERK: If you are not buying something, you are going to have to leave.
YOU: I am looking for a gift. If I find something I like, then I'll buy it.
CLERK: Well, all right then. As long as you're shopping.

(Assertive)—This is an assertive response because
1. you stated your right to shop without getting the clerk mad at you.
2. the clerk will probably be more helpful now.

CLERK: If you are not buying something, you are going to have to leave.
YOU: I'm just looking.
CLERK: Are you going to buy something or not?

YOU: Maybe.

> (Passive)—This is a passive response because
> 1. you only half stated your right to shop.
> 2. the clerk might still ask you to leave.

CLERK: If you are not buying something, you are going to have to leave.
YOU: Just try and make me! I know you can't do that.
CLERK: I'm sorry; unless you plan to buy something, you're going to have to leave.
YOU: Who would want to shop in your crummy store!

> (Aggressive)—This is an aggressive response because
> 1. you have made the store clerk angry, and you didn't explain your reason for being there.
> 2. you might be asked to leave because of your bad attitude.

PRACTICE SCRIPTS

Situation 1. Someone borrowed a record from you a while ago. You've already asked for it back once.

YOU: Excuse me (name), could you make sure you bring my record in tomorrow?
OTHER: I'm sorry; I forgot the last time. I'll try to remember.
YOU: Please don't forget—I do want it back.

Situation 2. You just bought an ice cream cone and you got back the wrong amount of change.

YOU: Excuse me. I think you gave me the wrong change.
CLERK: Really? How much did you give me?
YOU: Well, I gave you 75 cents, which means I should get back 15 cents in change.
CLERK: Oh, I'm sorry, you're right. Here you go.

Situation 3. You are standing in the lunch line and someone cuts in front of you.

YOU: Hey! You can't cut in line. That's not fair to everybody else.
OTHER: Aw, who cares!
YOU: I care. I've been waiting for 10 minutes. I think you'd better go to the end of the line.

Situation 4.   Someone in class unfairly accuses you of talking while the teacher stepped out.

YOU: Ms. Jacobs, it wasn't me who was making the noise. There were several people talking, but I wasn't one of them.
TEACHER: Well, OK. I don't want this sort of thing happening in the future.

Situation 5.   You bought a new model and you notice that there is a part missing. You go back to the store.

YOU: Excuse me, ma'am, but I just bought this model and it's missing some parts. I would like to exchange it.
CLERK: Do you have the sales slip? I don't remember you buying it.
YOU: Yes, I have it right here.
CLERK: OK, there's no problem. Why don't you go back and get a new one.

Situation 6.   Your parents are having friends come over to the house for a party. They have told you that you have to go to bed two hours before your normal bedtime.

YOU: Dad, I don't really think that is fair for me to have to go to bed so early. Isn't there something else I can do?
PARENT: I don't know, this party is only for adults. I guess maybe you can watch the TV in your room. How's that?
YOU: That's great! Thanks.

Situation 7.   Your sister tells you that it is your turn to wash the dishes. You washed them yesterday and you know that it is not your turn.

YOU: Sis, that's not fair. I did them yesterday. It's your turn today.
SISTER: I really can't. I've got a lot of homework to do tonight. Can't you do them?
YOU: That's different. I'll do them tonight and you can do them tomorrow night. OK?
SISTER: Yeah, that's a good idea.

Situation 8.   You've been watching a movie on television when your father walks in and changes the station without saying anthing.

YOU: Oh, Dad, I've been watching the movie on Channel 9 for awhile, and I'd like to see what happens. Could we change it back please?

PARENT: The news is on and I'd really hate to miss it.

YOU: Well, just for tonight, could you possibly watch the late news?

OR

Well, would you mind watching the news on Channel 5 which comes on after the movie?

PARENT: OK, I guess that would be all right.

SUGGESTED HOMEWORK ASSIGNMENTS

1. Try to think of at least one situation at school and at home where you should have stood up for your rights.
   a. Why didn't you?
   b. How could you have said something? (Give at least one good and one bad example for each.)
   c. What would be the best way to settle the problem or to be assertive in each case?
2. Make up one situation in which it would be easy and one situation in which it would be difficult to stand up for your rights. How would you settle these problems? What makes this solution good?
3. List as many as possible of the "good" things that can result from standing up for your rights. Use your own experience to help you come up with answers.

MODULE 9: CONVERSATIONS

Every day, conversations are held about every topic imaginable. Conversations can be formal and informal, they can be task-oriented or have no particular orientation at all, they can be hours long or last only a few seconds, and they can range in content from extreme importance to insignificance. Whatever the case, one fact is clear: conversations serve as the primary vehicle of information exchange between two or more people. Thus, it is not difficult to understand why an individual who knows the intricacies of conversing has a distinct social advantage over one who does not.

The scientific and educational literature extolls the virtues of being a good communicator and skilled interactor. Knowing how to participate in conversation is an invaluable asset. In fact, the number of adult "pop" psychology books available on how to become a better or more effective communicator supports this contention. Typically, most people are able to acquire the basic skills for social conversation through normal social, emotional, and intellectual development. Furthermore, those who get more practice generally become even more skilled and knowledgeable about the "fine art" of conversing.

The conversation itself comprises three phases: (1) *initiation*, (2) *maintenance*, and (3) *termination*. Successful conversing requires skill in each area. Often the initiation takes the form of an introduction, a greeting, or a question. The process of initiation gets the conversation under way and facilitates the inclusion of new participants. The body of the conversation is typically made up of the major portion of the dialogue. The last component, termination, is the conclusion of the conversation. This may either be done by mutual consent of the participants or an individual may withdraw from the conversation. Skill in conversational initiation, participation, and termination has a number of results. Participants not only tend to feel better about the conversation but also about the other participants, thus probably increasing the likelihood of future encounters.

For children, conversation is an essential mechanism of and vehicle for learning and social development. Peer interactions as well as child—adult (parents, teachers, etc.) interactions are based largely on dyadic and group communication. Thus, the more facile a child is in the art of conversing, the greater the contribution to his or her social, emotional, and intellectual development. A knowledge of how to participate in conversations contributes to the child's ability to gain as well as share information.

This module can be divided into three separate units; (1) initiating conversations; (2) maintaining conversations; and (3) terminating conversations. Also, after children practice the scripts, trainers may separate children into groups and have them discuss a television show or movie they have seen this increases spontaneity and the use of nonverbal cues. The participants should be individually "assigned" to contribute to the conversation by making appropriate comments, asking open-ended questions, and ending the conversation.

Sample Lecture on Conversations

For the past few sessions, we have practiced different social skills such as compliments, complaints, and standing up for your rights. Today, we are going to discuss and practice talking with others. We do it with most of the people we meet, old and young, strangers and friends. Not everyone, however, can do this easily. That is why we are going to discuss how we talk to people or, better yet, how we carry on conversations with others. You are probably wondering why it is *so* important to discuss something as simple as conversations. The truth is, taking part in conversations is easier for some people than it is for others because some people have learned and practiced these skills. Not only that, but there are different parts of conversation that could be more difficult than others. For instance, here are some questions to think about.

Discussion Questions

1. How many people know how to start a conversation?
2. How many of you know how to join a conversation that is already going on?
3. How do you keep a conversation going?
4. What do you do when everyone has run out of things to say?
5. How do you end a conversation?

You see, it is important to know more than just how to talk to somebody. It is also necessary to know how to start, join, and end conversation. Chances are that if you don't know how to start talking with another person or join in when others are talking, you won't be a part of very many conversations. In the same way, if you stop (disrupt) a conversation or leave one awkwardly, people may not be as willing to let you be a part of their conversations in the future. So, it *is* important to learn about how to start a conversation, keep it going, and end a conversation in a smooth, considerate, and intelligent way. For example, pretend that some of your classmates are talking about a TV show that you happened to see last night and you want to get in on the conversation.

DISCUSSION QUESTIONS

1. Can you give me a few examples of how you might join this conversation?
2. Which one of these ways is the best? Why?

What you might want to do is walk over to the group and, when there is a slight pause in the talking, say something like, "Are you talking about *Star Trek?* I saw that and really liked it a lot too." At this point, you have joined the conversation.

Next, you want to make sure that you participate in what's going on. You should listen and add comments to what is being said.

DISCUSSION QUESTIONS

1. Can you give me different examples of how you can now add to or take part in a conversation or what else could you say?
2. Why is it important to listen to what others are saying?

Probably, one of the best ways to be a part of what is going on and keep the conversation going is to listen to what is being said, ask questions, and make statements that have to do with what others are talking about. So, using the same example, you could say, "You know, I don't understand why Mr. Spock did that. Did it make sense to anybody?" After hearing the others' responses, you could reply, "Oh, yeah, I didn't think of that. Maybe that's why. . . ." By asking questions and answering other people's questions you are keeping the conversation going. One important point is that you should always try to stick to the topic that the others are talking about. If you want to change it, wait until the conversation about one topic starts to end and then a new one can be started.

It is also important to know when and how to end a conversation or how to excuse yourself from one that is going on. Actually, it isn't that hard. What you have to do is to make sure that the other people know that you are finished or finishing so that they can finish, too.

DISCUSSION QUESTIONS

1. How can you let others know that you are finished talking?
2. How do you get out of a conversation if you have to leave?
3. Why is it important to let people know that you are finished talking or that you have to leave?

Using the same example as before, a nice way to end the conversation would be something like, "Well, next week I'll watch it more carefully. Maybe we can talk more about it then, OK?" Or if *you* have to leave, "I really wish I could talk some more, but I've got some other things I have to do. Maybe we can talk some more next week. See you later." In both these examples, the other people know that you enjoyed the conversation and their company and that you would like to talk with them again. This is important, because next week it will probably be easier to get the conversation going. Also, when you left the conversation, you did so on friendly terms with the others. This is good because they will probably want you to join them in the future.

RATIONALE FOR CHILDREN

Benefits.   When you take part in conversations
A. you get to meet and learn about new people and even make new friends.
B. you have the chance to tell others about things that you like.
C. you aren't left out of what is going on.
D. you can learn about things that are interesting and important that you didn't know about.

Pitfalls.   When you do not take part in conversations
A. you miss out on what is going on.
B. you don't get the chance to meet new and interesting people.
C. you lose the chance to share your thoughts and interests with others.
D. you could end up being left out of other activities, such as parties, games, and outings.

TRAINER'S SCRIPT[1]

Now that you have seen the importance of being able to (1) start and join a conversation, (2) keep it going, and (3) end or leave a conversation, it would be good for you to practice these skills in different situations. First, I'll show you a few more examples and then, afterwards, you can practice being a good conversationalist on your own.

---

[1] It would be important to point out to students that the passive and aggressive approaches, as presented in previous modules, would probably not result in establishing a conversation. The passive individual would avoid approaching a conversation and the aggressive individual would probably not be responded to.

JOINING, PARTICIPATING, AND LEAVING CONVERSATIONS

Situation 1. A group of people that you recognize from school are standing in line at the theater. You would like to join them.

YOU: Hi, aren't you guys from Highland school? My name is (name); I thought I recognized you.

PERSON A: Yeah, I've seen you in the cafeteria. I'm (name), and this is (name), and (name), and (name).

YOU: I'm really glad to run into you. I've been waiting for this movie for weeks and I didn't want to have to see it alone. Would you mind if I joined you?

PERSON B: Oh, no problem. The more the merrier.

YOU: Have any of you seen this before?
                              OR
   I hope it's good; have any of you heard anything about it?

(Assertive)—These are assertive responses because
1. you waited for a pause and began by introducing yourself.
2. you might have made some new friends and were able to join them for the movies.

YOU: Hey, I know you guys. Great, now I can watch the show with someone else.

PERSON A: (Looks over to the other group members) Well, uh, . . .

PERSON B: Yeah, I guess its OK.

(Aggressive)—This was aggressive because
1. you forced yourself on the others.
2. you're not sure that they really want your company.
3. you might have interfered with the groups plans.

Situation 2. There is a new girl in school that you would like to meet and talk with.

YOU: Hi, my name is (name). I noticed that you were new here and thought you might need some help.

OTHER: My name is (name). It's such a big school. I could use some help.

YOU: It's not too bad. Have you been able to find all your classes?

OTHER: No, not yet; but I'm glad I met you. I was kind of worried about making friends here.

YOU: I could meet you right here before lunch and I could introduce you to some of my friends.

OTHER: That would be great, thanks!

YOU: OK. See you later.

(Assertive)—These are assertive responses because
1. you helped to make someone else feel better.
2. you may have made a new friend.

Practice Scripts

Situation 1. You are shopping at the mall when you spot one of your teachers walking out of a store. You want your parents to meet him or her.

YOU: Excuse me, Mr. Smith. I saw you coming out of the store and I wanted you to meet my parents.
TEACHER: Certainly (name), I'd love to meet them.
YOU: Dad, Mom, I'd like to meet Mr. Smith, my Phys. Ed. teacher. Mr. Smith, these are my parents, Mr. and Mrs. (name).
TEACHER: How do you do? Your son/daughter is one of my better students.
YOU: Oh, thanks Mr. Smith, but that's because yours is one of my favorite classes.
PARENT: My son/daughter talks a lot about the P.E. class.
TEACHER: That's nice to know.
YOU: Well, I don't want to take up too much of your time. I'm glad my parents could meet you.
TEACHER: I'm very glad to have met them.
YOU: See you back in school. Bye.

Situation 2. You are late for your club meeting. The group is talking about next week's picnic. You want to join in.

YOU: Excuse me, I'm sorry I'm late. I guess you're talking about the picnic. Has anything been decided yet?
PERSON B: No, not yet. We really just started.
YOU: Oh, good. I was hoping I didn't miss too much. Has anybody said yet that the lake park would be a good place?
PERSON C: Not yet. So far, the city park and the beach have been discussed.
YOU: Well, I think the lake park would be good because. . . .

Situation 3. You are at a party and don't know anyone.

YOU: Hi, my name is (name). I feel kind of like a stranger. I don't know very many people here.

PERSON B: I'm (name). Maybe I could introduce you to a few other people.

YOU: I'd really like that. Do you know many of these people?

PERSON B: Some, but not everybody.

YOU: I guess there are a lot of people here. I really would appreciate meeting a few more people.

Situation 4. You would like to end a conversation with someone.

YOU: Well, it was nice speaking with you, but I really have to go now.

OR

I really enjoyed speaking with you. I've got to go now. Maybe we can meet again soon.

OR

Oh, I'm late for my class. I'd really like to finish speaking with you. Can we get together later?

OTHER: OK, I'll see you later.

YOU: Thanks, Bye.

Situation 5. After listening to a concert with your friends, you want to talk about it with them.

YOU: Did you people like the concert? What did you like about it?

OR

I thought the concert was great. How about you?

OR

You look like you didn't like the concert. What didn't you like?

OTHERS: Oh, I thought it was good. It was just too hot.

YOU: Yeah, I guess that didn't bother me too much. I'm glad you came.

Situation 6. A classmate has made something in art class and you would like to know how he or she did it.

YOU: I really like the art project you made last week. Did it take long to do?

CLASSMATE: Oh, thanks. No, it really was pretty easy.

YOU: Where did you learn to do that? I don't think we had that in art class.

CLASSMATE: My art teacher from last year taught me. He did a lot of things like that.

YOU: Do you think that maybe sometime you might be able to show me how to do it?

CLASSMATE: Yeah, I'd like to. It's really easy.

YOU: Great! Maybe next Monday in art class we could get together.
CLASSMATE: That sounds OK to me.
YOU: I'm looking forward to that. Well, I better go or I'll be late for math.
  Thanks. See you later.
CLASSMATE: Take it easy.

Suggested Homework Assignments

1. In the next few days, try to start at least one conversation with a friend at school, with a new boy or girl at school, and with an adult (parent, neighbor) at home. Pay attention to how to start the conversation, how the conversation is kept going, and how it is ended. Try to end at least one of these conversations.
2. Try to join in on a conversation that has already started. Pay attention to what you said to join in, how you kept yourself involved in the conversation, and how it ended.

Module 10: Empathy

When you relate a story or a personal experience to another person, you would probably like to know whether that person understands what you are saying. This is also true when you try to convey an emotion or a private experience. In these situations you can often tell whether your listener is aware of what you are saying by observing his or her response to you.

Empathy is the ability to relate accurately and honestly to another person's feelings and emotions. In doing so, we are able to achieve a subjective understanding of what the other person is experiencing. By being empathic, we share the emotions of another person—excitement, sadness, joy, exhiliration. We also communicate to others that we are listening to what they are saying as well as trying to feel what they are feeling. We are, in a sense, opening ourselves to them, as they are to us.

The ability to be empathic is an asset. It conveys that you are understanding, responsive, concerned, respectful, and trustworthy. Certainly, these attributes would lend themselves to enhancing one's social desirability. It almost goes without saying that friendships, especially intimate friendships, are virtually impossible without the element of empathic understanding.

For children, becoming empathic and learning how to communicate empathy is a measure of their social maturation. Friendships can become more meaningful; words like *trust, feelings,* and *understanding* take on real meaning; and—by gaining empathy—one moves away from being a social isolate. The objective of this module is, therefore, to teach young people how to communicate empathy and, it is hoped, to gain greater insights into the meaning and importance of empathy.

Sample Lecture on Empathy

Today we are going to discuss empathy. Empathy is being able to feel and understand what another person is feeling. For instance, if a friend of yours is feeling sad and maybe even crying, do you feel sad? If a classmate is laughing really hard about something, do you find that you also tend to laugh or smile? If someone you know gets very excited about good news, do you feel excited for him or her? If you answered yes to any of these questions, then what you have felt is a form of empathy.

Empathy really means understanding how a person is feeling or thinking and letting them know that you can share those feelings (feel like they do).

It is important to remember that for you to become "empathic," you need to learn how to feel for others. Learning empathy, like other skills takes time and practice. For instance, you should already know what it feels like to be sad, happy, lonely, excited, or even scared. You also should know what kinds of situations can make you feel those ways. You already know some of these things, which means that you probably have the ability to share feelings and be empathic.

DISCUSSION QUESTIONS

1. What kinds of things make people happy? Sad? Lonely? Excited? Scared?
2. Can you describe each of these feelings?
3. Do you ever feel sad–happy–scared–excited when someone tells you that type of story? Why?

Now that you know that you have some empathic ability, it's important to learn how to use it correctly. Usually, when you are empathic, you try to help someone feel better by letting them know that you understand or are *trying* to understand how *they* feel. For example, if a friend tells you that he is very sad because he lost his dog, it might make him feel a little better if you said something like, "I'm sorry to hear that; I really liked Sparky too. That's really sad news." By saying this, you are telling your friend that you share his sadness and would like to offer some comfort. In this situation, you are showing empathy. You honestly feel bad for your friend and you want to help make him feel better.

However, you don't have to have empathy just for sad or unhappy situations; you can also share in someone's happiness. For example, pretend that your sister has just found out that she won first prize in an art contest for a painting that she worked very hard on. She comes running up to you after school and jumps up and down with joy. "Guess what? I won the first prize! I'm so excited I can't stop shaking!" You share your sister's excitement, "Wow, that's great! Oh, I knew you'd win! That's great!" You feel excited for your sister and your reaction has let her know this. You probably helped to make her even happier.

1. Can anyone give me examples of other situations where empathy is important?
2. In each of these cases, what does your being empathic tell the person who is experiencing the emotion?

3. Do you think that you can always be empathic, no matter what the situation? Why? Why not?

There are several ways in which you can find out how other people are feeling. First, it is important to listen to what others say when they describe their feelings. This is probably the best way to understand how they are feeling. Also, it helps to observe the other person carefully. You can learn a lot from people's facial expressions (smiling, looking sad, etc.), their gestures, the way that they have their hands, arms, and bodies, and the ways that they behave.

RATIONALE FOR CHILDREN

Benefits. Being able to share someone's feelings

A. can help people feel better, like someone cares about them.
B. can make them happier because they can share their feelings with you.

Sharing someone's feelings or being empathic can

A. make you feel good knowing that you helped to make things better.
B. help you understand other people better.
C. help you learn from another person's experiences because you feel what they are feeling.
D. make it easier to become close friends because you have shared special feelings.

Pitfalls. If you are not empathic

A. people will not share their feelings and thoughts with you.
B. it is possible that others will be less willing to listen and try to understand you.
C. it may be hard to develop close friendships.
D. you will not be able to share other people's emotions and feelings.

TRAINER'S SCRIPT: EMPATHY

I hope that you understand what empathy is and how important it is to express to others. So that we can get a little more practice with it, I will first give you a few more examples that we will do together. Later, you will have a chance to practice being empathic on your own.

Situation 1.   Your father/mother has just announced to the family that he/she is receiving a promotion and a raise. He/She is extremely proud and happy.

PARENT: I wanted you all to be first to know that I got a raise and promotion today. Isn't that great news?
YOU: That's fantastic! I'm glad; you deserve it!
PARENT: Thanks (name), but without such a great family, this wouldn't have happened.
YOU: We're all really proud and happy for you.

   (Assertive)—These are assertive responses because
1. you've let your parent know that you are interested in what he or she said and felt.
2. you have let your parent know that you share in the good feelings.
3. you have expressed an honest feeling and probably made your parent even happier knowing that you understand.

PARENT: I wanted you all to be the first to know that I got a raise and promotion. Isn't that great?
YOU: Hum.

OR

   Oh.
PARENT: Well, you all helped make this possible!
YOU: Not really.

OR

   Oh, c'mon.

   (Passive)—These are passive responses because
1. by not sharing in the positive experience, you take away some of the excitement of the occasion.
2. you have expressed that you really don't care.

PARENT: I wanted you to be the first to know that I got a raise and promotion today. Isn't that great?
YOU: So what took you so long?
PARENT: Well, you all helped make this possible!
YOU: Yeah, it it weren't for us you would still be waiting for a raise.

   (Aggressive)—These are aggressive responses because
1. you have probably made your parent angry.
2. you have made a happy occasion less so.
3. you acted like you were selfish and self-centered.

Situation 2. Your brother's best friend moved away today. You know he's feeling pretty sad. You go up to him.

YOU: I'm really sorry you feel so bad, Tom. We all liked Bill a lot, it's sad to see him go away.
BROTHER: He was my best friend, you know.
YOU: I know. Maybe you can write or call him once in a while.
BROTHER: Yeah, I guess so.
YOU: I hope you feel better soon. Maybe we can do something later, OK?

> (Assertive)—These are assertive responses because
> 1. you have helped your brother feel a little bit better.
> 2. he probably appreciated your feelings.

YOU: I heard Bill left.
BROTHER: He was my best friend, you know.
YOU: Yeah.

> (Passive)—This is a passive response because
> 1. you didn't really help your brother to feel any different.
> 2. he probably thinks that you don't care about his feelings.

YOU: Oh, come on! Cheer up. This isn't the end of the world.
BROTHER: He was my best friend, you know.
YOU: So what. You've got lots of friends.
BROTHER: Not like Bill.

> (Aggressive)—This is an aggressive response because
> 1. you weren't very helpful.
> 2. you might have made your brother feel worse, or even mad at you.

PRACTICE SCRIPTS

Situation 1. You see a young child crying outside of a store. You want to help.

YOU: Oh, what's the matter? Why are you crying?
OTHER: I can't find my uncle. I'm only visiting and I'm lost.
YOU: You must be frightened. It's scary to be lost. Maybe we can find him. I'll help you look for him.
OTHER: Thank you.

Situation 2. Your dad is sitting alone at the kitchen table and look-ing a little sad.

YOU: What's the matter, Dad? Did something happen?
PARENT: Not really. Some things just aren't going right.
YOU: I really hate to see you feel this way. Is there anything I can do to cheer you up a little?
PARENT: Sure. Why don't we go out for a walk? That would be nice.

Situation 3. Your teacher just found out that she won the annual teaching award.

YOU: Congratulations, Ms. Taylor! I heard the good news at lunch today.
TEACHER: Thanks, that's very nice of you.
YOU: Well, I know all the kids are really excited and proud of you, and so am I. You must be really happy.

Situation 4. You have noticed that for the last few weeks one of your friends has not been acting like himself. You are a little worried.

YOU: How are you doing (name)? Is something wrong? You haven't been yourself lately.
FRIEND: I haven't been feeling too well. I went to see the doctor and he said I'll have to go the hospital for some tests.
YOU: Oh, gee, I'm sorry to hear that. I guess you're probably a little worried. Do you know how long you'll be there?
FRIEND: Probably not too long.
YOU: Can I help somehow? I feel bad that I didn't say something earlier.
FRIEND: Thanks, you already made me feel a little better. I didn't think anybody cared.

Situation 5. You are talking with some friends about the monster movie you just saw. One of your friends says:

FRIEND: Boy, I sure got scared when that hand came up.
YOU: Yeah, I know what you mean, it made me jump, too.
FRIEND: I really had trouble keeping my eyes open.
YOU: Oh yeah! In fact, I missed the next scene because mine were closed.

Situation 6. A classmate loses the election for class president and feels kind of bad.

YOU: Too bad that you didn't win today; I thought you would.
CLASSMATE: So did I. I wonder what went wrong?

YOU: Try not to feel too bad. It's always hard to lose. I lost a class election last year and took it pretty bad.

CLASSMATE: Really? What happened?

YOU: Actually, I got over it pretty quickly.

CLASSMATE: Well, that's good. That makes me feel a little better.

Situation 7.   One of the kids in your class comes in smiling and very happy about something that happened in gym.

YOU: You look happy. What happened?

OTHER: I was picked for the all-star team.

YOU: That's great! You must really be excited.

OTHER: I am. I can't wait until practice starts.

SUGGESTED HOMEWORK ASSIGNMENTS

Newspapers have lots of stories about people who are experiencing all kinds of emotions (feelings). Find one example of a sad story, a happy story, and a story where someone gets exciting news. Pretend you know the person and try to figure out a way to empathize with his or her feelings. Write down what you would say. What effect do you think you might have had on the other person?

Module 11: Nonverbal Social Skills

An important part of being a skilled communicator is being able to use nonverbal signals to illustrate or emphasize what is being said. When verbal components and nonverbal cues are congruent, communication will be optimally clear.

Nonverbal cues help to provide feedback and information exchange between people in addition to conveying the affect and intensity of the verbal message. Researchers have found that nonverbal communication plays an important role in guiding interactions and in defining relationships among people. It also signals changes in speaker–listener roles. Thus, it is easy to understand how deficient nonverbal skills can affect not only the content of what is said but also the flow of conversation.

Generally, the nonverbal component of the communication should support the verbal component. Inconsistencies between the two modes are likely to result in misunderstandings, ineffective communication, double messages, and discomfort on the part of those interacting. In addition to learning the important nonverbal cues and gestures, it is necessary to recognize the interrelationship between nonverbal and verbal communication. For children, as with adults, skill in the use of nonverbal communication is essential. The youngster who has developed this aspect of his or her social skills will be a more effective communicator.

Note: This module can be accompanied by "charades." Cards are made up with situations involving expression of feeling and requiring use of nonverbal gestures (e.g., "You are happy to see your friend when he returns from vacation"), which children can then act out. You might also suggest that children describe a movie they've seen recently and comment on nonverbal gestures of both speaker and listener.

SAMPLE LECTURE ON NONVERBAL SKILLS

Today, we are going to talk about something that we all use and see other people using when they are speaking—nonverbal communication or talking without words. Let me show you what I mean. Imagine that a friend of yours is walking toward you while you are out playing or shopping. As your friend gets closer to you, you smile, wave, and say

"Hi." However, your friend just looks up at you and says "Hi" without any expression on his or her face. How would you feel? Well, your friend has *said* as much as you, but you probably *communicated* more. What is missing from your friend's communication?

The things that you have noticed as missing or wrong are what we call nonverbal signals. Almost every time we speak with other people, we are constantly giving and receiving nonverbal signals. When you smile, frown, look surprised, look sad, look angry, wave, and make lots of other expressions and gestures, you are communicating without words. By doing these things, you make it easier for other people to understand *exactly* what you mean. For instance, if you told somebody, "I'm mad!" and you only looked a little mad, that person might not be as impressed as if you really looked angry. If you were to tell a friend that his joke was funny but had no smile on your face, your friend might have trouble believing you.

DISCUSSION QUESTIONS

1. Can you give me other examples of nonverbal signals?
2. Does nonverbal communication help to get a point or message across?
3. How does it help to get the message across?
4. What would happen if you did not use nonverbal signals when you had something to say?

There are many different types of nonverbal signals, and all of them are important. However, because some of these signals are used more than others, there are about five signals that are really good to know about. They are *eye contact, facial gestures, hand and arm gestures, posture,* and the *distance that you stand or sit from the other person.* Let me give you an example of each of these. When we talk about eye contact, we mean looking at the other person when we are speaking with them. Facial gestures refer to expressions that you make with your face. When you smile, you are making a facial gesture. By hand and arm gestures, we mean things you say with your hands and arms. For instance, when you wave "Hi" or "Bye" to another person, you are using a hand and arm gesture.

Your posture is also a form of nonverbal communication because you can give different messages just by the way you are standing or sitting. For instance, if you are talking to someone and she is slouched in her chair looking at the floor, she is sending you a message like "I'm bored" or "I'm tired." The last type of nonverbal signal that we will talk about is what is called "proximity," or how close or how far you are from another person. Even though we may not be aware of it, we use this signal a lot. For example, if you were talking to a friend and he backed away from you slowly, wouldn't you think he was trying to tell you something?

DISCUSSION QUESTIONS

1. How many different examples can you give me of each of the following:
   Eye contact
   Facial gestures
   Head and arm gestures
   Posture
   Proximity (how close or far
       you are from the other person)
2. What does each mean?
3. For some of the examples that you have given, can you explain how or why they are important?

As you probably realize, it is common to use several different non-verbal signals at the same time. By doing this, you can make what you are saying even *more* understandable. However, it is very important to remember that when you use any of these signals, they should match what it is that you are trying to say. When this does not happen, not only will people have a harder time understanding what it is that you are saying but they may also think that *you* are confused. So, just as it is important to think carefully about what you are saying, it is also very important to think of how you are going to say it nonverbally. If the two fit, you've done a good job; if they don't match, your communication may not be clear.

RATIONALE FOR CHILDREN

Benefits.   Using nonverbal communication the right way

A. can help make what you are saying easier to understand.
B. can make what you are saying more enjoyable or interesting to listen to.
C. can make it easier to express difficult ideas or feelings.
D. helps people to know when it is their turn to speak and when the conversation is over.

Pitfalls. By not using nonverbal communications or using them incorrectly

A. you'll find it difficult to get your message across.
B. it might be harder for you to keep people's interest in what you are saying.
C. your conversations can seem awkward and make you feel uncomfortable.
D. you could give others the wrong impression or message.
E. you make it easier for others to misunderstand you.

TRAINER'S SCRIPT

I'm going to show you some examples of how people use nonverbal signals. When I finish, you will practice some on your own.

The following examples contrast the *appropriate* use of nonverbal signals with *inappropriate* and *poor* use of nonverbal signals. The ridiculousness of some of the examples shows the importance of proper usage.

Situation 1. You are extremely happy about receiving a gift from your parents that you've wanted for a long time.

YOU: (with appropriate nonverbal signals: smiles, eye contact) Thanks, Mom and Dad. This is really great! It's just what I wanted.
PARENT: Well, you really deserved it.
YOU: Thanks again.

(Appropriate)—This is an appropriate use of nonverbal communication because

1. you are correctly expressing that you are happy (i.e., smiling, eye contact).

YOU: (with *no* nonverbal signals: deadpan expression and flat affect) Thanks, Mom and Dad. This is really great. It's just what I wanted.
PARENT: Well, you certainly don't look too excited.
YOU: I am.

(Unclear)—The communication is unclear because

1. what you are saying is not the same as your nonverbal message.
2. it makes you look like you're faking it.

YOU: (with the *opposite* nonverbal signal: frown, shoulders down, no eye contact) Thanks, Mom and Dad. This is really great. It's just what I wanted.

PARENT: What's the matter? Aren't you feeling well?

YOU: No, I feel just fine.

(Inappropriate)—This is an inappropriate use of nonverbal communication because

1. it appears that you are being forced to say this.
2. you are acting like you might not really mean it.

Situation 2.   You are excited about a big exotic fish that you saw at the aquarium. You are telling your friends about it.

YOU: (with appropriate nonverbal signals: smiles, eye contact, hand gestures, close proximity) Boy, it was big! It was as big as a horse.

FRIEND: Wow! That was big.

(Appropriate)—This is an appropriate nonverbal response because
1. your hand gestures express the "bigness" of the fish.
2. you appear to be excited.

YOU: (with *no* nonverbal signals: expressionless, no vocal intonation) Boy, was it big. It looked like the size of a truck.

FRIEND: How big?

YOU: Really big.

(Unclear)—This is unclear because
1. your gestures didn't match what you are saying.
2. you are not acting excited about the size of the fish.

YOU: (With the *wrong* nonverbal signals: frown, looking away, no gestures) Boy it was big. It looked like the size of a truck.

FRIEND: What? How big?

YOU: You know, about this big.

FRIEND: What are you talking about?

(Inappropriate)—This is an inappropriate response because
1. you gave your friend the impression that you really don't know what "big" is.
2. your friends won't believe you because what you're saying doesn't match your hand gestures.

PRACTICE SCRIPTS

Note: Students should be encouraged to concentrate on developing their own nonverbal routines to accompany the practice scripts. Some guidelines for appropriate nonverbal behaviors are provided.

Situation 1.   A friend of yours was in the hospital for a little while. Now she is back in class. You walk over to your friend and stand next to her. You are glad that she is back in school. You look at her and smile.

YOU: Welcome back! Are you feeling OK now?
FRIEND: Oh, sure. What's been going on?
YOU: Well, we all really missed you. Not too much has happened.
FRIEND: It's good to be back.

Situation 2.   You just heard some sad news about one of your class-mates. You want to say something to him. You walk over to your class-mate and stand by him. As you speak, you look into his eyes. Your facial expression is a serious and concerned.

YOU: I'm really sorry about what happened, (name). Is there anything I can do to help?
CLASSMATE: Thanks. Things will get better soon.
YOU: Well, if you want someone to talk to, give me a call, OK?
CLASSMATE: Yeah. Thanks.

Situation 3.   You have just run into a friend whom you haven't seen in a while. Facing your friend, you have a surprised though happy look on your face. (Suggested nonverbal behaviors: surprised look, smiling, eye contact, and body turned toward other.)

YOU: Hey (name), how have you been? It's great to see you again.
FRIEND: Yeah! How have you been doing?
YOU: Pretty good! Wow, I'm really surprised to see you!

Situation 4.   You are telling some friends about a roller coaster ride that you were just on. While talking to your friends, you have an excited look on your face. You are smiling and using hand gestures to show what the ride was like. (Suggested nonverbal behaviors: eye contact, smiling, hand gestures.)

YOU: It started by going up this really steep climb, and then you got to the top, you could see the whole park.
FRIEND: How fast were you going?
YOU: It was slow then. But when we went over the top, we just shot right down the track. I had to grab on to the rail.
FRIEND: Wow! That sounds like fun!

Situation 5.   Somebody asks you for directions to the gas station. In explaining the directions, you are using hand gestures to show right and left turns, etc. (Suggested nonverbal behaviors: eye contact, hand gestures.)

YOU: Let me see. Go straight down this road until you get to an intersection. There are two churches there. Take a left turn and stay on the road for three blocks. The station will be on your right.
OTHER: Thanks.

Situation 6.   You are describing a scary scene from a movie that you saw. You have a scared look on your face and your voice is low, almost at a whisper. You are using your hands and body movements to show what happened. (Suggested nonverbal behaviors: a scared look, gestures, voice intonation.)

YOU: They opened the door and the room was completely dark inside. It was really spooky. They walked into the room and, all of a sudden, the door slammed behind them.
OTHER: Then what?
YOU: Then the guy said, "Shhhh, did you hear that?"

Situation 7.   Somebody has unfairly accused you of cheating on a test. You are directly facing the other person and looking into his eyes. You have an angry expression on your face.

YOU: That's not true! I didn't cheat! I never would.
OTHER: But I saw you.
YOU: What exactly did you see? I think *you're* making this up.
OTHER: Why should I do that?
YOU: I don't know, but I'm getting a little angry?

Situation 8.   You are buying gift wrap and are describing how much paper you will need. You use hand gestures to show the size of the box. (Suggested nonverbal behaviors: eye contact, hand gestures.)

YOU: I need enough paper for a box about this long and this wide.

Situation 9.   You see an interesting insect and are calling your friends over. (Suggested nonverbal behaviors: eye contact, hand gestures.)

YOU: Hey! Come over here and look at this!

Situation 10.   Your teacher has just told you that you won a class art contest. You have an excited and happy expression on your face. (Suggested nonverbal behaviors: excited facial expression, eye contact.)

YOU: That's fantastic!

Suggested Homework Assignments

1. Watch a television show at home with the sound turned off. Write down what you think is being said based on the nonverbal signals you are observing.
2. Observe other students at school and people at home and write down the ways that they are communicating nonverbally.
3. Observe two people who are talking with each other. Write down the different nonverbal behaviors they use to let each other know that they are listening and paying attention.
4. Find pictures in magazines and newspapers of people who are letting each other know how they feel about the other using nonverbal communication. What are they trying to communicate?

Module 12: Status Difference Interactions

Status differences generally involve the hierarchial structures that develop within groups, assigning higher levels of prestige to certain individuals or subgroups than to others. These status differences are derived from such variables as the degree to which an individual is held in esteem or affection, an individual's authority and power within a group, and the individual's age.

Status difference interactions play an important role in our everyday communications. When we ask a boss for a raise, interview for a job, or even speak to a store (restaurant) manager, we are engaging in a status difference interaction. In all of these examples, the way that we would approach the other person is somewhat different from the way we would address a peer. Whether it be out of respect for a person and his or her position or because of established protocol, the need often arises to adjust what is being said as well as how it is said to fit the status of the person being addressed.

Typically, adults encounter other adults in a variety of social interactions, often limiting status difference relationships to their job. For children, however, interactions with adults are not only frequent but they usually require respect because of status difference. These child–adult interactions include encounters with parents, teachers, neighbors, counselors, relatives, and other adults. Communications with parents are probably the most frequent and of greatest consequence initially; thus they serve as the vehicle for developing skills in status difference interactions. In fact, researchers have concluded that children tend to generalize the status difference relationship from their parents to other adults. The child's development of this skill can contribute to the ease and success with which he or she relates to the adult world.

Sample Lecture on Status Difference Interactions

Today we are going to talk about status difference interactions. By this we mean how you talk to people whose status is different from yours, like your parents, your teachers, and other adults. As I'm sure you realize, you don't talk to adults in the same way that you talk to other children. Chances are that if you were angry at your mom or dad, you wouldn't say the same thing as you would to one of your classmates. If you did, you would probably get into trouble.

What makes talking to adults different from talking to your friends and classmates is that they are in charge or in a position of authority; they are in control of things. Because of this, we are expected to treat them with respect. For example, if adults do or say something that you are not happy with, you shouldn't jump up and down and scream or say that you are going to tell on them. That would be pretty silly! However, there are ways that you can tell an adult that you are upset with him or her that are appropriate and effective. In some ways, this section is similar to that on standing up for your rights. Here, however, you are dealing with adults.

Discussion Questions

1. Can anyone tell me what is meant by "status difference" interactions
2. How many different examples can you give of people who have a status different from yours? Why is their status different?
3. Would you interact differently with these people than with your friends?

It's easy to see that learning how to speak with adults in a way that is socially appropriate can be beneficial. It will help you to get along better with adults and make it easier for them to speak with you and understand you. Later on, when it is time to get a job or even if you just want a job for the summer, it will probably help if you know how to talk with your employer. Can you imagine what might happen if you asked a store manager for a job in the same way that you asked your best friend for a favor? You would probably end up not getting the job. It is important to remember that if you treat adults with respect, they will be more likely to treat you with more respect. But just like with requesting favors, people will not always do as you ask them, even if you treat them respectfully. If this is the case, think again about what you are doing. Then, if you still think that it is important, try again.

Rationale for Children

Benefits.   By being skillful in status difference interactions

A. you can get along better with adults (i.e., your parents and your teachers).
B. you have a better chance at getting jobs or requesting favors from adults.
C. you will be treated in a more grown-up way.

D. adults will pay more attention to you.

E. you might find it easier to get along with older kids.

Pitfalls. By not having skill in status difference interactions

A. you may have trouble communicating with adults (i.e., your parents and teachers).

B. you may find that adults will be less willing to listen to you.

C. you may become embarrassed in speaking with adults.

D. you may have trouble getting a job.

E. older children (i.e., your brothers or sisters or your neighbors) may not want you to hang around.

TRAINER'S SCRIPT

Situation 1. Your parents don't want you to go to a party at your friend's house. They want you to take care of your younger brother/sister. You want to go to the party.

PARENT: You know that I wanted you to stay home tonight. You have to baby-sit this evening.

YOU: Oh gee, I've been waiting for that party for a long time. I don't mind baby-sitting, but this party is special.

PARENT: Well, we've had plans for some time now. I'm sorry but we have no choice.

YOU: All right then. It's too bad, but there will be other parties.

PARENT: Next time, we'll make sure you can go, OK?

(Assertive)—This is an assertive response because
1. you have expressed your point of view.
2. you were courteous and respectful.

PARENT: You know that I wanted you to stay home tonight. You have to baby-sit this evening.

YOU: Oh gee.

PARENT: I'm sorry, but we've already made plans, so stop fussing.

(Passive)—This is a passive response because
1. you didn't let your parents know your reasons.
2. you acted like a "complainer."

PARENT: You know that I wanted you to stay home tonight. You have to baby-sit this evening.

YOU: What? Again? Why don't you hire a baby-sitter?!
PARENT: Don't raise your voice to me! Stop talking back!

> (Aggressive)—This is an aggressive response because
> 1. by being rude, you have made your parents angry.
> 2. you hurt your chances to go to the party.
> 3. you didn't say why you didn't want to baby-sit.

Situation 2. Your uncle has been playfully teasing you, but you don't like it very much. You want to let him know that this bothers you.

YOU: Excuse me, Uncle Harry, I know you're just kidding, but that embarrasses me and bothers me a little.
UNCLE: I'm sorry, I didn't think it bothered you.
YOU: I know that; that's why I knew I could tell you.

> (Assertive)—This is an assertive response because
> 1. you have made it clear that you are unhappy but have done so in a courteous and respectful manner.
> 2. your uncle will probably stop teasing you.

YOU: (You just let your uncle continue until you get so upset you go to your room. Your uncle never realizes that something is wrong.)

> (Passive)—This is a passive response because
> 1. you didn't explain your feelings.
> 2. your uncle probably thinks that you are being rude.

YOU: Would you stop teasing me! It's not nice to do that.
UNCLE: Well, you don't have to be rude about it!
YOU: Just the same, I don't like it.
UNCLE: I think you had better learn some manners!

> (Aggressive)—This is an aggressive response because
> 1. your disrespect and rudeness may have hurt your uncle or made him angry.
> 2. you have probably made things worse for yourself.

PRACTICE SCRIPTS

Situation 1. Your teacher compliments you on the high score that you got on test.

TEACHER: You did a very nice job on the test (name).

YOU: Thank you. I studied very hard for it.
TEACHER: Well, your hard work shows. Keep up the good work.
YOU: Thank you. I'll try.

Situation 2.   You are on the school dance committee and have to ask your principal for permission to use the gym for the dance.

YOU: Excuse me, sir. I am a member of the dance committee and would like to know if we can get your permission to use the gym.
PRINCIPAL: I'll be able to give you an answer if you write down all the information that I need.
YOU: OK, I'll get the rest of the committee to help me write out our plans.

Situation 3.   You don't understand a math problem that your teacher has been discussing. You want to ask for some help.

YOU: Excuse me, Mr. White, but I had some trouble understanding that last problem. Could you explain it again, please?
TEACHER: Sure. What was it that you had trouble with?
YOU: Well, if you could start from the beginning, that would help.

Situation 4.   Your mother has scolded you for breaking a glass and you feel it wasn't your fault. You want to say something.

YOU: Mom, I don't mean to talk back to you, but I don't feel that I should have been scolded. I didn't even know that the glass was broken.
PARENT: I'm sorry, I thought that you were trying to keep it a secret.
YOU: No, I really didn't know.

Situation 5.   Your father has prepared one of your favorite dishes for dinner and you want to let him know that you appreciate it.

YOU: Thanks, Dad. I know you know that this is my favorite dish.
PARENT: Well, you deserved it; you've been working hard.
YOU: You really didn't have to do this, though. Thanks.

Situation 6.   You disagree with your teacher on a question that she marked wrong on your test. You want to explain your side.

YOU: Excuse me, Ms. Jones, but I think that one of the problems you marked wrong is right. I think my answer is right.
TEACHER: Let's see. I really don't think so. You might have misunderstood the question.

YOU: I'll read it again. I thought that I had the right answer, but I could be wrong.

TEACHER: Check it first, then we can discuss it later.

Situation 7.   Your friends are all getting allowances, and you feel that it is time to ask your parents for one.

YOU: Dad, do you think I could earn an allowance for doing chores around the house?

PARENT: What do you have in mind?

YOU: I thought I could do some extra work on the lawn and in the garage.

PARENT: OK, let's see what we can afford for an allowance.

YOU: That's great! Thanks!

Situation 8.   There is a special dance coming up soon and you want to buy some new clothes, but you don't have enough money. You want to ask your parents to help you out.

YOU: Mom, do you think you could let me borrow some money so I can get some new clothes for the dance? I would really appreciate your help.

PARENT: Do you really need something new? You have so many things to wear.

YOU: I know, but this is a special dance.

PARENT: Well, OK, I think that something could be worked out.

YOU: Great! Thanks.

Situation 9.   You would like to get a weekend job at the local grocery store to earn a little spending money. You ask to speak to the store manager.

YOU: Excuse me, Mr. Smith, but are there any jobs available on weekends? I would like to work part time so I can earn some money.

MANAGER: We don't really have any jobs right now, but if you give me your name and phone number, we'll call you when we have an opening.

YOU: That sounds good, thanks.

Situation 10.   An adult neighbor is also the coach of a Little League team and you would like some pointers on your pitching.

YOU: Mr. Jones, since you know a lot about baseball, do you think that you could show me how to pitch a curve ball?

COACH: Sure. How about this weekend?

YOU: Thanks. I'll bring my mitt and ball.

SUGGESTED HOMEWORK ASSIGNMENTS

1. Write down three examples of status difference interactions that you have observed or participated in. Include one example from your home, one example from school, and one from your neighborhood (or shopping, etc.).
2. Write down one example of a status difference interaction in which somebody behaved inappropriately. What did he or she do wrong? How could he or she have done better?

Module 13: Sex Difference Interactions

By the time most people reach adulthood, they are not as likely to feel trepidation, anxiety, and awkwardness in sex difference interactions as they did during their childhood and adolescence. As adults, we have greater skill and confidence in the area of mixed-sex social interaction. However, this is not true of all adults, nor do all adults have the same level of skills. Researchers have shown that a lack of social skills in mixed sex interactions can be a major factor contributing to social anxiety in adults. Fortunately, treatment programs designed to teach these skills have helped to reduce anxiety and incompetence in heterosexual social encounters.

Although the importance of mixed sex interaction does not become fully evident until adolescence, it is generally believed that the psychosocial groundwork for these skills begins to develop at a much earlier age. Whereas sex role development begins early in childhood and progresses through adolescence, it is during the preadolescent years that both physical and behavioral manifestations of sexuality become most apparent. Thus, the development of skills in sex difference interactions between youngsters can serve as an important aid in heterosocial development.

The purpose of this module is to develop skills in the area of heterosocial interaction. These skills will help to prepare the youngster to expand the scope of his or her peer interactions. Thus, the focus is on mixed-sex interactions concerning interpersonal communication.

Sample Lecture on Sex Differences Interactions

Today, we are going to talk about one type of peer interaction, which means talking with and hanging around with others your age, like your classmates and friends. Girls are usually comfortable talking to and being with other girls and boys are usually comfortable with boys, but girls and boys can learn to be just as comfortable with each other. So, when we talk about peer interaction we are also talking about boys speaking with girls and girls speaking with boys.

DISCUSSION QUESTIONS

1. Does anyone know why it seems more comfortable for a boy to talk to a boy or a girl with a girl?
2. (Boys) What stops you from speaking more with girls?
3. (Girls) What stops you from speaking more with boys?
4. What kinds of things can you talk about?

Today, we will try to help everybody here become better friends with everyone else, both boys and girls. We will also try to get rid of some of the things that can get in the way of these friendships. Everyone can learn and share things with everyone else, and it shouldn't matter whether we're talking about boys or girls, men or women. But sometimes we just don't know how to talk to another boy or girl. For example, Mary needs to borrow a pen because hers ran out of ink. There are no other girls sitting close by, and she can't get out of her seat during class. Mary doesn't want to ask the boy next to her because she is shy. What should she do?

DISCUSSION QUESTIONS

1. Why do you think that Mary is so shy?
2. Would she be as shy if a girl were sitting next to her?
3. Is it hard for girls in your class to talk to boys or boys to girls?
4. Can you give me another example in which a boy has the problem speaking?
5. What kinds of problems could not speaking to boys and girls cause?

RATIONALE FOR CHILDREN

Benefits.   By having skills in talking to or playing with both boys and girls

A. you can feel more comfortable speaking with boys or girls.
B. you can get to know more people and make more friends.
C. other people will feel more comfortable talking to you.

Pitfalls.   By not having skills in sex difference interactions

A. you may have trouble meeting and making new male and female friends.
B. (For boys) you might have trouble talking with girls socially.
C. (For girls) you might have trouble talking with boys socially.

D. you may have trouble or feel awkward speaking with the boys and girls in your class.

Trainer's Script[2]

You see, things would be a lot easier and you might even have more friends if you didn't let things like this bother you. Everyone is a little shy at first, but you can have more fun and be much more comfortable once you get over this. Let me give you a few more examples of problems and situations in which it would be good to know how to talk with people of the opposite sex. Afterward, you can practice some on your own.

Situation 1. There's a new kid in school and you notice that he or she is kind of confused about classroom numbers.

YOU: Hi, my name is (name). I guess that when you're new it's easy to get confused and lost.
OTHER: Yeah, this sure is a big school. My name is (name).
YOU: Well, it's pretty easy to get to know your way around. What's your homeroom number? I'll show you where to go.
OTHER: Gee, thanks, that'll help a lot.

(Assertive)—This is an assertive response because
1. you have helped someone out of a problem.
2. you might have made a new friend.

YOU: I guess you're kind of lost, huh?
OTHER: Yeah, this is a pretty big school.
YOU: Oh. Well, see you around.
OTHER: OK.

(Passive)—This is a passive response because
1. you didn't help the new student out.
2. you may have made him or her feel worse about being confused just because you couldn't talk to them because they were of the opposite sex.

YOU: You must be new here. You really look lost and out of place.
OTHER: Well, it is a big school.
YOU: It's not that big.
OTHER: It is to me.

---

[2] Set up practice scenarios so that they are all mixed sex interactions. The scripts devised for previous modules can be used for this section if practice dyads involve both sexes.

(Aggressive)—This is an aggressive response because
1. you failed to help the new person.
2. you were rude and not very considerate.

Situation 2. You are having a party but forgot to invite one of your classmates, a person you would like to come. You want to ask your classmate after school.

YOU: Say (name), somehow I forgot to invite you to my party. I didn't mean to. Do you think that you could still come?
CLASSMATE: Sure, I'd like to come to your party. I was wondering why I wasn't invited.
YOU: Well, it was a silly mistake. I'm glad you can come.

(Assertive)—This is an assertive response because
1. you excused yourself for your mistake.
2. you politely invited your friend to the party.

YOU: I'm having a party you know (name).
CLASSMATE: Yeah, I guess I heard something about that.
YOU: I guess you can come.
CLASSMATE: I'll have to see.

(Passive)—This is a passive response because
1. you didn't explain the reason for not inviting your friend in the first place.
2. it looks like you don't really want to invite your friend.

YOU: I hope you didn't think that I forgot to invite you to my party.
CLASSMATE: I wasn't sure.
YOU: Thanks a lot! I thought we were friends.
CLASSMATE: I was wondering if there was a problem.
YOU: Well, you can come.

(Aggressive)—This is an aggressive response because
1. you didn't apologize or explain your mistake.
2. the new invitation was rude and not very friendly.
3. you questioned your classmate's friendship.

PRACTICE SCRIPTS

Situation 1. You are playing a game of volleyball and you want to ask another person to join your team.

YOU: Hey (name), come on, we need another player. Would you like to be on our side?

OTHER: Sure. I'm not that good though.

YOU: That's OK. You're probably as good as any of us.

OTHER: OK! Where do you want me to play?

Situation 2. Someone in your class borrowed a pen from you but didn't return it. You want to ask to get it back.

YOU: Excuse me (name), but could I get that pen back that you borrowed? I need it.

OTHER: Oh, I forgot that I had it. Sure, I'll get it.

YOU: Thanks.

OTHER: Here it is, thanks for letting me borrow it.

Situation 3. You need a book for a report that you are writing, but you notice that it has been checked out by a person you don't know very well. You want to ask that person when he or she expects to be done with it.

YOU: Excuse me, my name is (name). Are you (name)?

OTHER: Yes, why?

YOU: Oh, I found out that you checked out a book that I'm looking for and I wanted to know when you might be finished with it.

OTHER: Actually, I don't need it anymore. If you want it, you can take it.

YOU: Great! Thanks.

Situation 4. There's someone in your class who you think is interesting (funny, smart, etc.); you want to get to know her or him better.

YOU: That was a really interesting story you told the class today. Do you have any more like that one? I'd like to hear them.

OTHER: Sure, but I really don't have time right now.

YOU: How about if I meet you after class tomorrow?

OTHER: Sure. I know some other people who would probably like to come along.

YOU: OK, I'll see you then.

Situation 5. You are sitting on the bus and a boy or girl from your school sits down across the aisle from you. You want to start a conversation.

YOU: Hi, my name is (name). I recognize you from school. Do you live around here?

OTHER: Yeah, I've seen you at school, too. I just moved here from across town.

YOU: I thought you were new here. What's your name?

OTHER: I'm (name). You're the first person I've met from this neighborhood. Are there other kids around here?

YOU: Sure. Listen, if you like, you can walk with a group of us to school tomorrow.

OTHER: Great! Where should I meet you?

Situation 6. As chairperson of the student dance committee, you have to ask other students to help you put up decorations. There's a person in your class that you would like to ask because you've heard that he or she has done this before.

YOU: Excuse me (name). I heard that you helped with the class party last year and that it turned out really well.

OTHER: Who told you that?

YOU: Some kids from your class. Do you think you would want to help us decorate for the dance next week?

OTHER: Sure. We'll need some good ideas for decorations.

YOU: Well, let's meet on Friday afternoon at 3 to talk about it some more.

OTHER: OK, I'll be there.

YOU: Thanks!

Situation 7. There's someone in school who, you've heard, has been saying some bad things about you. You want to find out whether this is true.

YOU: Hi (name), I'd like to ask you something kind of important, OK?

OTHER: Sure, what's up?

YOU: Well, I was told that you've told some other people some bad things about me, and I wanted to know if that's true.

OTHER: I did, but I was only kidding.

YOU: Even if you were kidding, that wasn't very nice to say. Besides, *they* didn't think you were kidding.

OTHER: I'm sorry. I didn't mean for this to happen. I'll tell them that I was kidding.

YOU: OK, thanks.

HOMEWORK ASSIGNMENTS

1. Write down an example of sex difference interaction between children that you have seen on television or in the movies. De-

scribe the interaction. What happened? What could have made it better?

2. Write down an example of sex difference interaction between adults from a TV show or movie that didn't work out because one of the people had poor social skills. What should that person have done? How would things have ended differently if the person had good social skills?

3. Begin at least one conversation at school with someone of the opposite sex with whom you might become a friend.

MODULE 14: DECISION MAKING

RATIONALE FOR TRAINER

"It's so hard to decide." "I just can't make up my mind." These are phrases that we hear quite often. You would think that a simple decision like what to wear, what to do, or what to buy would be easy to make. For many people, this is not true. The problem, however, becomes much more troublesome when there is a choice to be made, the outcome of which can have important consequences. This would include career decisions, a decision involving a large amount of money (like buying a car or a house), or decisions involving personal or monetary risk. Whatever the decision might be, the ability to decide intelligently without ruminating, procrastinating, or vacillating is a vital skill.

What is it, then, that makes some people better decision makers than others? Researchers suggest that those individuals who are good at making decisions have the ability to organize relevant choices efficiently and to rank them according to their benefits and drawbacks. When this is done, the skilled decision maker chooses what is seemingly the best course of action and then acts. This combination of skilled organizing, choosing, and acting is what makes up decision making. Of course, even the best of decision makers can occasionally err in making the "right" choice. However, it has been demonstrated that people who mull and ponder over their options and choices as well as those who are impulsive in their decision making are less effective than the individual who approaches decisions in a determined yet organized fashion.

Socially, decision makers are generally regarded positively and are recognized as being capable, self-confident, and organized. Many times, individuals who have been singled out for their decision-making abilities are chosen as group, club, or activity leaders. Thus, a high premium (i.e., social status) is associated with this ability. The child who has learned the skills of decision making is often recognized by his or her peers, teachers, and parents as being more mature and intelligent. Functionally, this ability helps the child to eliminate or reduce the inconvenience, anxiety, and awkwardness of being indecisive, thus improving the overall quality of his or her social interactions.

SAMPLE LECTURE ON DECISION MAKING

Today we are going to talk about decision making. You are probably wondering why this is an important topic to talk about. Actually, knowing how to make decisions is not always very easy. I'm sure that all of you here can remember a time when you could not make up your mind or decide on something. You also probably felt a little silly or maybe even frustrated and angry with yourself because you couldn't decide. So you see, most people at some time or another have been in a situation where they have had trouble making a decision.

You are constantly faced with having to make decisions about what to wear, what to get for lunch, what movie to go to, and who you want to go with. These things are probably not that hard to decide. From time to time, you also have more important decisions to make. Some of these include decisions about what kind of job you eventually want to get, decisions about whether or not to "go along" with your friends when they are doing something that may not be right, and whether or not you should invite somebody (a date) to go out with you. I think you'll agree that things like these *are* a little more difficult to decide.

DISCUSSION QUESTIONS

1. Can anyone give me examples of decisions that you are faced with every day?
2. Have you ever had trouble making a decision on one of these? Which?
3. How did you feel while you were trying to make up your mind but couldn't?
4. How does not making up your mind affect you?

What should you do when you have to make a decision? Even though you have decided on many different things, some important and some not, there is a basic method you use for deciding. First, you have to make sure that you know what your choices are. This involves thinking about all the important ways that you can choose to behave or think. Second, you have to figure out the benefits and the consequences about each of your top choices. Third, you should begin to get a pretty good idea of what you ought to do. Then comes the hard part, doing it. The more practice you get in doing the first three steps, the easier it becomes to "do it."

For example, there are three different movies that you want to see and you have to choose one of them. You can't seem to make up your mind. So what you have to do is: (1) think about your choices—going to see Movie 1, Movie 2, Movie 3, or not going at all; then (2) figure out what is good and bad about each movie—Movie 1 looks good but nobody else wants to see it with you, Movie 2 should be good but it's more expensive than the others, Movie 3 had good previews and it's playing just a few blocks away, and you definitely don't want to sit at home tonight; (3) choose one thing to do—you decide to see Movie 3. Now, all that remains for you is to (4) go to the movie and have a good time.

DISCUSSION QUESTIONS

1. Can you give me some examples of decisions that are hard to make?
2. In each case, what are your choices?
3. What is good and bad about each choice?
4. In each case, which is the best choice?

RATIONALE FOR CHILDREN

Benefits.   The ability to make decision quickly, efficiently, and intelligently

A. can help reduce your feeling of frustration when you have to make a choice.
B. can help you become more effective in social situations.
C. help you to avoid wasting time in trying to make decisions.
D. can increase your chances of having your opinion respected by others.

Pitfalls.   By not being able to decide

A. you can lose out on good opportunities and experiences.
B. other people might have less confidence in you.
C. you end up wasting time.
D. you can end up feeling frustrated with yourself.
E. others might end up "deciding" for you.

TRAINER'S SCRIPT

Now that you've gotten to this point, it is important to remember that part of making any decision is doing what you have chosen to do. Let me give you a few more examples of situations in which you are faced with a decision and how you can make up your mind. After this, you can practice making decisions on your own.

Situation 1. Your parents have asked you to take your younger brother with you to the movies. You really don't want to. It is a tough decision to make.

1. Your choices are:
   a. Take your brother.
   b. Don't take your brother.
   c. Don't go to the movies.
2. The good and bad results are:
   a. You'll make your parents happy but you might not have as good a time at the show.
   b. You'll feel bad because your parents might be disappointed in you, and your brother might feel that you don't like him.
   c. You really want to go to the show.
3. Your choice is:
   a. You'll take your brother—that way your parents will be happy and maybe you'll have a great time anyway.
4. Your action is:
   a. Go to the show with your brother.

Situation 2. You are shopping for a birthday card for your father and you are having trouble deciding which one to get.

1. Your choices are:
   a. Card A
   b. Card B
   c. Card C
2. The good and bad results are:
   a. Card A—you like this one but it might be too silly for your father.
   b. Card B—your father will like this, it has a picture of his favorite hobby; but you think that it is old-fashioned.
   c. Card C—this one is really nice; you like and you think your father will, too. It is kind of expensive though (30 cents more than the others).
3. Your choice is:
   a. You decide on Card C because it is a nice birthday card and you know your father will like it; besides, 30 cents isn't really that much more.
4. Your action is:
   a. Buy Card C.

PRACTICE SCRIPTS

The following present examples in which decisions have to be made. Have each person make up his or her own scenario based on the example. Be sure to emphasize that he or she should carefully follow the procedure of:

1. identifying the choices.
2. deciding what is good and bad about each.
3. choosing one.
4. acting.

Initially, have the students verbalize how it is that they are making their decision. After a while, have them do it in their heads and ask them to explain what they did after they have made a choice.

Situation 1.   Your family is going to the movies together on Saturday night. You have also been invited to a party by some of your friends. What are you going to do?

Situation 2.   For next year, you have a choice between taking a class that you really want and taking a class that all your friends are going to be in. Which one will you choose?

Situation 3.   Three different people have asked you to sit with them at lunch. You like them all and you don't want to hurt anybody's feelings. You also know that they don't really care for each other. Who are you going to sit with?

Situation 4.   Your grandparents have given you a choice between getting one small present for your birthday and another for Christmas or one expensive present for Christmas. Which one of these choices will you take?

Situation 5.   There are three ways you could earn money during your summer vacation. Your parents will give you $15 a week to baby-sit with your younger sister. Your next door neighbors (your parents' friends) will pay you $20 a week to help clean their house. The manager at the supermarket will let you work bagging groceries for tips (between $10 and $30 a week). All these jobs involve the same amount of time. Which will you choose?

Situation 6.   You just got $5 for your allowance. One of your friends is having a birthday soon and you have to decide whether to get your friend a present or get the T-shirt that you want that costs $4.80. What will you do?

Situation 7. There are three records (toys, books) that you really want to buy, but you only have enough money for one. Which one will you get?

Situation 8. Your parents have offered to take you and two of your friends to the beach for the day. You have three very close friends and you don't want to hurt anybody's feelings. Which ones are you going to invite to come along?

Situation 9. Someone in class has cheated on a test and you know who it is. You are in a bad position because you know the person pretty well, but you also know that cheating is very wrong. The teacher is upset with the class and you think this is not fair. What are you going to do?

Situation 10. Your best friend gave you a sweater for your birthday. She or he thinks that it is a great looking sweater and has one just like it. You think that it is pretty ugly. You can return it to the store if you do so within the next two days. What are you going to do?

Suggested Homework Assignments

1. Try to remember a time when you made a wrong or bad choice and see if you can imagine the decision that you had to make. Using the procedure that you have been practicing, choose, again, what to do. Did you make the same choice? Why? Did you choose differently? Why?
2. Observe people around you when they are in a situation where they have to make a decision. Were any of these people impulsive (deciding without really thinking about it)? Did any of them have to think about the choices over and over again to make a decision? Did any of them procrastinate (unnecessarily put off making a decision)? Why would making a quick yet intelligent decision have helped these people?

Module 15: Group Interactions

Rationale for Trainer

By group interactions we mean situations in which three or more individuals are communicating with each other. It is precisely this that makes group interactions somewhat more difficult than dyadic interactions. That is, there are more people to address verbally and nonverbally and to whom you must attend. In one-to-one conversations, it is generally easier to keep track of what is being said and the manner in which it is said. In group interactions, this process becomes more complicated.

In the group interaction, rules that govern dyadic communication are expanded. Each participant must learn how to share the speaker's platform and avoid monopolizing it. At the same time, participants must make sure that they are included in the interaction. Furthermore, each participant must share the responsibility of keeping his or her contributions relevant to the group's interest.

Group interactions also tend to increase an individual's sensitivities and insecurities about social participation. The person who is reluctant to engage in dyadic social interaction is usually even more reticent in a group. In fact, it is not unusual for a person to be able to participate in social dyads and still experience anxiety and insecurity in group interactions.

For the child and adolescent, social skills in group interactions are an important part of successful psychosocial development. For children perhaps more than for adults, peer-group activities are an important component of everyday life. School activities, play, team sports, clubs and extracurricular activities all involve some form of group encounter. The child who is unable to enjoy these activities because of deficient social skills is socially handicapped. The skilled youngster is able to develop self-confidence and a sense of security in most social situations. Thus, the development of skills in group interactions has important short- and long-term consequences for the children.

Sample Lecture on Group Interactions

Today we are going to talk about group interactions. By group interactions we mean situations in which three or more people are interacting or talking with each other. I'm sure that almost every day you are in situations where you are with a group of friends or classmates, talking together and doing things. This is a group interaction, and learning how to talk and behave when you are part of a group is very important. Just as knowing how to speak with another person is important, so is having social skills in group interaction.

Because you are often with groups of people, not having these skills may lead you to experience some uncomfortable and possibly embarrassing situations.

DISCUSSION QUESTIONS

1. How many different examples of group interactions can you think of?
2. Are group interactions an important part of what you do every day? Why?
3. What would happen if you didn't have skills in group interaction?
4. Why are these skills important to you?

Basically, there are three main points that you should be aware of in group interactions. First, it is very important that you *listen to what the other people have to say*. This will not only let *you* know what is going on but also let *them* know that you are interested in what they have to say. Second, you should *be assertive (speak up) when you have something that you want to say*. If you don't do this, the other people won't know what you're thinking and you won't be able to tell them about things you feel are important. On the other hand, you have to be careful about talking too much and not giving the other people a chance to speak. When this happens, people will begin to lose interest in what you have to say. It is also important to make sure that what you have to say is connected with what the group is discussing or doing. Third, when you are participating—speaking and listening—in a group interaction, it is important that you *include as many of the other group members as possible*. If you end up paying attention to or speaking with just one person, the other people may begin to lose interest. If there is someone in particular that you want to speak with, arrange to do so afterwards.

DISCUSSION QUESTIONS

1. When you are speaking with a group of people, why is it important
   a. to listen carefully to everyone?
   b. to speak up when you have something relevant to say?
   c. to try to include all the group members in the interaction?

2. What kinds of things can happen when these rules are not followed?

RATIONALE FOR CHILDREN

Benefits. Social skills in group interactions or being comfortable with a group of people can help you

   A. meet more people and make more friends.
   B. participate more easily in group activities (i.e., games, sports, clubs, etc.).
   C. share your ideas with a larger number of people.
   D. keep up with what is going on with your friends and classmates.
   E. participate more easily in classroom discussion.

Pitfalls. By not having social skills in group interactions

   A. you may find it difficult to participate in group activities.
   B. you may be left out of group activities (i.e., games, sports, clubs, etc.).
   C. you may have difficulty meeting new people and making new friends.
   D. you may feel anxious and embarrassed about speaking in class.

TRAINER'S SCRIPT

To help you better understand what we are talking about, I am going to give you an example of how you should participate in a group interaction. I'll show you the kinds of things that can go wrong and ways to deal with them. After this, you will practice some group interactions among yourselves.

Situation 1. You and some of your friends are discussing some plans for next Saturday's picnic.

FRIEND A: We should have a lot of fun because the park has a swimming pool, too.
YOU: Really? That's great, but I hope it doesn't rain or anything.
FRIEND B: Yeah, that could ruin everything.
FRIEND C: Maybe we should get one of the covered picnic areas?
YOU: That's a good idea. That way we'd be OK even if it rained.
FRIEND B: Yeah, but I think that it costs money to use those picnic areas.
FRIEND A: How much? Maybe we could get everybody to share the cost.

YOU: We could try; I think it depends on how much it costs. Why don't we call and find out?

FRIEND A: That's a good idea, I'll give the park a call.

FRIEND B: OK. Let's meet tomorrow and make our final plans, all right?

> (Assertive)—These are assertive responses because
> 1. you have added useful information.
> 2. you have made good suggestions.
> 3. you have helped to keep the conversation going.

FRIEND A: We should have a lot of fun because the park has a swimming pool, too.

YOU: Really? Actually, I don't like to swim that much. Last year I almost drowned at the beach. That was really scary. What if it rains? Hey, why don't we go out and play ball?

FRIEND B: I hope it doesn't rain. That could ruin everything.

YOU: Maybe we could get everybody to go to the movies instead of a picnic. There's a movie that I would really like to see.

FRIEND C: No, let's plan on a picnic. Besides, we could get one of those covered picnic areas.

YOU: I guess no one wants to play ball.

FRIEND B: Don't those areas cost money? I think they do.

FRIEND C: Do you know how much? Maybe we could split the cost.

YOU: I hope it's not too much. I'm trying to save as much money as I can for a new record. It's the one they've been playing on the radio.

FRIEND A: Maybe we should call the park, huh? I'll give them a call.

YOU: Hey (name), remember the last time you and I went to the park? Remember that. . . .

> (Inappropriate)—These are inappropriate responses because
> 1. your comments have taken away from the theme of the conversation.
> 2. you are forcing your own plans and ideas on the group.
> 3. you act like you don't care about other people's ideas.

PRACTICE SCRIPTS

The following examples are suggested topics for a group discussion and interaction. Students can use these topics to structure their own scripts. It is important to pay attention to the rules of group interaction described earlier.

1. Listen carefully to all participants.
2. Speak up when you have something relevant to say.
3. Try to include all group members in the conversation.

Situation 1.   You and some friends are talking about a television show that was on last night. You want to let them know that you enjoyed it and why you enjoyed it.

Situation 2.   You are a member of the class dance and party committee, and you are meeting to discuss plans for the Halloween celebration. Include in your discussion whether or not to wear costumes and what kinds of snacks you want to have.

Situation 3.   Some kids from your neighborhood have gotten together to plan a neighborhood softball team. You are discussing where you can play and who is going to pick the teams.

Situation 4.   You are discussing with your classmates what to get your teacher for a birthday present. Suggest several different types of gifts.

Situation 5.   You are with a group of your relatives (i.e., uncles, aunts, cousins) and are talking about where to have a family get-together. The adults want to know what the children think.

Situation 6.   Your teacher has asked the class where they would like to go for the spring field trip. She has suggested the museum, the park, and a clothing factory. As a group, you have to help decide on one of these.

Situation 7.   Your scout unit is planning a fund raising event and you are discussing what to do. Some of the suggestions include a car wash, a bake sale, and a cookie sale.

Situation 8.   You are discussing what movie to see with several of your friends. Each of you wants to go to a different movie. As a group, discuss and decide on one movie.

SUGGESTED HOMEWORK ASSIGNMENTS

1. Join in the next group interaction that you find to be of interest. Observe one other participant and pay attention to see if he or she

follows the three main rules. Afterward, write down what you thought of the interaction.

a. Did he or she follow the rules?

b. If not, what was done wrong?

c. What could have been done to improve the interaction?

2. Write down the ways in which you behave differently in group interactions than when you are speaking with just one other person. Why are these differences important?

Module 16: Coping with Conflict—Training in Conflict Resolution

Almost all theories regarding children's psychological development include some element of conflict, whether it be intrapersonal, interpersonal, or societal. It is not surprising, then, that conflict plays an important role in an individual's psychosocial development. In this case, conflict can encourage social exploration and communication as parts of the process by which resolution is sought. However, conflict, by definition, begins with disagreement or misunderstanding, and therefore can lead to negative consequences. Thus, it is the manner in which conflict is addressed that determines its social utility. Peaceful resolution of a conflict contributes to understanding and open communication; entrenchment of differing positions results in further social deterioration.

Throughout history, conflict in its many forms has been an important force in the development of individuals and societies. Within the last century, however, much systematic analysis has been undertaken to explore the processes involved in conflict resolution. Logically, many of the processes involved in resolving interpersonal conflict are similar to those that play a role in the resolution of social, ideological, and international conflicts. The differences rest on the willingness of the involved parties to practice restraint and to engage in rational, open communication.

In human interaction, the ability to resolve conflict is regarded as a mature and desirable skill; it can also be of enormous benefit to the individual. Because conflict is an integral part of social interaction, the ability to cope with it effectively contributes to a healthier, more productive social environment. In many societies, individuals who are able to resolve conflict are highly regarded as humanitarians and protectors of the social conscience. Thus, the skill involved in conflict resolution focuses not only on a particular process of resolution and change but also on attitudinal considerations. Both, however, are important and should serve as integral features of each individual's psychosocial development.

It is also important to point out that arguments and disagreements are often the result of a need for social confirmation of our beliefs and attitudes. When our opinions are not shared, we feel a dissonance that needs to be resolved. An important aspect of social maturation is the understanding and the ability to accept the fact that some degree of ambiguity or incongruence will always exist. In other words, people need to learn, realize, and feel comfortable with the idea that not all issues are resolvable.

Sample Lecture on Conflict Resolution

Today we are going to discuss what is known as "conflict resolution." By this we mean the way in which people solve problems they are having with other people. These problems, or conflicts, can be about anything and might involve a disagreement, a misunderstanding, or a difference of opinions and beliefs. For instance, if a friend of yours disagrees with you over a rule in a game you are playing, that is a conflict. If your parents expected you to be home an hour before you thought you had to be home, that could result in a conflict. If one of the members of a group you are with wants to do one thing and you want to do another, that is a conflict.

Each of the situations that I've just described could easily get out of hand and become a real problem. Actually, any time that you have a disagreement or a misunderstanding with someone it can, if you lack the necessary skills in conflict resolution, build up to a serious situation. When this happens, you may find yourself arguing—not talking—or even fighting about the issues involved. This is how you end up losing friends, making enemies, or getting into trouble with your parents and other adults. So it's easy to see why it's important to learn how to discuss, control, or resolve these problems before they become serious.

Discussion Questions

1. Can anyone give examples of different conflicts that occur with your friends? Your family? Your classmates?
2. What happens when these get out of hand? How do you feel? How does the other person feel?
3. What happens if you "resolve" these conflicts before they become serious?
4. Can you resolve conflicts even when they are serious? Why?

Learning how to resolve conflicts is not always that difficult, but there are several things you should keep in mind. Most important, you have to remember to think about how you are acting and try to stay calm. This is probably the hardest thing to learn, because it can be so easy to get angry at the other person. When this happens, you will be more likely to resolve your argument if you can discuss your anger in a skilled manner. So when you first realize that there is a problem, take some time to think before you say or do anything.

When you are ready to try and resolve the conflict, there are some steps that will help to make it a little easier. First, you should talk to the others involved and find out what they have to say, how they feel, or what they want. This will give you a chance to tell them what your side is. If you don't do this, you won't know what the problem is all about and you'll make it almost impossible to resolve the conflict in an acceptable way. Second, it is important to decide how different your ideas or viewpoints really are. If they are not that different, you may be able to work out some agreements. If your views are very different, see if each party can give in a little so as to resolve some of your differences. This will help to make the situation a little better and perhaps let you work out some of the other problems later on. However, if your differences are too great and you still disagree, you may want to say, "We see things differently so it may not make much sense to keep arguing about this." Third, once you've made an agreement on how to resolve the conflict, *do* what you agreed to do. If you wait to see what the other person is going to do or change your mind, you may ruin any agreement or resolution that has been made. By doing what you have agreed to, you show the other person that you have respect for the agreement and that you are trustworthy. Last of all, when the conflict has been resolved or while it is being resolved, make sure that you keep in touch with the other person or persons. This will help to ensure that the resolution works out the way you've planned and will also enable you to avoid a similar argument or problem in the future.

DISCUSSION QUESTIONS

1. Can someone give me an example of a conflict they have recently had?
   a. What were the two opposing opinions or stories?
   b. On what points could each side give in or compromise?
   c. If there is more than one point or issue, which one would you work on first? Second? Third? Why?
   d. How would you resolve this conflict?
2. Why is it important to talk with one another in order to resolve conflict?

RATIONALE FOR CHILDREN

Benefits. Skill in coping with and resolving conflict can help you

A. solve problems that come between you and others.
B. take care of your problems or issues with others without risking your friendship.

C. begin to understand others better.
D. allow others to understand you better.
E. let others know that you are open-minded, tolerant, and respect-ful.
F. win more respect from other people.

Pitfalls. By not having skills in conflict resolution

A. you will find yourself involved in more arguments, disagree-ments, and fights.
B. you may find it hard to make and keep friends.
C. you may have more difficulty in getting along with your family, friends, and playmates.
D. you may easily see small problems between yourself and others escalating into big problems.
E. you may get less respect from others.

TRAINER'S SCRIPT

Now that you have an idea of what is involved in resolving conflicts, I'm going to demonstrate how this is done. Later, you will have a chance to practice resolving some conflicts that you have made up on your own.

Situation 1. You are with a group of friends preparing to go to the movies. You have suggested going to a movie that everyone says is good. Somebody else is strongly set on going to a different movie.

YOU: Why don't we go to see *The Monster That Ate Pittsburgh?* I heard that it's really great.
FRIEND A: Yeah, I heard it was good too.
FRIEND B: I'd rather see *Return of the Moon Men!* I saw the previews and it looks really good. C'mon, let's see it instead.
FRIEND C: I'd prefer that movie, too. My favorite star is in it.
YOU: OK, I think that both movies would be all right to see. Why don't we see one tonight and the other next week?
FRIEND B: That's all right with me, but can we see *Return of the Moon Men* tonight? I think it's ending this week.
FRIEND A: Will *The Monster That Ate Pittsburgh* be around next weekend?
YOU: Oh, sure! It just started three days ago. So why don't we go to *Return of the Moon Men* tonight, and next Saturday we'll go to *The Monster That Ate Pittsburgh.*
FRIEND B: Great! Let's go.

(Skilled conflict resolution)—This is an appropriate response because

1. you have contributed important information to the conversation.
2. you helped to reach a solution that would be fair.
3. everyone benefits from having solved the problem together.

YOU: Why don't we go to see *The Monster That Ate Pittsburgh?* I hear that it's really good.

FRIEND A: Yeah, I heard it was good too.

FRIEND B: I'd rather see *Return of the Moon Men!* I saw the previews and it looks really good. C'mon, let's see it instead.

FRIEND C: I'd prefer that movie, too. My favorite star is in it.

YOU: Oh, c'mon. I know you'll like *The Monster That Ate Pittsburgh* better. I really want to see it.

FRIEND B: Yeah, but we can see it some other time! This is the last few days that *Return of the Moon Men* is playing.

YOU: So what! This movie is better anyway.

FRIEND B: I doubt it.

YOU: Well, I'm going to see it! I don't want to see your movie.

FRIEND B: Good! I didn't want to go with you anyway.

YOU: Who wants to go see *The Monster That Ate Pittsburgh?* Let's go!

FRIEND B: Who wants to go and see *Return of the Moon Men?* We'll go without them!

(Poor conflict resolution)—This was an inappropriate response because

1. you did not see or understand the other people's wants and feelings.
2. you were being too pushy.
3. a mutually beneficial solution was not found.

Situation 2.   A classmate is angry at you and you are not sure why. You are not very close friends, but you feel a little uncomfortable about the whole situation. Things are already getting a little unfriendly. You go up to your classmate.

YOU: Listen (name), I wish I knew why you were mad at me about. I'd like to try to make things better.

CLASSMATE: Oh, sure you would. You're just a big tattletale. Leave me alone!

YOU: Honestly (name), I don't know what you're talking about. Please do me a favor: explain what happened.

CLASSMATE: As if you didn't know!

YOU: I really don't know.

CLASSMATE: I suppose somebody else told the teacher about me?

YOU: I never talked to the teacher about you. I don't even know what happened. You can ask (teacher's name).

CLASSMATE: Well, if you didn't, who did?

YOU: I don't know, but I'll go with you if you want to ask the teacher. I don't want you to be mad at me. There's no reason for you to be.

CLASSMATE: No, I'll find out alone.

YOU: Well, I hope things are OK between us. I'd rather have you as a friend than an enemy.

CLASSMATE: OK, I'm sorry I got so mad.

YOU: That's all right. I'm glad things are better.

(Skilled conflict resolution)—This is an appropriate response because

1. you have shown respect for the other person.
2. you are trying to resolve this problem.
3. you probably managed to save a friendship by discussing the problem and learning what really happened.

YOU: Listen (name), I wish I knew what you were mad at me about. I'd like to try to make things better.

CLASSMATE: Oh, sure you would. You're just a big tattletale. Leave me alone!

YOU: I don't know what you're talking about, but you've got the wrong person.

CLASSMATE: I'll bet.

YOU: All right, that's it! I tried to be nice. If you don't like it, that's too bad.

CLASSMATE: Well, just stay out of my way.

YOU: Don't worry about it; I wouldn't hang around you.

(Poor conflict resolution)—This is an inappropriate response because

1. you made your classmate more angry by getting mad yourself.
2. you failed to explain what really happened.

PRACTICE SCRIPTS

This section offers scenarios in which conflict resolution skills are desirable. Have the participants develop their own scripts, making sure to incorporate the major steps discussed.

1. Stop and think before you say or do anything.
2. Speak with the other person or persons to find out what the problem is.
3. Reach some agreement on how to handle the problem.
4. Do what you have agreed to do.

Situation 1. Your parents have asked that either you or your brother/sister baby-sit tonight. You both have other things that you want to do. Resolve this problem.

Situation 2. You are playing a game with some friends and somebody accuses you of not playing fairly. You really don't think that you've done anything wrong. Resolve this problem.

Situation 3. Your parents are mad at you because they feel that you did not do all of your chores. They have decided not to give you your allowance. You are not sure of what it is that you failed to do and feel that they are reacting unfairly. Resolve this problem.

Situation 4. You are unhappy about something that a classmate has said about you. You want to know why these things were said and let your classmate know that you are unhappy about this. You would like to resolve this problem.

Situation 5. You and a friend find a ticket that will get one of you into a movie free. You both claim that you saw it first. Resolve this problem.

Situation 6. You accidentally spill paint on a classmate's sweater. Your classmate are very upset because the sweater is a new one; you are accused of having spilled the paint on purpose. You know that this is not true. Resolve this problem.

Situation 7. Your teacher suspects that you have copied from another student's paper during a test. She is a little angry with you. You know that you didn't cheat and feel somewhat angry at being accused of this. Resolve this problem.

Situation 8. You and some friends are discussing a television show. You end up arguing about what actor played the main character. Everyone feels that he or she is right. Resolve this problem.

SUGGESTED HOMEWORK ASSIGNMENT

1. There are always conflicts between people being portrayed in movies on television. Write down what happens in one of the

conflicts. Were good resolution skills used? Why? Why not? What should the participants have done instead?

2. Think about the last conflict you had with someone that didn't work out very well. What went wrong? What could you have done to make things work out better? How would better conflict resolution skills have changed what happened?

6

Clinical and Logistical Issues in Social Skills Training with Children

Special Issues in Training

As previously mentioned, social skills training programs for children focus on two primary areas: the remediation of specific social skills deficits and the development and refinement of normative social abilities as a preventive measure. In both instances several issues can arise related to the design, implementation, and ramification of the type of intervention. Clinicians, teachers, and childcare workers involved in social skills training with children, typically report that they encounter occasional clinical and logistical problems which might hinder the effectiveness of the program. In this chapter, therefore, we address the more common problem areas so as to provide a basic troubleshooting guide for social skills trainers.

Of course, novel concerns will also arise as training in social skills is offered to larger and more diverse populations. Consequently, it is advisable for trainers and program designers to seek out and review relevant data regarding the subjects' social, cultural, and psychological environment. It is also imperative that the knowledge and approval of parents, school staff, and, importantly, the child be obtained regarding the design and modification of intervention format and content.

Although trainers will need to tailor the social skills training program individually to the needs of the specific population with whom they are working, it may be helpful first to review the clinical issues presented in this chapter. The primary objective of the chapter is not to serve as a substitute for proper training and supervision of trainers. Likewise, many complex clinical issues cannot be effectively dealt with in just one chapter. However, trainers should not hesitate to seek out supervision and/or consultation with local psychologists and educators who are more experienced and who can provide invaluable clinical expertise and feedback, should it be needed. Fortunately, the program described in the text has been applied in a wide variety of settings (schools, clinics, hospitals) and across varied populations (normal, maladjusted, aggressive withdrawn, high-risk, and psychiatric outpatient children). As a result of these various applications, several clinical issues have been identified and subsequently resolved. As a convenience to trainers, we have detailed the major clinical issues needing consideration, which if not adequately addressed, might limit the program's efficacy.

AGE RANGE OF THE GROUPS

In designing the modules, it became necessary to develop consistency regarding the age-level abilities of the targeted population, keeping approximately within an eight- to twelve-year-old range. Similarly, when utilizing scenarios for discussion and practice, it is necessary to adapt these according to the cognitive abilities, social maturation, and skill levels of the children. In general, except when working with special populations, the ages of youngsters in the group can serve as a satisfactory gauge of the homogeneity of these variables. Also, except when group composition is determined by target areas of skill deficiency, it is strongly suggested that groups be reasonably homogenous with respect to age. Experience and research suggest that a disparity of ages within a population, if there are no additional unifying themes or content areas, can adversely affect outcome. For example, a five-year-old and an eleven-year-old youngster would have less common ground upon which to base practice in social interaction than two children of the same age. We have found that combinations of third and fourth, fourth and fifth, and fifth and sixth graders are most successful if merging of different grade levels is necessary.

SEX RATIO OF THE GROUP

The social skills training modules featured in Chapter 5 assume a mixed-sex composition of the training groups. However, these modules can easily be adapted for same-sex groups, as they emphasize generalized communication skills more than heterosocial interaction. The one exception, Module 13, entitled *Sex Difference Interactions*, focuses on developing and refining interactional skills specifically related to heterosexual social communication.

However, there are advantages and disadvantages to the various possible ways of composing the training group. Ideally, a balanced sex group composition would provide greater flexibility and breadth in developing role-play scenarios as well as a more balanced feedback from the subjects regarding idiosyncratic, sex-role-based concerns. On the other hand, at some ages in some groups, boys and girls may be very willing to interact with each other socially. Therefore it is important to keep the ages of the subjects in mind and to consider their input when designing heterosocial scenarios.

ETHNIC AND CULTURAL DIFFERENCES

Because attitudes within schools often reflect prevalent societal attitudes and expectations, ethnic and cultural differences within the training population can provide valuable subject material. Children, sometimes exposed to rigid and narrow perspectives, can explore other viewpoints and address these and related issues in the context of social skills training. It is the responsibility of the trainer to ensure that the various attitudes and perspectives of the training population are equally represented and integrated into the program design. The best means for achieving this is to encourage all participating youngsters to contribute ideas for training and practice scenarios. In addition, throughout training the content of group discussion should be monitored to identify issues related to ethnic and cultural differences. Once these are identified, two concerns become salient. If such differences are overlooked, the norms and behavioral styles of one group may be inadvertently imposed on another.

First, disregard for minority, ethnic, or cultural differences may communicate a message of insensitivity, disrespect, or ignorance of the child's social environment. Clearly, if training is to lead to mutual respect, understanding and acceptance of individual differences is mandatory. Children and their families may be resistant to training programs that do not address genuine cultural differences. Thus, failure to recognize and accept legitimate alternative cultural styles may result, at the very least, in a socially invalid program. In a more serious vein, the ethical and psychological ramifications of such an oversight could be quite deleterious and lead to possible mistrust, resentment, or opposition to ongoing or prospective social competency programs. Conversely, exploration, discussion, and the role playing of various culturally influenced responses facilitate greater cross-cultural generalization, decrease prejudice, and augment intracultural pride. Moreover, expanded ethnic awareness among group members is a positive and desirable goal which enhances a variety of prosocial behaviors.

GROUP SIZE

Social skills training with children appears to be optimally effective as part of a group intervention. However, training methods can easily be adapted for work with individuals, dyads, and small groups as well. The teaching and training strategies described in earlier chapters of this book have been selected and designed for group instruction. Some strategies (e.g., behavior rehearsal and role playing) assume the participation of two or more children. However, for individual social skills training, the trainer can assume the role of the "other" and effectively utilize the training modules.

For larger groups or in-class instruction, teaching assistants and aides, if available, can play an important role. Although instruction, modeling, and discussion can be conducted with larger groups, behavior rehearsal and more intimate discussion demand a small-group format. For this reason, assistants and aides can facilitate discussion in the smaller groups and supervise practice strategies. Typically, these groups are made up of 4 to 6 children. Overall, the groups' size in previous programs ranged from 5 to 30 children. However, there is no obstacle to altering class size to suit the needs and resources of the school, clinic, or institution. Trainers must recognize that use of the program with larger groups (e.g., over 20 members) may present problems if aides or co-trainers are not available.

The major difficulties to be overcome in running a large group unaided include (1) the problem of giving each and every participant praise and positive feedback; (2) the need to adapt the "scripts between trainers" phase of the module; (3) possible difficulties managing the larger number of children without help, given increased noise and interaction; (4) possible reduction in comprehension on the part of group members due to increased distractions and decreased opportunity to ask the trainer questions related to the module; and (5) difficulty ascertaining and ensuring the social validity of responses and topics due to large number of participants. Thus, it is our suggestion that, in working with large groups, either aides or co-trainers be enlisted (and trained accordingly) or extra time be allotted to deal with the above issues. It has been our experience that the use of co-trainers is the most beneficial and manageable strategy for running larger groups or even small ones. The use of co-trainers allows for increased modeling, praise, feedback, and stimulation; it also facilitates group management and participation. Should a co-trainer or aide not be readily available, it is important for the sole trainer to know the module well, to practice repeatedly in advance, and to avoid reading the entire module to the group. These steps will reduce possible boredom while also enhancing both trainer and trainee spontaneity and excitement. Likewise, the use of humor, enthusiasm, warmth, authenticity, and kindness are even more vital when performing training alone, as there is no one to help "refine" the process or to serve as a sounding board. Similarly, the use of creativity is not in any way discouraged merely because one uses modules. Thus, "sole" trainers need to maintain group attention, interest, and enthusiasm as outlined above in order to ensure training effectiveness. However, the use of co-trainers does not contraindicate the use of these therapeutic ingredients. Yet, trainers acting alone need to pay more attention to these facilitating strategies to compensate for the absence of the second trainer.

FREQUENCY OF GROUP MEETINGS

Although the frequency and length of the training sessions can sometimes be determined by the trainer, often these variables are dictated by logistics within the training environment. Within the school setting, supplanting curricular classroom time with social skills training can cause difficulties. However, as educators increasingly acknowledge the value of the classroom in the social and affective education of children, they will be more willing to include this type of intervention in their curriculum.

Previous applications of this social skills training program have occurred in school settings (Mannarino, Michelson, Marchione, & Martin, 1983; Michelson & Wood, 1980a; Sugai, 1978), medical and psychiatric settings (Michelson *et al.*, 1981), and community residence programs (Sugai, 1978). In most cases, the training sessions have been organized either on a once- or twice-weekly basis (each session lasting from 45 to 60 minutes). Both schedules were satisfactory in achieving training objectives and did not interfere with other daily activities. It should also be noted that variations in the content and format of the modules influence the time needed for module implementation. The characteristics of the children and trainer experience may also affect the amount of time needed. Furthermore, although children can benefit from exposure to all of the modules, regardless of their prior experience level, trainers should feel free to select content areas to meet the specific needs of their children. In this case, the amount of time necessary for the implementation of the program would vary according to the determined needs of the child or group.

Importance of Parental Cooperation

The social skills training program is not intended to replace the role of the parents as agents of socialization. Instead, the program is supplementary and is most effective with the support and input of parents. To this end, their cooperation in the implementation of the program and in supporting their children's participation is of critical importance.

Our experience in designing and implementing social skills training with children suggests that the most likely way to secure and maintain parental support is to familiarize parents with the program's content, to stress the supplementary nature of the program, and to integrate parents' ideas and concerns into the design of the program whenever possible. Typically, parents have little objection to a program that lends itself to sound and normative development of their children. When presented with a description of the benefits and possible risks to the child and a cursory review of the literature regarding the importance of normal affective and social development, parents are generally cooperative and supportive.

Importance of School Staff Cooperation

Because school staff members are often involved in the identification of youngsters with problems related to the development of social skills and with the implementation and administration of the training programs, their cooperation is essential. Teachers, counselors, and administrators are all involved in either designing or implementing a successful social skills training program and may play major roles in the actual instruction, evaluation, and assessment of the program and the children within it. These individuals also serve an important function as liaisons to parents and the community. To encourage and support their efforts, it is important that communication remain open to all levels of the school system affected by the social skills training intervention and that the program be flexible enough to accomodate their specific concerns.

Maintaining Attention during Training

At times, maintaining the attention of children in the training program can be a problem. However, because the content areas address the specific needs and social anxieties of these children and because the scripts and scenarios are taken directly from their own experiences, interest levels tend to remain high.

In the event that interest and participation begin to dwindle, there are several strategies that can help to reestablish attention. First, the trainer can draw students into the discussion or activity by posing stimulating questions regarding the particular topic or by soliciting examples drawn from the children's personal experience. Second, the trainer can have the child initiate discussion or pose questions that present a more immediate and personal social skills-related concern that tends to demand additional elaboration and disclosure. In this situation, the trainer plays an important role in facilitating the presentation of these ideas and in the group response. Third, the trainer can place additional responsibility with the children by having them assume the roles of discussion leaders and peer tutors. This strategy utilizes peer pressure in a supervised, constructive fashion while providing the children with a positive sense of responsibility and leadership. Fourth, in the event that these procedures fail to increase attention during training, it might prove to be necessary to institute a program of external, material reinforcement to reward youngsters for their participation. However, this last strategy typically is not necessary. As a check, it is encouraged that the content material and methods of presentation of the training modules be reexamined to determine if they do, in fact, address the needs and abilities of the participating youngsters. Finally, humor, warmth, and authenticity are stimulating to children and should always be incorporated in the training program.

WHEN TRAINING FAILS

As has been the experience of the authors, it is possible that some of the participants in the training program may not demonstrate improved social skills. These youngsters warrant additional attention, especially in identifying areas of skills deficiency and possible reasons why there has not been any improvement.

Assessment of the child through observation, self-report, and peer report can help delineate areas in which further remediation or restructuring of strategies and objectives might prove helpful. The problem to be addressed will generally fall into one of three areas to be described. First, it is possible that a child's peers, parents, and others in his or her social environment will not reinforce the skill being developed. In this case, social validity may be the primary issue. If the skill is not useful or acceptable in the child's daily milieu, the intervention may have to be redesigned to accommodate these social parameters.

Second, there are realistic limitations on the amount of time available for a program of social skills training, particularly in a group setting. This may have resulted in insufficient time for the child to assimilate, integrate, practice, and apply what he or she has been taught. If this proves to be a factor and if the time and resources are available, a simple solution would be to provide additional training and practice in designated areas of social skills deficiency.

Third, aside from the more obvious indicators of social skills deficiency such as asocial or antisocial behavior, a youngster's lack of responsiveness to training may have a more subtle etiology. The presence of emotional, cognitive, and medical problems can inhibit the effects of training and further complicate the accurate evaluation of a child's social problem. Social skills trainers should consider these possibilities when working with a youngster who is not responding to the training intervention, especially as these problems may not be readily observable. In this event, professional consultation with others more skilled in the assessment of cognitive, emotional, or medical problems is mandated.

When To Make A Referral

In the course of social skills training, two situations can occur that would warrant caution and additional professional consultation. First, as described in the preceding section, when a youngster is not responding to the social skills intervention and continues to manifest significant skills deficiencies that are not related to inappropriate behavior or skills targeting or to ineffective training strategies, then emotional, cognitive, and/or medical disability must be considered. Such a disability may, of course, not be causally related either. However, it would be best to leave this determination up to a professional skilled in the diagnosis and possible remediation of these problems.

Second, through discussion, role play, or self-disclosure, a youngster may reveal information or present concerns that are not related to or cannot be addressed in the context of social skills training. These problems may be related to the child's physical or mental health, concerns regarding parents or other family members, questions of abuse, or school difficulties. As these factors become evident, it is important that trainers who are not experienced in these matters avoid tackling such issues and instead seek out appropriate professionals for evaluation and/or consultation.

Ethical Considerations and Guidelines

Many ethical issues surround the assessment and training of children's social skills. These questions include the following: Who trains the trainers? On what bases or criteria are children selected for training? What are the possible negative consequences of teaching children social skills? Who determines which skills are important? For *whom?* Do children have the right to refuse participation in social skills groups? Do parents have the right to refuse to allow their child to participate in training? These and many other difficult issues should be given serious consideration prior to the initiation of any social competency program. Trainers should recognize their responsibility to achieve maximum synchrony between the children's, parents', teachers', peers', and society's norms, objectives, and aspirations—a difficult task at best!

Trainers should recognize their own limitations and seek additional training and experience when necessary. Likewise, trainers have an ethical obligation to avoid making unwarranted or exaggerated claims to either the children or their parents. Indeed, children and their parents should be informed of the nature of the training, its possible benefits, and its potential adverse effects. For example, it is not uncommon for recently trained children to become more assertive with their parents or siblings. Although the child may just be acting assertively, reactions to the new behaviors may range from subtle rejection to physical punishment. Trainers must realize that individual family norms may depart radically from middle-class notions of appropriate social skills. Trainers have an ethical responsibility to inform children and their parents of the possible behavioral changes, why they are considered important to the child's welfare, and how they can be reinforced and maintained in the natural environment.

Trainers must also remember that their own behavior serves as a model to the trainee. Thus, trainers should always strive to be open, direct, honest, empathic, and appropriate in their expression of opinions, beliefs, feelings, and needs. This is equally true in regard to social interaction with children, parents, teachers, and colleagues.

Trainers, particularly teachers, need to recognize the limitations of social skills training in remediating major psychological or psychiatric disorders including hyperactivity, learning disabilities, childhood psychoses, and organic brain syndrome. Trainers are obliged to recommend alternative evaluations and treatments for children who manifest serious psychological dysfunctions. This is not to say that social skills training cannot be used as an effective adjunct to more intensive and specialized treatment. However, it is important to recognize that social skills training is not a panacea for all childhood disorders. Trainers should consult with specialists to request further evaluation when in doubt regarding the appropriateness of applying social skills training versus utilizing another therapeutic strategy.

Trainers should recognize the continuous need to adapt and modify existing modules in order to achieve maximum social validity, effectiveness, and generalization. Minority-group children may have different expressions and colloquialisms, which—although not present in the trainer's vocabulary—are vital to the success of the child's peer relations. Therefore, trainers need not rigidly enforce the "King's English" when and where alternative or slang responses would more likely be understood and accepted. Which social skills are taught and for whom are they beneficial are questions that need to be considered. Trainers must also be aware of possible difficulties in teaching social skills to children of differing cultural, religious, and family backgrounds. Occasionally, such skills as "standing up for your rights," "refusal," or "asking why" can be perceived by a few parents as disrespectful, sacrilegious, or even subversive!

The following is a statement by expert assertion and social skill trainers regarding the use of assertion training strategies. Although the recommendations do not, in total, relate to solely the teaching of *children's* social skills, they do offer guidelines for defining trainer and training characteristics.

PRINCIPLES FOR ETHICAL PRACTICE OF ASSERTIVE BEHAVIOR TRAINING

With the increasing popularity of assertive behavior training, a quality of "faddishness" has become evident, and there are frequent reports of ethically irresponsible practices (and practitioners). We hear of trainers who, for example, do not adequately differentiate assertion and aggression. Others have failed to advocate proper ethical responsibility and caution to clients (e.g., failed to alert them to and/or prepare them for the possibility of retaliation or other highly negative reactions from others).

The following statement, "Principles for Ethical Practice of Assertive Behavior Training," is the work of professional psychologists and educators (Alberti, Emmons, Fodor, Galassi, Galassi, Garnett, Jakubowski, & Wolfe, 1976) who are actively engaged in the practice of facilitating assertive behavior (also referred to as assertive therapy, social skills training, personal effectiveness training, and AT). We do not intend by this statement to discourage untrained individuals from becoming more assertive on their own, and we do not advocate that one must have extensive credentials in order to be of help to friends and relatives. Rather, these principles are offered to help foster responsible and ethical teaching and practice by human services professionals. Others who wish to enhance their own assertiveness or that of associates are encouraged to do so, with awareness of their own limitations and of the importance of seeking help from a qualified therapist/trainer when necessary.

We hereby declare support for and adhere to the statement of principles, and invite responsible professionals in our own and other fields who use these techniques to join us in advocating and practicing these principles

A. *Definition of assertive behavior*. For purposes of these principles and the ethical framework expressed herein, we define assertive behavior as that complex of behaviors, emitted by a person in an interpersonal context, which express that person's feelings, attitudes, wishes, opinions or rights directly, firmly, and honestly, while respecting the feelings, attitudes, wishes, opinions and rights of the other person(s). Such behavior may include the expression of such emotions as anger, fear, caring, hope, joy, despair, indignance, embarrassment, but in any event is expressed in a manner which does not violate the rights of others. Assertive behavior is differentiated from aggressive behavior which, while expressive of one person's feelings, attitudes, wishes, opinions or rights, does not respect those characteristics in others.

While this definition is intended to be comprehensive, it is recognized that any adequate definition of assertive behavior must consider several dimensions:

1. *Intent:* behavior classified as assertive is not intended by its author to be hurtful of others.
2. *Behavior:* behavior classified as assertive would be evaluated by an "objective observer" as itself honest, direct, expressive and non-destructive of others.
3. *Effects:* behavior classified as assertive has the effect upon a receiver of a direct and non-destructive message, by which a "reasonable person" would not be hurt.
4. *Socio-cultural Context:* behavior classified as assertive is appropriate to the environment and culture in which it is exhibited, and may not be considered "assertive" in a different socio-cultural environment.

B. *Client self-determination*. These principles recognize and affirm the inherent dignity and the equal and inalienable rights of all members of the human family, as proclaimed in the "Universal Declaration of Human Rights" endorsed by the General Assembly of the United Nations.

Pursuant to the precepts of the Declaration, each client (trainee, patient) who seeks assertive behavior training shall be treated as a person of value, with all of the freedoms and rights expressed in the Declaration. No procedure shall be utilized in the name of assertive behavior training which would violate those freedoms or rights.

Informed client self-determination shall guide all such interventions:

1. the client shall be fully informed in advance of all procedures to be utilized;
2. the client shall have the freedom to choose to participate or not at any point in the intervention;
3. the client who is institutionalized shall be similarly treated with respect and without coercion, insofar as is possible within the institutional environment;
4. the client shall be provided with explicit definitions of assertiveness and assertive training;
5. the client shall be fully informed as to the education, training, experience or other qualifications of the assertive trainer(s);
6. the client shall be informed as to the goals and potential outcomes of assertive training, including potentially high levels of anxiety, and possible negative reactions from others;
7. the client shall be fully informed as to the responsibility of the assertion trainer(s) and the client(s);
8. the client shall be informed as to the ethics and employment of confidentiality guidelines as they pertain to various assertive training settings (e.g., clinical vs. non-clinical).

C. *Qualifications of facilitators.* Assertive behavior training is essentially a therapeutic procedure, although frequently practiced in a variety of settings by professionals not otherwise engaged in rendering a "psychological" service. Persons in any professional role who engage in helping others to change their behavior, attitudes, and interpersonal relationships must understand human behavior at a level commensurate with the level of their interventions.

General qualifications. We support the following minimum, general qualifications for facilitators at all levels of intervention (including "trainers in training"—preservice or inservice—who are preparing for professional service in a recognized human services field, and who may be conducting assertive behavior training under supervision as part of a research project or practicum):

1. Fundamental understanding of the principles of learning and behavior (equivalent to completion of a rigorous undergraduate level course in learning theory);
2. Fundamental understanding of anxiety and its effects upon behavior (equivalent to completion of a rigorous undergraduate level course in abnormal psychology);
3. Knowledge of the limitations, contraindications and potential dangers of assertive behavior training; familiarity with theory and research in the area.
4. Satisfactory evidence of competent performance as a facilitator, as observed by a qualified trainer, is strongly recommended for all professionals, particularly for those who do not possess a doctorate or an equivalent level of training. Such evidence would most ideally be supported by:
   a) participation in at least ten (10) hours of assertive behavior training as a client (trainee, patient); and
   b) participation in at least ten (10) hours of assertive behavior training as a facilitator under supervision.

Specific qualifications. The following additional qualifications are considered to be the minimum expected for facilitators at the indicated levels of intervention:

1. Assertive behavior training, including non-clinical workshops, groups, and individual client training aimed at teaching assertive skills to those persons who require only encouragement and specific skill training, and in whom no serious emotional deficiency or pathology is evident.

a) For trainers in programs conducted under the sponsorship of a recognized human services agency, school, governmental or corporate entity, church, or community organization:

  (1) An advanced degree in a recognized field of human services (e.g., psychology, counseling, social work, medicine, public health, nursing, education, human development, theology/divinity), including at least one term of field experience in a human services agency supervised by a qualified trainer; or

  (2) certification as a minister, public school teacher, social worker, physician, counselor, nurse, or clinical, counseling, educational, or school psychologist, or similar human services professional, as recognized by the state wherein employed or by the recognized state or national professional society in the indicated discipline; or

  (3) one year of paid counseling experience in a recognized human services agency, supervised by a qualified trainer; or

  (4) qualifications under Items b2 or b3 below.

b) For trainers in programs including interventions at the level defined in this item, but without agency/organization sponsorship:

  (1) An advanced degree in a recognized field of human services (e.g., psychology, counseling, social work, medicine, public health, nursing, education, human development, theology/divinity) including at least one term of field experience in a human services agency supervised by a qualified trainer; and

  (2) certification as a minister, social worker, physician, counselor, nurse, or clinical, counseling, educational, or school psychologist, or similar human services professional, as recognized by the state wherein employed or by the recognized state or national professional society in the indicated discipline; or

  (3) qualification under Items b2 or b3 below.

2. Assertive behavior therapy, including clinical interventions designed to assist persons who are severely inhibited by anxiety, or who are significantly deficient in social skills, or who are controlled by aggression, or who evidence pathology, or for whom other therapeutic procedures are indicated:

a) For therapists in programs conducted under the sponsorship of a recognized human services agency, school, governmental or corporate entity, church, or community organization:

  (1) An advanced degree in a recognized field of human services (e.g., psychology, counseling, social work, medicine, public health, nursing, education, human development, theology/divinity) including at least one term of field experience in a human services agency supervised by a qualified trainer; or

  (2) certification as a minister, social worker, physician, counselor, nurse, or clinical, counseling, educational, or school psychologist, as recognized by the state wherein employed or by the recognized state or national professional society in the individual discipline; or

  (3) qualification under Item b3 below.

b) For therapists employing interventions at the level defined in this item, but without agency/organization sponsorship:

  (1) An advanced degree in a recognized field of human services (e.g., psychology, counseling, social work, medicine, public health, nursing, education, human development, theology/divinity) including at least one term of field experience in a human services agency supervised by a qualified trainer; and

      (2) certification as minister, social worker, physician, counselor, nurse, or clinical, counseling, educational, or school psychologist, as recognized by the state wherein employed or by the recognized state or national professional society in the indicated discipline; and

      (3) at least one year of paid professional experience in a recognized human services agency, supervised by a qualified trainer, or

      (4) qualification under Item d below.

3. Training of trainers, including preparation of other professionals to offer assertive behavior training/therapy to clients, in school, agency, organization, or individual settings.

    a) A doctoral degree in a recognized field of human services (e.g., psychology, counseling, social work, medicine, public health, nursing, education, human development, theology/divinity) including at least one term of field experience in a human services agency supervised by a qualified trainer; and

    b) certification as a minister, social worker, physician, counselor, nurse, or clinical, counseling, educational, or school psychologist, as recognized by the state wherein employed, or by the recognized state or national professional society in the indicated discipline; and

    c) at least one year of paid professional experience in a recognized human services agency, supervised by a qualified trainer; and

    d) advanced study in assertive behavior training/therapy, including at least two of the following:

      (1) At least thirty (30) hours of facilitation with clients;

      (2) participation in at least two different workshops at professional meetings or professional training institutes;

      (3) contribution to the professional literature in the field.

We recognize that counselors and psychologists are not certified by each state. In states wherein no such certification is provided, unless contrary to local statute, we acknowledge the legitimacy of professionals who are otherwise qualified under the provisions of Items 2a and 2b and would be eligible for certification as a counselor or psychologist in another state.

We do not consider that participation in one or two workshops on assertive behavior, even though conducted by a professional with an advanced degree, is adequate qualification to offer assertive behavior training to others, unless the additional qualifications of Items 2a and 2b are also met.

These qualifications are presented as standards for professional facilitators of assertive behavior. No "certification" or "qualifying" agency is hereby proposed. Rather, it is incumbent upon each professional to evaluate himself/herself as a trainer/therapist according to these standards, and to make explicit to clients the adequacy of his/her qualifications as a facilitator.

D. *Ethical behavior of facilitators.* Since the encouragement and facilitation of assertive behavior is essentially a therapeutic procedure, the ethical standards most applicable to the practice of assertive behavior training are those of psychologists. We recognize that many persons who practice some form of assertive behavior training are not otherwise engaged in rendering a "psychological" service (i.e., teachers, personnel/training directors). To all we support the statement of "Ethical Standards for Psychologists" as adopted by the American Psychological Association as the standard of ethical behavior by which assertive behavior training shall be conducted.

We recognize that the methodology employed in assertive behavior training may include a wide range of procedures, some of which are of unproven value. It is the responsibility of facilitators to inform clients of any experimental procedures. Under no circumstances should the facilitator "guarantee" a specific outcome from an intervention.

E. *Appropriateness of assertive behavior training interventions.* Assertive behavior training, as any intervention oriented toward helping people change, may be applied under a wide range of conditions, yet its appropriateness must be evaluated in each individual case. The responsible selection of assertive behavior training for a particular intervention must include attention to at least the following dimensions:

1. *Client:* The personal characteristics of the client in question (age, sex, ethnicity, institutionalization, capacity for informed choice, physical and psychological functionality).
2. *Problem/Goals:* The purpose for which professional help has been sought or recommended (job skills, severe inhibition, anxiety reduction, overcome aggression).
3. *Facilitator:* The personal and professional qualifications of the facilitator in question (age, sex, ethnicity, skills, understanding, ethics—see also Principles 3 and 4 above).
4. *Setting:* The characteristics of the setting in which the intervention is conducted (home, school, business, agency, clinic, hospital, prison). Is the client free to choose? Is the facilitator's effectiveness systematically evaluated?
5. *Time/Duration:* The duration of the intervention. Does the time involved represent a brief word of encouragement, a formal training workshop, an intensive and long-term therapeutic effort?
6. *Method:* The nature of the intervention. Is it "packaged" procedure or tailored to client needs? Is training based on sound principles of learning and behavior? Is there clear differentiation of aggressiveness, assertiveness and other concepts? Are definitions, techniques, procedures and purposes clarified? Is care taken to encourage small, successful steps and to minimize punishing consequences? Are any suggested "homework assignments" presented with adequate supervision, responsibility, and sensitivity to the effect upon significant others of the client's behavior change efforts? Are clients informed that assertiveness "doesn't always work?"
7. *Outcome:* Are there follow-up procedures, either by self-report or other post-test procedures?

F. *Social responsibility.* Assertive behavior training shall be conducted within the law. Trainers and clients are encouraged to work assertively to change those laws which they consider need to be changed, and to modify the social system in ways they believe appropriate—in particular to extend the boundaries of human rights. Toward these ends, trainers are encouraged to facilitate responsible change skills via assertive behavior training. All those who practice, teach, or do research on assertive behavior are urged to advocate caution and ethical responsibility in application of the technique, in accordance with these Principles.

Sample Assessment Instruments

Sample A: Social Skills Observation Checklist

The Social Skills Observation Checklist (Figure 1) measures expressive and receptive behaviors in five social skill content areas: (1) expressing and responding to positive statements (e.g., compliments, praise), (2) expressing and responding to negative statements (e.g., complaints, criticism), (3) giving and following instructions and/or requests, (4) starting and maintaining conversations and listening to others during conversation, and (5) expressing and responding to feelings and/or sympathetic statements, such as "I'm sad" or "you sure look happy."

Each of the five content areas are divided on the checklist into expressive and receptive sections. The first assesses how well a child can *express* compliments, complaints, feelings, and so on to adults or peers, whereas the second rates how well the child *responds* to others (adults or peers) when they make such statements.

For each content area and its expressive and receptive sections, specific behavioral components are listed which constitute a particular social skill. These components describe the minimal necessary "ingredients" to complete the associated social skill. For each of these components, the observer records whether the child did or did not make the specified response.

In its current state, the Social Skills Observation Checklist is rather general in scope and can provide adequate information regarding social skills in major areas of functioning. This checklist can also be "individualized" for specific children or target behaviors by providing a specific type of behavior to be observed. Most of the specific components are behaviorally stated or described and some include examples for further clarification. However, for a particular child or special group of children, these components may require further specification to be added to their definitions on the checklist so as to allow for more accurate recording of target behaviors. For example, under "Expressing Positive Statements," Component 2 requires that the child "state *what* deserves special attention"; but if a focus was to measure only the expression of positive statements which compliment another person for helping with a task, then this component could be further defined to measure only these types of statements.

These specific components are placed on the checklist in the order that they would likely occur during an interaction, so as to make the observation process a little smoother. However, at this point, it does not matter whether the child performs the components in

Name:_____

Date:_____

Circle One: Pretraining   During Training   Posttraining

P = Peer/Child Interaction
A = Adult/Child Interaction

	Yes	No

1. Positive statements (compliments, praise, etc.)
   A. Expressing positive statements
      1. Eye contact (during 60% of interaction).
      2. State what deserves special attention (e.g., "You did a good job cleaning the dishes").
      3. Explains or gives rationale as to why it is appreciated (e.g., "Now I don't have to do them later").
      4. States praise, affection, encouragement, appreciation, or support (e.g., "Thanks for your help").

   B. Responding to positive statements
      1. Eye contact (during 60% of the interaction).
      2. States feeling about compliment (e.g., "I'm glad you appreciate my help").
      3. Statement of appreciation or thanks (e.g., "Thanks for saying so").

   Totals

2. Negative statements (compliments, criticism, etc.)
   A. Expressing negative statements
      1. Eye contact (during 60% of the interaction).
      2. States *what* the problem is or concerns (e.g., "You did not get the dishes done").
      3. Explains feeling about problem (e.g., "I don't appreciate it when you leave a mess").
      4. Asks for a response or feedback to problem or feelings (e.g., "What do you think can be done about this").
      5. States steps to be taken for solution (e.g., "Why don't you finish your work, then finish washing the dishes, and then go play").

   B. Responding to negative statements
      1. Eye contact (during 60% of the interaction while listening to complaint).
      2. Asks for clarification or more details (e.g., "Do you mean the dishes on the table?").
      3. Expresses understanding of others feelings or position (e.g., "I can see that you are upset about this mess").
      4. States thoughts, feelings or accepts responsibility (e.g., "I guess I should have washed these too").
      5. Summarizes steps to solutions (e.g., "I'll wash them when I finish my homework").

   Totals

FIGURE 1. Social Skills Observation Checklist.

3. Requests/Instructions
   A. Giving requests/instructions
      1. Eye contact (during 60% of the interaction).   1.
      2. States *what* needs to be done (e.g., "The dishes need to be
         washed").   2.
      3. States *who* should do it (e.g., "I think Joe should do them
         today").   3.
      4. Provide *rationale* for request/instructions (e.g., "Joe hasn't
         done them all week").   4.
      5. Asks for feedback concerning request/instructions (e.g., "Do
         you think that's OK, Joe?").   5.

   B. Following requests/instructions
      1. Eye contact (during 60% of the interaction).   1.
      2. Gives feedback/seeks clarification (e.g., "Which dishes to you
         want cleaned?").   2.
      3. Acknowledges requests/instructions (e.g., "You want me to
         wash them today").   3.
      4. States compliance or states refusal and rationale for refusal
         (e.g., "OK, I'll do them" or "No way, I did them twice last
         week, it's not my turn").   4.
                                                                  Totals

4. Engaging in conversations
   A. Starting and maintaining conversations
      1. Eye contact (during 60% of the interaction).   1.
      2. Introductory greeting/statement (e.g., "Hi, how is it going?"). 2.
      3. States own thoughts, opinions, or information (e.g., "This
         new record is really great").   3.
      4. Asks for others' thoughts, opinions, or information (e.g.,
         "What do you think of this group?").   4.
      5. Summarize major points of the conversation (e.g., "This is
         their best record yet, you should listen to it").   5.
      6. Closing or concluding statement (e.g., "Maybe you'll hear it
         tonight, see you on Tuesday and we'll talk about it").   6.

   B. Listening to Others During Conversations
      1. Eye contact (during 60% of the interaction).   1.
      2. Asks questions about topic (e.g., "What do you mean about
         _____?").   2.
      3. Gives feedback, opinions, reactions, feelings (e.g., "That's
         great," "How interesting," "Who cares?").   3.
                                                                  Totals

Continued

any specific order. Rather, observers merely record whether or not a particular component occurred at any time during the interaction.

Recording occurrences or nonoccurrences of specified social behaviors is accomplished by the observer (or observers) by marking a *P* or an *A* in the box opposite the
defined components of the skill area. A *P* denotes that the behavior occurred during an
interaction between the target child and another peer (e.g., friend, playmate, another

5. Feelings/empathic statements
   A. Expressing feelings/empathic statements
      1. Eye contact (during 60% of the interaction).   1.
      2. States feelings or describes emotional state (e.g., "I'm upset
         because I wrecked my bike").   2.
      3. Asks for feedback/reactions to feelings (e.g., "Do you know
         how it feels to wreck your favorite bike?").   3.

   B. Responding to feelings/empathic statements
      1. Eye contact (during 60% of the interaction).   1.
      2. Provides feedback/empathy (e.g., "Yeah, what a drag, sorry
         to hear about that").   2.

                                                                                 Totals

                                        Grand   Grand
                                        totals   totals
                                         (all   (see
                                        areas)   areas)

student). An *A* denotes that the behavior occurred during an interaction between the child and an adult (e.g., teacher, staff member, store clerk, stranger, etc.).

For example, if the child started a conversation with a *peer* by introducing himself, then, on the Social Skills Observation Checklist, section 4 (Engaging in Conversations), Component 2 (Introductory greeting/statement), the observer would record a *P* in the "yes" box. If a similar conversation were started with an adult, then the observer would record an *A* in the "yes" box. However, if the child engaged in a conversation with another peer or adult and did *not* include an introductory greeting/statement, then a *P* or an *A* would be recorded in the "no" box. Note that if the child does not engage in any conversation, all the boxes in Section 4 would be left blank. Therefore, a mark (either *P* or *A*) in a "yes" or "no" box indicates which components of a social skill area were included when the social behavior was attempted and no marks in any of the boxes indicates that the entire social behavior was not attempted or observed. This distinction can prove important, because the first measure tells you that the social behaviors are at least being attempted and also which "ingredients" are being used by the child; the latter signifies that the social behavior is not occurring at all during the observation period.

Before presenting the assessment steps for naturalistic observation, a brief note is in order regarding the use of multiple observers. If only one observer was used during assessment, then the results could reflect this observer's opinions, biases, expectancies, and guesses. To avoid reliance upon one observer and to demonstrate that the observations made are valid, a common research method is to employ two or more observers (called co-observers) who independently observe and record the child's behavior at the same time. Using more than one observer allows for comparisons to be made between the observers to make sure that they *independently* agree about what they have observed (technically referred to as "interobserver agreement").

If one observer records that the child started 10 conversations while a second observer (e.g., a co-observer) also records 10 conversations, then they are in 100% agreement regarding their observations of the child's social behavior. However, the observers often do not agree (usually because they are using different definitions or criteria regarding what constitutes a conversation); one may record 10 conversations while the other records only 5. This results in only 50% agreement between observers, which is too low to be accepted as a reliable observation. The generally accepted standard is to achieve from 80 to 100% agreement between all the observers. Sometimes this requires extensive practice by the observers, along with discussions to clarify the definition of the behavior to be observed. A consensus must be reached on how to decide whether the behavior has occurred. Once all the observers are averaging from 80 to 100% in their agreement with each other, the collection of data through the naturalistic observation procedure can begin.

Assessment Steps for Naturalistic Observation

1. Photocopy enough observation sheets for each child.
2. Enter name and date on the observation sheet for each child. Indicate on each sheet whether the assessment is occurring before, during, or after training by circling "pretraining," "during training," or "posttraining."
3. Read list of behaviors to be observed and discuss with a co-observer the definition and examples of each response.
4. Practice with one subject and a co-observer for 15 minutes; discuss how each response would be coded (e.g. an A or a P in a "yes" or "no" box).
5. For 15 minutes, independently observe and record the responses of a child while a co-observer independently does the same thing with the same child.
6. Compare your observations with the co-observer's observations. Divide the number of agreements between you and the coobserver by the total of your agreements and disagreements, then multiply by 100. This will calculate the interobserver reliability percentage.

$$\frac{\text{Agreements}}{\text{Agreements} + \text{Disagreements}} \times 100 = \quad \%$$

7. If the reliability is below 80%, then further discussion, practice, and consensus among observers are required. After 80% agreement (reliability) is achieved, observation assessment procedures can be started.
8. Select a setting (such as a classroom, playground, etc.) and collect observations by recording responses between the child and other peers (P) and adults (A). Do this by making a P or A in either the "yes" or "no" box for each component.
9. The observation period can be for a specified length (e.g., 15 minutes, or you can collect observations until there are at least two child/peer and two child/adult observations for each individual component. This may cause problems if the child rarely engages in some of the content areas. If the child never produces a response for a content area (e.g., never gives a compliment), a percentage cannot be calculated and the category will be left blank (or coded X). The fact that no responses were observed in a particular social area, however, does provide information as to the low frequency of this class of social behaviors for this subject.
10. Upon completion of the observations, individually sum the "yes" and "no" responses for each category and determine the number of A's placed in the "yes" boxes and the number of P's placed in the "yes" boxes and determine the number of A's and P's placed in the "no" boxes. Divide the number of yesses for the A codes by the sum of the "yes" plus "no" A responses to determine a

percentage for *A* (interacting with adults). Do the same thing with *P* codes. These two percentages represent the percent of correct social skills behavior used in interactions with adults and other peers (*P*). You should determine percentages for interaction with both adults and peers for the five content areas, which will result in ten percentage scores ranging from 0 to 100%. An example of how the scores are presented in a summary table is located in Figure 2 of Sample A.

11. The content areas with the lowest percentage scores are the ones that need the most focused training. Some areas may be identified which do not require any significant training efforts. You should be able to identify the social skill performance deficits and strengths of the child and adapt your training efforts to maximize effectiveness.

12. During and upon completion of the training, the observation procedures should be replicated and the results of pretraining compared with during training and posttraining. This comparison procedure can demonstrate the training's effectiveness and can show areas that still need improvement.

SAMPLE B: SOCIAL SKILLS ROLE-PLAY TEST

The Social Skills Role-Play Test measures the same behaviors and utilizes many of the same procedures as the Social Skills Observation Checklist (Sample A). This assessment procedure collects data on expressive and receptive behaviors in the five social skill

Content area	Pretraining		During training		Post-training	
	Peer	Adult	Peer	Adult	Peer	Adult
1. Positives	*X*	30	60	60	60	70
2. Negatives	*X*	50	40	40	50	60
3. Requests	20	40	70	70	90	90
4. Conversation	20	60	50	50	70	80
5. Feelings	20	60	80	80	90	90
Total correct (%)	12	48	60	68	70	78

(Table header: "Training phase" spans Pretraining, During training, and Post-training columns)

FIGURE 2. Example of a summary table depicting some possible scores for a child on the Social Skills Observation Checklist. The pretraining observation data for this child indicate that most of the interactions with peers were deficient (even nonexistent for "positive statements" and "negative statements," coded *X*) and moderately low for interactions with adults. Improvements were made during training and further improvements could be seen at the end of the training. Overall, the child's use of social skills went from 12 to 70% with peers and 48 to 78% with adults. It appears that the training was effective and that there were no major social skill deficits remaining.

areas, can be "individualized" to focus on specific target behaviors or children, and involves multiple observers to ensure interobserver reliability.

This assessment technique differs from the naturalistic observation method in the following ways: (1) observation situations are only role plays in which the child is to pretend it is a real situation and (2) identical situations are presented to each child by using written "scripts" which the peer (P) or adult (A) "confederates" read for each scene (see Figures 3 and 4). Since the situation is controlled, it is easy to audio- or videotape the child's responses and have the observers do the ratings at their convenience.

The Behavioral Assertiveness Test for Children (BAT-C) is also included in this section to provide examples of role-play scenes (see Figure 5) and more elaborate target behavior definitions (see Figure 6). Discussion regarding the use of this instrument can be found in Chapter 2 and more extensive administration and scoring procedures can be obtained from Bornstein, Bellack, and Hersen (1977).

Assessment Steps for the Social Skills Role-Play Test

1. The same observation sheets provided for the Social Skills Observation Checklist can be used for the Social Skills Role-Play Test. Observation sheets should be reproduced for each child.
2. Each sheet should be marked with the date and designated pretraining, during training, or posttraining, depending upon whether the assessment is occurring before, during, or after training.
3. The observers and confederates (an adult and/or a peer) who will be interacting with the child should read the social skills role-play scripts that follow and become familiar with their content. The user may wish to change the wording of the scripts or replace items with relevant examples to improve the simulated conditions. For example, instead of saying "pretend I have done something which has pleased you, and you are going to compliment me for it," a specific example could be provided, such as "While over at the main building, I bought you a coke and I brought it over for you." *Note:* If examples are substituted, they *must* be used identically for all children (at least if comparative research is being conducted).
4. Observer and confederates should also assess reliability as described in Steps 3 through 7 for naturalistic observation (see previous section, Sample A). This can be accomplished by having any person who is *not* going to be a subject (another staff, volunteer youth, etc.) act as a practice subject. This serves a dual purpose, as the confederates can then practice giving the script while observers assess their reliability and work on accurate coding of the child's responses.
5. After adequate interobserver reliability (80% agreement) has been achieved and the confederates are fluent in their roles, role-play observation procedures can begin. It should be noted that the confederate should use exactly the same words, examples, instructions, voice tone, eye contact, and so on for every child. It is important that the confederates' delivery be consistent and standardized throughout the assessment.
6. It should take approximately 5 to 20 minutes to put each child through the role-play situations, depending upon the number of scenes. If possible, have subjects refrain from discussing the situation with others until all subjects have been assessed. Otherwise, one subject may influence another's responses.
7. The observers record the subjects' responses by putting an A or a P in either the "yes" or "no" box on the observation sheet depending upon whether the con-

1. A. Expressing positive statements
      CONFEDERATE: "Pretend that I have done something that you like: _____ (e.g., I drew a
      nice picture) and you compliment me for it."
      CHILD: (Allow 30 seconds for initiation of a response, then continue script.)

   B. Responding to positive statements
      CONFEDERATE: "Now I will give you a compliment that you might deserve and you
      respond back to me. (Using eye contact) That is a really nice _____ (article of
      clothing, e.g., shirt, necklace, etc.). When you wear it you look better and will
      probably receive other compliments."
      CHILD: (Allow 30 seconds for initiation of a response, then continue script.)

2. A. Expressing negative statements
      CONFEDERATE: "Pretend I have done something that makes you angry or upset like:
      _____ (e.g., I have broken your pencil) and express a complaint to me about it."
      CHILD: (Allow 30 seconds for initiation of a response, then continue script.)

   B. Responding to negative statements
      CONFEDERATE: "Now I will give you a complaint and pretend that you deserve it, and
      you respond back to me. (Using eye contact) The way you _____ (e.g., did your work
      today was terrible. It makes me feel that you don't care and you don't want to try).
      What do you think about that?"
      CHILD: (May respond with a solution, apology, or request clarification, etc.)
      CONFEDERATE: "I think that the solution for you will be _____ (e.g., to put extra effort
      into your work and I will be sure to give you plenty of praise when you do)."

3. A. Giving requests and instructions
      CONFEDERATE: "Pretend that there is something you would like me to do for you like:
      _____ (e.g., lend you a book) and ask me to do it."
      CHILD: (Allow 30 seconds for initiation of a response, then continue script.)

   B. Following requests and instructions
      CONFEDERATE: "Would you do me a favor?"
      CHILD: (May acknowledge request or ask for clarification.)
      CONFEDERATE: (Allow 30 seconds for initiation of a response) "I would like you to:
      _____ (e.g., pick up all the paper on the floor in the room. That way this place will
      look better). What do you think?"
      CHILD: (Allow 30 seconds for initiation of a response, then continue script.)

4. A. Starting and maintaining a conversation
      CONFEDERATE: "Let's have a simple conversation, a couple of minutes long, about
      anything *you* want to talk about. Pretend that I have just walked into the room and
      sat down and now *you* start the conversation."
      CHILD: (Allow 30 seconds for initiation of a response, then continue script.)
      Note: If the child asks for your name (or opinion, etc.), continue the conversation for
      about two minutes.

   B. Listening to others during a conversation
      CONFEDERATE: "Now it is my turn to choose a topic and I would like to talk about _____
      (e.g., my favorite TV show). I really like *Sesame Street*. What do you think about it?"
      CHILD: (Allow 30 seconds for initiation of a response, then continue script.)

FIGURE 3. Social Skills Role-Play Script.

---

5. A. Expressing feelings/empathic statements
   CONFEDERATE: "Pretend that you are feeling sad about _____ (e.g., losing a game). Try to express your feelings to me."
   CHILD: (Allow 30 seconds for initiation of a response, then continue script.)
   Note: If the child expresses feelings, then provide feedback to those feelings and wait 30 seconds for further responses by the child.

   B. Responding to feelings/empathic statements
   CONFEDERATE: "Now I will express my feelings to you. It makes me mad when _____ (e.g., nobody wants to do what I want to do around here. It makes me feel unimportant because nobody would help me. I wish that people would pay more attention to what I need to get done, and then I would be glad to help them do what they need to do").
   CHILD: (Allow 30 seconds for initiation of a response, then continue script.)

	Training phase					
Content area	Pretraining		During training		Post-training	
	Peer	Adult	Peer	Adult	Peer	Adult
1. Positives	43	57	100	100	86	100
2. Negatives	30	20	70	40	60	30
3. Requests	50	70	90	90	90	90
4. Conversation	66	100	100	100	100	100
5. Feelings	20	40	40	60	60	60
Total correct (%)	42	57	80	78	79	76

FIGURE 4. Example of a summary table depicting the possible scores for a child on the Social Skills Role-Play Test. The pretraining observation data for this child indicate that two types of interactions with both peers and adults were deficient ("negatives" and "feelings"). Several other social skill areas were moderately low (43 to 66%) and one, "conversation with an adult," was completely adequate (100%). During-training results showed improvement in all areas. Some of the posttraining results showed a slight decrement from during-training results (e.g., "positive statements with peers" dropped from 100 to 86%, "negative statements" from 70 to 60%, etc.) This may indicate that the training was too brief and that the skills were not learned adequately. Further retraining or "booster sessions" on a follow-up basis may be needed to maintain the social skills learned in the initial training. Several of the other skill areas reached high levels of performance and were maintained at or near these levels at the end of training.

1. NARRATOR: Imagine you're sitting with a boy in class. You tell a story. He thinks it's good and so do you. He says:
   PROMPT: "That was a neat story."

2. NARRATOR: Pretend that you're watching your favorite TV program. Your friend comes over and turns on something you don't like and he says:
   PROMPT: "I'm going to watch this instead."

3. NARRATOR: You draw a picture in art class and the boy next to you says:
   PROMPT: "Wow, that's really great."

4. NARRATOR: You're reading a comic during recess. Pretty soon another kid takes the comic and says:
   PROMPT: "I want to read it by myself."

5. NARRATOR: Pretend you're racing one of the guys and you beat him. He says:
   PROMPT: "Gee, you're really fast."

6. NARRATOR: Imagine it's your turn to play the video game. Your friend leaves it on the table for you. But someone else gets there first and says:
   PROMPT: "I'm taking this."

7. NARRATOR: Imagine you're playing ball with some of your friends and you've made a good catch. One of your friends says:
   PROMPT: "Hey _____, that was a good play."

8. NARRATOR: Pretend that you're standing near the TV. Suddenly your brother or sister comes by and pushes you and says:
   PROMPT: "Get out of my way."

9. NARRATOR: You've been working really hard on a project that's coming up. One of the boys says to you:
   PROMPT: "That's a really neat project you did."

10. NARRATOR: Someone else makes a mistake and blames it on you. He says:
    PROMPT: "You're the one who did it."

11. NARRATOR: Imagine you're getting dressed to go on a special outing. Your friend says:
    PROMPT: "_____, you look very nice today."

12. NARRATOR: Your friend is teasing you. He keeps calling you names. You're getting tired of it. He says:
    PROMPT: "What's the matter? Can't you take a joke?"

13. NARRATOR: Imagine you just finished decorating your room with posters and other stuff. A friend says to you:
    PROMPT: "Wow, _____, you really did a good job."

14. NARRATOR: You forgot something you were supposed to bring and someone says:
    PROMPT: "You're so dumb! You'd forget your head if it weren't screwed on!"

FIGURE 5. Role-play scenes for the Behavioral Assertiveness Test for Children (BAT-C).

15. NARRATOR: You worked hard making the popcorn for the movie and someone says:
    PROMPT: "_____, this is very good."

16. NARRATOR: While you're trying to watch TV, someone keeps running in front of the screen. When you tell him to stop, he says:
    PROMPT: "You're gonna have to make me. C'mon, make me."

17. NARRATOR: You let a friend borrow a toy and he tells you how much he appreciates your kindness.
    PROMPT: "_____, you were very nice to lend me that toy."

18. NARRATOR: Imagine you're sitting outside during recess. Someone walks by and kicks you and says:
    PROMPT: "Move. You're in my way."

19. NARRATOR: Imagine that you've just finished a hard homework assignment and one of your friends comes over and says:
    PROMPT: "_____, it looks like you did a nice job."

20. NARRATOR: Imagine one of the kids in class is swearing at you. You don't like it. He says:
    PROMPT: "I feel like swearing at you. I'm gonna keep swearing."

21. NARRATOR: You are playing with a friend and he says:
    PROMPT: "Playing with you is lots of fun."

22. NARRATOR: You're working with another kid in the classroom. The two of you are sharing a book. Someone takes the book and says:
    PROMPT: "I want to look at the book myself."

23. NARRATOR: Imagine that someone you like says to you:
    PROMPT: "I think you are a very nice person."

24. NARRATOR: You're playing a board game. One of your friends comes over, takes the dice and says:
    PROMPT: "I need these."

federate giving the prompt was an adult or a peer, respectively (see explanation given in Sample A, Social Skills Observation Checklist). Since the role-play observation script is designed to portray each of the components only once in a specific order, there should be only one *A* or *P* marked for each specific component.

8. As each subject enters the room for assessment, the experimenter or confederate(s) should briefly explain the assessment procedures and provide the child with general instructions to "respond promptly to the pretend or role-play situations as you would in everyday life."

9. Upon completion of the role-play assessment for the subjects, the observation sheet should be summated and scored separately for responses to adult (*A*) and peer (*P*) confederates. For example, this is accomplished for "responding to an adult confederate" by counting the number of components for each content area (i.e., seven components for "positives") and then determining the percent of correct responses by dividing the number of components into the number of *A*'s in the "yes" boxes (e.g., five *A*'s in the "yes" boxes out of seven components

1. *Eye contact*
   Length of time from beginning of subject's verbal reply to termination of subject's response that the subject maintains eye contact is measured in seconds. If subject makes no verbal reply, make no entry other than a dash (—) for eye contact. If subject has a speech pause of three seconds or more (which terminates timing of speech duration), terminate timing of eye contact until subject begins to speak again.

2. *Response duration*
   Length of time (in seconds) that the subject speaks to partner is recorded for each scene. Speech pauses of greater than three seconds terminate timing (i.e., timing stops at the end of the last spoken word) until the subject begins speaking again.

3. *Voice intonation*
   Subject's verbal affect is scored on a five-point scale, with 1 indicating a very flat, unemotional tone of voice and 5 indicating a full and lively intonation appropriate to each situation.

4. *Smiles*
   Lip corners drawn back and up, with or without teeth showing. Recorded on a dichotomous occurrence or nonoccurrence basis for each scene after delivery of prompt to termination of response. If subject makes no verbal reply, note whether smiling occurred during first five seconds after delivery of prompt.

   ✔ = smile occurred   × = smile did not occur

5. *Accept help*
   Verbal content indicating acceptance of help is recorded on a dichotomous occurrence or nonoccurrence basis for each applicable scene. The following are examples of target behavior occurrence: "Thanks," "OK," "that's nice of you," "I sure would like to help," "Yes." Examples of nonoccurrence of the target behavior include such refusal statements as: "I can do it myself," "Leave me alone," "No thanks." the subject has to show verbal evidence of wishing to accept the help offered; no response at all or simply nodding the head would be scored as nonoccurrence of the target behavior.

   ✔ = help accepted   × = help not accepted

6. *Appreciation*
   Verbal content indicating that the subject expresses gratitude or thankfulness for the partner's behavior (e.g., if the subject thanks the prompter for offering the help, for doing a favor, or for giving a compliment). "OK" would count as an example of "accepting help" but would *not* count as an example of expressing appreciation. "Thank you" counts as an example of *both* accepting help *and* expressing appreciation.

   ✔ = appreciation expressed   × = appreciation not expressed

7. *Praise*
   Verbal content indicating that the subject expressed approval, admiration, or was complimentary toward the partner's behavior (e.g., the subject tells a peer that a new outfit looks good or that it is great that the peer won the quiet worker award).

   ✔ = praise given   × = praise not given

FIGURE 6. Target behavior definitions for the Behavioral Assertiveness Test for Children (BAT-C).

8. *Affect statement*

Any statement by a child describing or evaluating his or her own state (other than intellectual or physiological). The response class includes affect statements that begin with the pronouns *I* or *we* and statements beginning with *it* or *that* but which still reflect the child's affect. The following are examples of affect statements: "I am satisfied," "I'm happy," "We enjoyed it," "I like you," "I don't like that," "I am upset," "I'm sorry for you," "I feel good," "It makes me happy," "It makes me feel good," "That makes me angry," "That makes me upset."

Incomplete statements (in the sense that the object of the affect is not mentioned) like "I love . . ." or "We don't like . . ." are still counted as affect statements. However, quotations in which affect is ascribed to the speaker by another individual (e.g., "My mother said I was angry") and nonaffect statements like "It was nice" and "I want it" are not counted as responses in this class.

✔ = occurrence   × = nonoccurrence

9. *Noncompliance*

Verbal content indicating adaptive noncompliance is rated on a dichotomous occurrence or nonoccurrence basis for each applicable (male/female negative) scene. Noncompliance is scored if the child resists the unreasonable request of the prompter (e.g., doesn't allow the peer to change a television channel in the middle of a TV show). Noncompliance requires an active verbal code in order to be scored.

✔ = noncompliance occurred   × = noncompliance did not occur

10. *Request for new behavior*

Verbal content requesting new behavior from the interpersonal partner is scored on an occurrence or nonoccurrence basis for each applicable scene. Responses scored in this category require more than simple noncompliance and more than a request for a simple termination/cessation of the response or exact reversal of the offending behavior (e.g., "Stop that"; "You took it . . . put it back"). The subject has to show evidence of wanting the partner to change his/her behavior (e.g., the subject asks partner to play elsewhere, asks peer who cut into a school line to step to the end of the line.) The basic paradigms into which most requests for new behavior will fall are the following: "Let's discuss it," "Move somewhere else or engage in a competing behavior to the one you're now engaged in," "Let's share," and "Wait now and you'll get it later." The child does not have to phrase the negotiating position in the form of a question or to be extremely polite in advancing the request for new behavior: "Why don't you quit swearing at me and maybe we can both play a game," "You can have it when I've finished looking at it," "After I've finished watching my show you can watch yours," "Ask nicely," "I'm going to watch the TV show I want to watch; then I'm going to turn the channel and you can watch what you want to watch."

11. *Overall social skill*

All scenes are rated individually for overall social skill on a 5-point scale, with 1 indicating a socially very unskilled and 5 indicating a socially very skilled response.

---

yields 71% correct responses for the "positives" content area). This same procedure would be repeated for the *P*'s (responding to peer confederates) to determine the percentage of correct responses for each content area. After completing the percentage correct for each content area, determine the percentage correct for all areas combined. This should yield an overall percentage score that reflects general social skills ability. Examples of the percentage scores are presented in a summary table and can be seen in Figure 4.

10. The content areas with the lowest percentage scores are the ones that need the most focused training. Some scores that do not require any significant training efforts may be identified. You will be able to identify the social skills performance deficit and strengths of each child and provide in-depth training to maximize effectiveness.

11. During and upon completion of the training, the observation procedures should be replicated and the results of pretraining compared with those obtained during training and posttraining. This comparison procedure can be accomplished by displaying the data on graphs, tables, and so on. An example of a table that allows comparison of pretraining, during training, and posttraining percentage scores is presented in Figure 4.

12. One method used by clinical researchers to check on whether training generalized to nontargeted areas of social functioning is to administer certain scenes only pre and post (without providing any training for those specific scenes) and measure the improvements.

Sample C: The Children's Behavioral Scenario (CBS)

The CBS is a contrived "candid camera" method of social skills assessment designed to obtain seminaturalistic data in a standardized manner. The CBS may be used as a general screening device to identify socially incompetent children for training, as it is easy to conduct and highly efficient [e.g., Wood, Michelson, & Flynn (1978) tested approximately 140 children in five days]. In addition to being a "deceptive" contrived interview, this assessment technique is different in that it also tries to provide information as to whether the child's social behavior is passive, assertive, or aggressive. (The reader is referred to Chapter 2 for additional discussion of this technique.)

Basically, the child is exposed to an interview that contains stimuli, prompts, and questions to elicit social responses. There are also a number of neutral, "filler" questions to reduce the child's suspicion and anxiety and allow for rapport building between the interviewer and the respondent. After the child enters the room, the interviewer typically greets him or her with a warm smile, a handshake, and an introduction. The child's social performance from this moment until he or she exits (about 15 minutes later) is carefully observed and scored across many dimensions of social skills.

During the interview, the interviewer (I) acts out a prepared script (see Figure 7) in a specified order. This script was designed to elicit social skill responses from the child which can be recorded and rated by observers. They include greeting others, making requests, giving and receiving praise, giving complaints, expressing empathy and feelings, refusing unreasonable requests and blame, and initiating and terminating conversations.

Although the interview script presented in Figure 7 has been empirically validated, trainers should feel free to modify, add, or delete items to tailor or "individualize" the assessment to the specific characteristics or needs of the children, setting, or program. Interviewers may also wish to modify some of the examples slightly, such as getting one's finger caught in the attaché case (to stub one's toe, etc.) so as to reduce the possibility that children will discuss similarities of the interview outside the room. This became rather obvious to one of the authors when confronted by the 100th child tested, who asked "Are you guys gonna hurt your finger with me too?"

Child's Name:_____   Date:_____
Interviewer:_____   Assessment (circle one):   Before training
                                                                          During training
                                                                          After training
         Interviewer's Script (I)   Response Components and Coding Format

Scene: Child enters a medium-sized room   Components: Scene provides a one-to-one
  with the interviewer present behind a   interaction between child and adult in
  desk. There is only one chair present, but   which various areas of assertive behavior
  it is covered by interviewer's attaché case   may be observed and assessed.
  lying flat on the seat. There are various
  papers in piles on the desk; the inter-   Child's response coding format and
  viewer appears casually though not lei-   taxonomy:
  surely dressed and relatively moderate in   −2 = very passive behavior
  expression throughout the interview.   −1 = partially passive
                                                    0 = assertive response
                                                    1 = partially aggressive
                                                    2 = very aggressive behavior

I: (Says neutrally) "Hi, my name is _____   Component: Responding to greeting

_____.   (1) Response coding:
        (first)   (last)   −2 = no response.
                                                   −1 = nod and/or "Hi."
                                                    0 = nod or "hi" *and* returns name.
                                                    1 = (rude response) "So what."
                                                    2 = (very rude) "Who cares!"

I: (Whether or not child has given his name)   Comment: No response specifically coded;
  "How do you spell your name?"   information used to verify child's name for
                                                  data collection.

                                               Child: (spells name) "_____"

I: "I'm part of a group of people who are   Comment: Response not specifically scored.
  talking with children in schools about   Interviewer is providing rationale for
  their hobbies, their school, and things like   interview.
  that."

I: (Begins to look in desk drawers and   Component: Making requests
  through papers for certain form) "Why
  don't you have a seat while I look for   (2) Response coding:
  something?"   −2 = stands, says nothing.
                                                   −1 = sits on corner of chair (moves the
                                                        attaché case less than 3 inches.
                                                    0 = *asks* to move case, moves case and
                                                        sits down.
                                                    1 = moves case without asking or re-
                                                        marks, "What's this doing here?"
                                                    2 = sits on case, or knocks it off chair, or
                                                        rude remark, "What dummy left this
                                                        here?"

                                               Comment: If child hasn't moved case and
                                                 sat down after 30 seconds, child is asked
                                                 to do so.

FIGURE 7. Interview script and response coding for the Children's Behavioral Scenario (CBS).

I: "What is your favorite hobby?"

Comment: Response not specifically coded. Question used as "filler" for interview.

I: "Can you think of something that's good about this school and why?"

Component: Making positive statements

(2) Response coding:
  −2 = no response or shakes head "No."
  −1 = "Not much," "It's OK," or "Everything."
   0 = "I like _____."
   1 = "Good, but not as good as others."
   2 = "It's good because I'm in it!" or "This school's lousy!"

I: "Can you think of something nice to say about another student?"

Component: Making positive statements

(4) Response coding:
  −2 = No response.
  −1 = "Don't know," or "Some kids are OK."
   0 = specific compliment.
   1 = "_____ is nice, but I'm nicer."
   2 = "Yea, I'm great" or "The other students are creeps."

I: "You seem like a very nice person."

Component: Receiving positive statements

(5) Response coding:
  −2 = "No, I'm not."
  −1 = No response of irrelevant comment.
   0 = "Thanks."
   1 = "I'm great", or "better than most."
   2 = "I'm the best" or puts down others.

I: "What's your favorite sport to watch or play?"

Comment: Response not specifically coded. Filler question for interview.

I: "Can you think of something you don't like about this school and why?"

Component: Making negative statements

(6) Response coding:
  −2 = No response
  −1 = "Nothing really"
   0 = Specific complaint and reason.
   1 = Complaint and no reason
   2 = "It's lousy!"

I: "Can you think of something you don't like about another student and why?"

Component: Making negative statements

(7) Response coding:
  −2 = No response
  −1 = "They're O.K."
   0 = Specific reason, i.e. "_____ tells lots of lies."
   1 = "This school is full of creeps."
   2 = "_____ is a real creep!"

I: "What class do you like the most?"

Comment: Response not specifically coded. Interview filler.

I: "By the way, I like your (some part of physical appearance; e.g., shirt, dress, etc.)."

Component: Receiving praise

(8) Response coding:
 −2 = No response of "This old rag?"
 −1 = "It's O.K."
  0 = "Thanks."
  1 = "It's my favorite!"
  2 = "It's the best!"

I: (Looks in desk drawer for something and appears to slam his finger in the drawer and expresses pain without eye contact) "Ow! that hurt!" (Shakes hand and grimaces for period of 30 seconds.)

Component: Expressing empathy

(9) Response coding:
 −2 = no response.
 −1 = "What happened?"
  0 = "Are you all right?" "Can I help?" etc.
  1 = "Tough luck!"
  2 = Laughs, "What a dumb thing to do."

I: "We might start a new program in the schools to make them cleaner. Would you give up your whole recess time every day to pick up paper and trash instead of playing for the next three months?"

Component: Responding to unreasonable requests

(10) Response coding:
 −2 = no response
 −1 = "Doesn't sound like much fun."
  0 = "No, I'd rather not."
  1 = "No way!"
  2 = "You're crazy!!!"

I: (Asks subject to record his response on a sheet marked "Yes" and "No"; interviewer places volunteer form in front of subject) "I need you to mark down yes or no so we can keep count." (Interviewer then hands subject a pencil, eraser first, and conceals that the pencil lead is broken off.)

Component: Making negative statements

(11) Response coding:
 −2 = no response.
 −1 = "I must have broken it."
  0 = "This pencil's broken."
  1 = "What a lousy pencil."
  2 = "You gave me a broken pencil, dummy!"

I: (Acknowledges broken pencil) "You kids are always breaking my pencils!"

Component: Responding to negative statements

(12) Response coding:
 −2 = "Sorry."
 −1 = no response.
  0 = "I didn't break it." or "It was already broken."
  1 = "Lousy pencil."
  2 = "You're crazy!!"

Continued

I: "Well, it doesn't matter. We aren't going to have children pick up the trash. We will hire some people to do it, so you don't have to volunteer. Just forget about it."

Comment: When child leaves interview, he will not spread the word that such a request will be made to others.

I: "Shuffles papers in and out of drawer for 30 seconds) then says, "Well, how are you feeling today?"

Component: Expressing feelings

(13) Response coding:
   −2 = no response.
   −1 = "OK," or "All right."
    0 = "OK" *and* returns question.
    1 = "What's it to you?"
    2 = "None of your business!!" or "Feel super."

I: (Removes pack of sugarless gum with two pieces remaining. Removes and eats one and places the other on the desk, midway to subject.)

Component: Making requests

(14) Response coding:
   −2 = no response.
   −2 = hints about gum.
    0 = asks for gum.
    1 = demands gum.
    2 = tries to reach and take gum.

(If subject has asked for gum, interviewer says he is saving it for later and it's his last piece; if subject does not request gum, then interviewer unwraps last piece and eats it too at the end of interview.)

Comment: Child will leave the interview with the impression that there is no more gum to be had so that he/she will not inform others of its possible availability.

I: "What's your favorite TV program?"

Comment: Response not specifically coded.

I: "Would you go over to the door and open and close it a couple of times?" (Regardless of child's response) "The door wasn't working right earlier, and I just wanted to check it."

Component: Responding to requests asking why

(15) Response coding:
   −2 = does it.
   −1 = "Well, OK" and does it.
    0 = "Why?" before doing it.
    1 = "Sounds silly."
    2 = "This is stupid."

Comment: Statement provides rationale for unusual request.

I: "If you could make any change in this school, what would it be and why?"

Component: Making requests

(16) Response coding:
   −2 = no response.
   −1 = "Things could be better."
    0 = specific request.
    1 = "This place stinks."
    2 = "Burn the place!"

I: "What do you think about the weather here?"
"Who's your favorite TV star?"
"What was going on in class when you left?"

I: "Thanks for talking to me. Now return to your class and have a good day." (Child leaves room to return to class.)

Comment: No specific response coding. These questions provide filler and ending for interview.

Component: Termination of conversation

(17) Response coding:
   -2 = no response.
   -1 = "I'll try."
    0 = "Goodbye."
    1 = "Sure."
    2 = "Later, jerk."
Responses during the interview to filler questions, etc., are rated in the following components.

General component: Initiating conversation

(18) Response coding:
   -2 = no initiation.
   -1 = occasional questions.
    0 = Appropriate questions, requests, etc.
    1 = inappropriate remarks.
    2 = rude or very inappropriate responses.

General component: interruptive behavior

(19) Response coding:
    0 = none or appropriate
    1 = occasional
    2 = frequent and very inappropriate (off the subject or "attacking")

General component: Answering questions

(20) Response coding
   -2 = no answer.
   -1 = "Don't know."
    0 = specific answer.
    1 = "What's the difference!"
    2 = "None of your business."

Continued

Figure 7 (*Continued*)

Social Behavior Scores/Ratings	− (Passive)	0 (Assertive)	+ (Aggressive)
Content areas			
1. Positive statements (Items 3, 4, 5, 8)			
2. Negative statements (Items 6, 7, 11, 12)			
3. Requests/Instructions (Items 2, 10, 14, 15, 16)			
4. Conversations (Items 1, 17, 18, 19, 20)			
5. Feelings/Empathy (Items 9, 13)			
Totals			

	Training phase								
	Before training			During training			After training		
Content areas	−	0	+	−	0	+	−	0	+
1. Positive statements (3, 4, 5, 8)		3	+1		4			4	
2. Negative statements (6, 7, 11, 12)	−8			−2	6			8	
3. Requests/Instructions (2, 10, 14, 15, 16)	−1	3	+1		5			5	
4. Conversations (1, 17, 18, 19, 20)		5			5			5	
5. Feelings/Empathy (9, 13)	−4			−4			−4		
Totals	−13	11	+2	−6	20	+0	−4	22	+0

Figure 8. Summary table for the Children's Behavioral Scenario (CBS). The before-training scores indicate that this child has major deficiencies in "making and responding to negative statements" and "expressing and responding to feelings/empathic statements." For both of these social skill components, this child provided only "very passive" responses (e.g., −8, −4), which were inappropriate. During- and after-training results show an improvement in handling "negatives" but no change in "feelings/empathic statements." Further training in this particular area may still be required.

ASSESSMENT STEPS FOR THE CHILDREN'S BEHAVIORAL SCENARIO

1. Reproduce a CBS script/coding form (Figure 7) for each child to be interviewed.
2. Complete Steps 2 through 6 listed for the Social Skills Role-Play Test (Sample B).
3. The observer(s) should circle a score (0, +, or −) for each of the 20 components as they occur during the interview (or videotape the CBS and do the ratings later).
4. After child leaves the room, add up all the minus scores (passive responses), plus scores (aggressive responses), and all zero scores (assertive responses) separately; enter the totals on the last page of the form.
5. An example of a summary table is presented in Figure 8. It shows the content areas from which the child's pluses, minuses, and zeros were obtained and lends itself to the isolation of specific deficits and strengths.
6. *Note:* If data are collected before and after training, the same interviewer should be used both times (to ensure consistency).

SAMPLE D: INFORMANT REPORT OF YOUTH'S BEHAVIOR: CHILDREN'S ASSERTIVE BEHAVIOR SCALE (CABS)

The informant report method of assessing children's social skills relies upon the judgments and ratings provided by members of the child's social environment. Informants are usually such persons as teachers, neighbors, parents, friends, classmates, and staff members, but an informant could be anyone who has substantial interaction with or opportunities to observe the child behaving and responding in social situations.

As indicated in Chapter 2, informant reports are subject to several limitations. One of the main concerns that surfaces in utilizing this assessment procedure is the degree of "biased reporting" by the informants. For example, one teacher who likes a child may report all "assertive" responses while another teacher who dislikes the child (perhaps from a single previous incident) may report the same child as always aggressive. At present, the only solution to solving these discrepancies is first, to instruct all informants to be *objective* and accurate as possible and, second, to utilize additional assessment measure to substantiate informants reports.

This informant report (see Figure 9) has been designed to be consistent with the previous samples in terms of content areas covered. Various items are included to measure expressive and receptive responses in the same five social skill areas: positive statements, negative statements, requests/instructions, conversations, and feelings/empathic statements. Therefore, in utilizing one or more of the other measures, it should be easy to compare the content areas and totals across all the measures with the informant report ratings.

ASSESSMENT STEPS FOR THE INFORMANT REPORT OF YOUTH'S BEHAVIOR (CABS)

1. Read the instructions on the first page to the informants and to yourself and make sure that they are easy to understand and are explained to each informant.
2. Reproduce one test form for each informant and enough answer sheets (Figure 10) to report on all children. Each informant can use one test form for all children by completing a different answer sheet for each child.
3. Instruct informants to answer each question honestly and accurately and not just to mark answers randomly on the answer sheet. Collect all materials after testing.

Described in this questionnaire are various situations and possible responses that a youth would use. From your observations over the past two months, please select the response that best describes the youth's usual response to the given situations. Please consider each situation and its alternative responses in an accurate and objective manner. You will be asked to answer how the youth would react to (1) another youth and (2) an adult. Thus, for each question two answers are required; one relating to how the youth responds to another youth and, second, how the youth responds to an adult (parents, teachers, staff members, volunteers, etc.). Complete confidentiality will be maintained and all information will be used strictly for clinical purposes. Therefore, it is essential that your answers are based specifically upon the youth's behavior.

DO NOT WRITE ON THE TEST. WRITE ON THE ANSWER SHEET ONLY

1. Someone says to the youth, "I think you are a very nice person."
   The youth would usually:
   (a) Say, "No, I'm not that nice."
   (b) Say, "Yes, I think I am the best."
   (c) Say, "Thank you."
   (d) Say nothing and blush.
   (e) Say, "Thanks, I am really great."

2. Someone does something that the youth thinks is really great.
   The youth would usually:
   (a) Act like it wasn't that great and say, "That was all right."
   (b) Say, "That was all right, but I've seen better."
   (c) Say nothing.
   (d) Say, "I can do much better than that."
   (e) Say, "That was really great."

3. The youth is working on something he or she likes and thinks is very good. Someone says "I don't like it!"
   The youth would usually:
   (a) Say, "You're a dummy!"
   (b) Say, "I think it's good."
   (c) Say, "You're right," although you don't really agree.
   (d) Say, "I think this is great; besides, what do you know."
   (e) Feel hurt and say nothing.

4. The youth forgets something they were supposed to bring and someone says, "You're so dumb! You'd forget your head if it wasn't screwed on!"
   The youth would usually:
   (a) Say, "I'm smarter than you any day; besides what do you know!"
   (b) Say, "Yes, you're right, sometimes I do act dumb."
   (c) Say, "If anybody is dumb, it's you!"
   (d) Say, "Nobody's perfect. I'm not dumb just because I forgot something!"
   (e) Say nothing or ignore it.

5. Someone the youth was supposed to meet arrives 30 minutes late, which makes the youth upset. The person says nothing about why he or she is late.
   The youth would usually:
   (a) Say, "I'm upset that you kept me waiting like this."
   (b) Say, "I was wondering when you'd get here."
   (c) Say, "This is the last time I'll wait for you!"
   (d) Say nothing to the person.
   (e) Say, "You're a jerk! You're late!"

FIGURE 9. Informant Report of Youth's Behavior: Children's Assertive Behavior Scale (CABS).

6. The youth needs someone to do something for him or her.
   The youth would usually:
   (a) Not ask for anything to be done.
   (b) Say, "You have to do this for me!"
   (c) Say, "Would you please do something for me?" and then explain what you want.
   (d) Give a small hint that he or she needs something done.
   (e) Say, "I want you to do this for me."

7. The youth knows that someone is feeling upset.
   The youth would usually:
   (a) Say, "You seem upset; can I help?"
   (b) Be with them and not talk about his or her being upset.
   (c) Say, "What's wrong with you?"
   (d) Not say anything and leave them alone.
   (e) Laugh and say, "You're just a big baby!"

8. The youth is feeling upset, and someone says, "You seem upset."
   The youth would usually:
   (a) Say nothing.
   (b) Say, "It's none of your business!"
   (c) Say, "Yes, I am upset, thank you for asking."
   (d) Say, "It's nothing."
   (e) Say, "I'm upset, leave me alone."

9. Someone else makes a mistake and someone blames it on the youth.
   The youth would usually:
   (a) Say, "You're crazy!"
   (b) Say, "That wasn't my fault; someone else made the mistake."
   (c) Say, "I don't think it was my fault."
   (d) Say, "Wasn't me, you don't know what you're talking about!"
   (e) Take the blame or say nothing.

10. Someone asks the youth to do something, but the youth doesn't know what has to be done.
    The youth would usually:
    (a) Say, "This doesn't make any sense, I don't want to do it."
    (b) Do what the person asks and say nothing.
    (c) Say, "This is dumb, I'm not going to do it!"
    (d) Before doing it, say, "I don't understand why you want this done."
    (e) Say, "If that's what you want," and then do it.

11. Someone praises something the youth did as being terrific.
    The youth would usually:
    (a) Say, "Yes I usually do better than most."
    (b) Say, "No, that wasn't so hot."
    (c) Say, "That's right, because I'm the best."
    (d) Say, "Thank you."
    (e) Ignore it and say nothing.

12. Someone has been very nice to the youth.
    The youth would usually:
    (a) Say, "You have been really nice to me, thanks."
    (b) Act like the person weren't that nice and say, "Yea, thanks."
    (c) Say, "You have treated me all right, but I deserve even better."
    (d) Ignore it and say nothing.
    (e) Say, "You don't treat me good enough!"

13. The youth is talking very loudly with a friend and someone says, "Excuse me, but you are being too noisy."
    The youth would usually:
    (a) Stop talking immediately.
    (b) Say, "If you don't like it, get lost," and keep on talking loudly.
    (c) Say, "I'm sorry, I'll talk quietly," and then talk in a quiet voice.
    (d) Say, "I'm sorry," and stop talking.
    (e) Say, "All right" and continue to talk loudly.

14. The youth is waiting in line and someone breaks in in front.
    The youth would usually:
    (a) Make quiet comments such as, "Some people have a lot of nerve," without actually saying anything directly to the person.
    (b) Say, "Get to the end of the line!"
    (c) Say nothing to the person.
    (d) Say in a loud voice, "Get out of this line you creep!"
    (e) Say, "I was here first; please go to the end of the line."

15. Someone does something to the youth that the youth doesn't like and it makes the youth angry.
    The youth would usually:
    (a) Shout, "You're a creep, I hate you!"
    (b) Say, "I'm angry, I don't like what you did."
    (c) Act hurt about it but not say anything to the person.
    (d) Say, "I'm mad. I don't like you!"
    (e) Ignore it and not say anything to the person.

16. Someone has something that the youth wants to use.
    The youth would usually:
    (a) Tell the person to hand it over.
    (b) Not ask to use it.
    (c) Take it from the person.
    (d) Tell the person he or she would like to use it and then ask to use it.
    (e) Make a comment about it but not ask to use it.

17. Someone asks to borrow something that belongs to the youth, but it is new and the youth doesn't want to lend it.
    The youth would usually:
    (a) Say, "No, I just got it and I don't want to lend it out; maybe some other time."
    (b) Say, "I really don't want to, but you can use it."
    (c) Say, "No, go get your own!"
    (d) Give it up even though he or she doesn't want to.
    (e) Say, "You're crazy!"

18. Someone is talking about a hobby the youth really likes, and the youth wants to join in and say something.
    The youth would usually:
    (a) Not say anything.
    (b) Interrupt and immediately start saying how good he or she is at this hobby.
    (c) Move closer to the group and enter into the conversation when possible.
    (d) Move closer and wait to be noticed.
    (e) Interrupt and immediately start talking about how much he or she likes the hobby.

19. The youth is working on a hobby and someone asks, "What are you doing?"
    The youth would usually:
    (a) Say, "Oh, just something" or, "Oh, nothing."
    (b) Say, "Don't bother me. Can't you see I'm working."
    (c) Keep on working and say nothing.
    (d) Say, "It's none of your business!"
    (e) Stop working and explain what he or she is doing.

20. The youth sees someone trip and fall down.
    The youth would usually:
    (a) Laugh and say, "Why don't you watch where you're going?"
    (b) Say, "Are you all right? Is there anything I can do?"
    (c) Ask, "What happened?"
    (d) Say, "That's the breaks."
    (e) Do nothing and ignore it.

21. The youth bumps his or her head on a shelf and it hurts. Someone says, "Are you all right?"
    The youth would usually:
    (a) Say, "I'm fine, leave me alone!"
    (b) Say nothing and ignore the person.
    (c) Say, "Why don't you mind your own business?"
    (d) Say, "No, I hurt my head; thanks for asking."
    (e) Say, "It's nothing, I'm OK."

22. The youth makes a mistake and someone else is blamed for it.
    The youth would usually:
    (a) Say nothing.
    (b) Say, "It's their mistake!"
    (c) Say, "I made the mistake."
    (d) Say, "I don't think that person did it."
    (e) Say, "That's their tough luck!"

23. The youth feels insulted by something someone has said.
    The youth would usually:
    (a) Walk away but say nothing about being upset.
    (b) Tell the person not to do it again.
    (c) Say nothing to the person, although the youth feels insulted.
    (d) Insult the person back and call him or her a name.
    (e) Tell the person he or she didn't like what was said and tell the person not to do it again.

24. Someone often interrupts the youth, who is talking.
    The youth would usually:
    (a) Say, "Excuse me, I would like to finish what I was saying."
    (b) Say, "This isn't fair; don't I get to talk?"
    (c) Interrupt the other person by starting to talk again.
    (d) Say nothing and let the other person continue to talk.
    (e) Say, "Shut up, I was talking!"

25. Someone asks the youth to do something that would keep the youth from doing what the youth really wants to do.
    The youth would usually:
    (a) Say, "I have other plans, but I'll do what you want."
    (b) Say, "No way! Find someone else."
    (c) Say, "OK, I'll do what you want."
    (d) Say, "Forget it, shove off!"
    (e) Say, "I've already made other plans, maybe next time."

26. The youth sees someone the youth would like to meet.
    The youth would usually:
    (a) Yell at the person and tell them to come over.
    (b) Walk over to the person, make an introduction, and start talking.
    (c) Walk over near the person and wait for them to start talking.
    (d) Walk over to the person and start talking about great personal accomplishments.
    (e) Not say anything to the person.

27. Someone the youth has not met before stops and says hello.
    The youth would usually:
    (a) Say, "What do you want?"
    (b) Say, "Don't bother me. Get lost!"
    (c) Not say anything.
    (d) Say hello, make an introduction, and ask who the stranger was.
    (e) Nod, say hi, and walk away.

Youth's Name:_____   Date:_____
Informant's Name:_____   Assessment:_____

How would the youth answer if "someone" in the question was (1) another youth or (2) an adult.

Another Youth	An Adult
1. a, b, c, d, e	1. a, b, c, d, e
2. a, b, c, d, e	2. a, b, c, d, e
3. a, b, c, d, e	3. a, b, c, d, e
4. a, b, c, d, e	4. a, b, c, d, e
5. a, b, c, d, e	5. a, b, c, d, e
6. a, b, c, d, e	6. a, b, c, d, e
7. a, b, c, d, e	7. a, b, c, d, e
8. a, b, c, d, e	8. a, b, c, d, e
9. a, b, c, d, e	9. a, b, c, d, e
10. a, b, c, d, e	10. a, b, c, d, e
11. a, b, c, d, e	11. a, b, c, d, e
12. a, b, c, d, e	12. a, b, c, d, e
13. a, b, c, d, e	13. a, b, c, d, e
14. a, b, c, d, e	14. a, b, c, d, e
15. a, b, c, d, e	15. a, b, c, d, e
16. a, b, c, d, e	16. a, b, c, d, e
17. a, b, c, d, e	17. a, b, c, d, e
18. a, b, c, d, e	18. a, b, c, d, e
19. a, b, c, d, e	19. a, b, c, d, e
20. a, b, c, d, e	20. a, b, c, d, e
21. a, b, c, d, e	21. a, b, c, d, e
22. a, b, c, d, e	22. a, b, c, d, e
23. a, b, c, d, e	23. a, b, c, d, e
24. a, b, c, d, e	24. a, b, c, d, e
25. a, b, c, d, e	25. a, b, c, d, e
26. a, b, c, d, e	26. a, b, c, d, e
27. a, b, c, d, e	27. a, b, c, d, e

COMMENTS:

FIGURE 10. Informant Report Answer Sheet (CABS).

4. Using the scoring key (Figure 11), score each response on the answer sheet.
5. Note that a *high score represents unassertiveness*, as each response is scored −2 for a very passive response, −1 for a partial passive response, 0 for an assertive response, 1 for a partially aggressive response, or a 2 for a very aggressive response. Therefore a negative score would mean a passive response and a positive score would denote an aggressive response.
6. Scoring of the informant report inventory is relatively simple.
   a. Overall scoring: Add together the raw or absolute values of scores for all responses, regardless of positive or negative values. This produces two basic

Youth's Name:_____   Date:_____
Informant's Name:_____

How would the youth answer if the "someone" in the question was (1) another youth or (2) an adult.

	Another Youth						An Adult				
	a	b	c	d	e		a	b	c	d	e
1.	−2	2	0	−1	1	1.	−2	2	0	−1	1
2.	−1	1	−2	2	0	2.	−1	1	−2	2	0
3.	2	0	−1	1	−2	3.	2	0	−1	1	−2
4.	1	−2	2	0	−1	4.	1	−2	2	0	−1
5.	0	−1	1	−2	2	5.	0	−1	1	−2	2
6.	−2	2	0	−1	1	6.	−2	2	0	−1	1
7.	0	−1	1	−2	2	7.	0	−1	1	−2	2
8.	−2	2	0	−1	1	8.	−2	2	0	−1	1
9.	2	0	−1	1	−2	9.	2	0	−1	1	−2
10.	1	−2	2	0	−1	10.	1	−2	2	0	−1
11.	1	−2	2	0	−1	11.	1	−2	2	0	−1
12.	0	−1	1	−2	2	12.	0	−1	1	−2	2
13.	−2	2	0	−1	1	13.	−2	2	0	−1	1
14.	−1	1	−2	2	0	14.	−1	1	−2	2	0
15.	2	0	−1	1	−2	15.	2	0	−1	1	−2
16.	1	−2	2	0	−1	16.	1	−2	2	0	−1
17.	0	−1	1	−2	2	17.	0	−1	1	−2	2
18.	−2	2	0	−1	1	18.	−2	2	0	−1	1
19.	−1	1	−2	2	0	19.	−1	1	−2	2	0
20.	2	0	−1	1	−2	20.	2	0	−1	1	−2
21.	1	−2	2	0	−1	21.	1	−2	2	0	−1
22.	−2	2	0	−1	1	22.	−2	2	0	−1	1

FIGURE 11. Informant Report—Scoring Key (CABS).

23.	−1	1	−2	2	0	23.	−1	1	−2	2	0
24.	0	−1	1	−2	2	24.	0	−1	1	−2	2
25.	−1	1	−2	2	0	25.	−1	1	−2	2	0
26.	2	0	−1	1	−2	26.	2	0	−1	1	−2
27.	1	−2	2	0	−1	27.	1	−2	2	0	−1

raw scores, one for responding to "another youth" and one for responding to "another adult." Since there is a maximum score of 54, individually divide the two total scores obtained by 54, multiply each sum by 100, and subtract each sum from 100. Thus you will have determined two scores that represent the percentage of *correct responses*. Example: If "another youth" raw score = 38, divide by 54, which equals .71. Multiplied by 100, this equals 71%. Subtracted from 100, it equals 29%. Therefore a raw score of 38 = 29% correct responses to "another youth." It is easier to determine the percentages of various scores with the help of a percentage conversion table.

b. Passive and aggressive scores can be obtained by adding up all the negative raw scores for a passive total and all the positive raw scores for an aggressive total. Example: A person may score 34 in responding to "another youth" which can be broken down into a negative 30 for a passive total and a positive 4 for an aggressive total. This information is useful in that it further describes a subject's inappropriate behavior as mostly passive with "other youths". After the scores for responding to "an adult" are completed, comparisons can be made between types of passive and aggressive responding by the subject to peers and adults.

c. Further information can be obtained by breaking the total scores down into the 5 content areas of positives, negatives, requests, empathy, and conversations. This is accomplished by using the following procedures to determine the percent scores of correct responses for each content area.

Positive = 1. Add together Questions 1, 2, 11, and 12 (using absolute values only).
    2. Divide total by 8.
    3. Multiply remainder by 100.
    4. Subtract result from 100.
    5. Final result is the percentage of correct responses for this content area.

Negatives = 1. Add together Questions 3, 4, 5, 15, 23, and 24 (using absolute values only).
    2. Divide total by 12.
    3. Multiply remainder by 100.
    4. Subtract result from 100.
    5. Final result is the percentage of correct responses for this content area.

Requests = 1. Add together Questions 6, 10, 14, 16, 17, and 25 (using absolute values only).
    2. Divide total by 12.
    3. Multiply remainder by 100.
    4. Subtract result from 100.
    5. Final result is the percentage of correct responses for the content area.

Conversations = 1. Add together Questions 13, 18, 19, 26, and 27 (using absolute values only).
2. Divide total by 10.
3. Multiply remainder by 100.
4. Subtract result from 100.
5. Final result is the pecentage of correct responses for this content area.

Feelings = 1. Add together Questions 7, 8, 9, 20, 21, and 22 (using absolute values only).
2. Divide total by 12.
3. Multiply remainder by 100.
4. Subtract result from 100.
5. Final result is the percentage of correct responses for this content area.

d. An additional level of analysis would be to determine whether the responses for each individual content area were aggressive or passive by considering the positive and negative scores. This would require repeating the procedures in section c for the positive/aggressive totals and negative/passive totals for each content area.

9. An example of the entire breakdown and summation of the scores from the Informant Report Inventory is presented in Figure 12.

	Training phase					
	Before training		During training		After training	
	Peer	Adult	Peer	Adult	Peer	Adult
Content area	+ −	+ −	+ −	+ −	+ −	+ −
Positives	+2 0	0 0	+2 0	0 0	0 0	0 0
Negatives	+10 0	+4 −2	+6 0	+4 0	+2 0	0 0
Requests	+3 −1	+3 −6	+1 −1	+1 −2	+1 −2	+1 −1
Conversation	+2 0	+2 0	0 0	0 0	0 0	0 0
Feelings	+6 −2	+2 0	+4 −2	0 0	+4 2	0 0
Totals	+23 −3	+11 −8	+13 −3	+5 −2	+7 −4	+1 −1
Absolute totals	26	19	16	7	11	2
Total (%) correct	52	65	71	88	80	97

FIGURE 12. Example of a summary table depicting ratings given to a child on the Informant Report (CABS). The before-training totals indicate that this child reported as behaving fairly aggressively with peers and a mixture of mild aggressive and passive responses to adults. Examination of the specific content-area scores shows that the main problem areas concerned "negative statements" in responding to both peers and adults, passive responses in "requests" involving adults, and aggressive responses to peers regarding "feelings/empathic statements." Scores during and after training reflect a change toward appropriate assertive responses in all areas.

10. It is not required that all possible scores be obtained. Just having the overall totals may suffice for your assessment needs. Whatever level of analysis of scores is determined before training, however, should also be accomplished after training and then compared to determine treatment effects. Comparison of "before" versus "after" scores on graphs can easily be done or inferential statistics (*t*-tests, ANOVA, etc.) can be utilized.

Sample E: Social Skills Sociometric Questionnaire

A sociometric technique is another form of informant report, as it relies upon ratings made by other members of a child's peer group. This usually means other classmates, friends, neighbors, and so on who serve as "informants" and report their ratings of the child's social status. Although not a direct measure of a child's social skills, the sociometric ratings can indicate which children are disliked or liked by most other children. In general, the children who are disliked usually have social skill deficits and vice versa for the children who are liked. Again, these informant reports are not "absolute" because they are affected by other factors (e.g., biases, physical appearance, etc.), and do have limitations (see Chapter 2). Thus they should be used as a quick general screening assessment or with other measures of social skills which can substantiate the results of the sociometric questionnaire.

Assessment Steps for the Social Skills Sociometric Questionnaire

1. Enter the names of the peers (e.g., classmates, dormitory residents, neighborhood children, etc.) on the Social Skills Sociometric Questionnaire (Figure 13).
2. Copy (with all names listed) enough before-, during-, and after-training forms for all children completing the questionnaire.
3. Read the instructions on the child's questionnaire thoroughly. Make any modifications needed to transmit instructions effectively (e.g., Have more examples included, comments, etc.).
4. Arrange the children in a suitable testing environment (nondistracting, quiet, adequate writing spaces, etc.) and pass out answer sheets/questionnaire forms as well as sharpened pencils.
5. Read the instructions to the children and answer all immediate questions.
6. Be sure to determine whether any of the children cannot read the required material. If this is the case, it may be necessary to administer the test verbally during a private session.
7. Have the children begin the questionnaire and then go from child to child to make sure that the answer sheet is being completed correctly. Instruct children to answer each question and not just to mark answers randomly on the answer sheet. Collect *all* materials after testing.
8. Upon completion of the testing, score the individual answer sheets. For each child named on the list, compile the frequency of 1, 2, and 3 ratings and compute a total score for each child by summing all the ratings. Also compute the "average rating" for each child by dividing the total rating by the number of people providing the ratings. See Figure 14 for an example of how the scores and average ratings are presented in a summary table.

Below is a list of other children. Beside each name you are supposed to circle a number which shows how much you like the person. Circle 1 if you *don't like* the person, circle 2 if you don't really like or dislike the person, and circle 3 if you *like* the person.

Circle one			Name of person
Don't like	Don't like or dislike	Like	
1	2	3	_____
1	2	3	_____
1	2	3	_____
1	2	3	_____
1	2	3	_____
1	2	3	_____
1	2	3	_____
1	2	3	_____
1	2	3	_____
1	2	3	_____
1	2	3	_____
1	2	3	_____
1	2	3	_____
1	2	3	_____
1	2	3	_____
1	2	3	_____
1	2	3	_____

FIGURE 13. Social Skills Sociometric Questionnaire.

9. The summary scores can be used to identify and select children for further evaluation and social skills training. For example, three to five children with the highest frequency of 1 ratings or those 25% with the lowest total rating or those with an average rating below 2.0 may be selected for further evaluation and observation. By ratings of their peers, these children have been identified as socially unpopular and may be candidates for social skills training. The during- and after-training ratings indicate whether their peers have changed their opinions of the subject's social behavior.

SAMPLE F: SELF-REPORT OF SOCIAL BEHAVIOR—CHILDREN'S ASSERTIVE BEHAVIOR SCALE (CABS)

The Children's Assertive Behavior Scale (CABS) has 27 situations (Figure 12) that cover the same content areas as the naturalistic observations and role-play tests. Each situation has five possible responses from which the child must choose the one that most accurately reflects his or her usual social behavior. One response is very passive, one partially passive, one assertive, one partially agressive, and one very aggressive. Therefore, the full range of responding from passive to assertive to aggressive is provided. In addition, the child is requested to respond twice, once if the other person in the situation were "another youth" and once if the other person were "an adult." This last request is optional and should be deleted if the child is not likely to discriminate between "another youth" and "an adult." In this case only the "another child" category is used. The reader

Subjects	Training phase											
	Before training				During training					After training		
	Frequency of rating			Total rating	Aver-age rating	Frequency of rating			Total rating	Average rating	Frequency of rating			Total rating	Aver-age rat-ing
	1	2	3			1	2	3			1	2	3		
John G.	15	4	1	26	1.3	10	9	1	31	1.5	7	10	3	36	1.8
Bob F.	3	10	7	44	2.2	0	13	7	47	2.3	0	10	10	50	2.5
Susan L.	5	10	5	40	2.0	3	13	5	44	2.2	2	14	5	45	2.2
Karen M.	0	12	8	48	2.4	0	10	10	50	2.5	0	8	12	52	2.6
Liz W.	0	0	10	50	2.5	0	10	10	50	2.5	0	9	11	51	2.5

FIGURE 14. Example of a summary table depicting possible scores for five subjects on the Social Skills Sociometric Questionnaire. In this example, 20 people rated five children before, during and after training. By examining the frequency of ratings, total rating, and average rating, it can be seen that one child, John G., was rated by most of the others as "disliked." In selecting candidates for social skills training, John G. would be at the top of the list. Two other children, Bob F. and Susan L., received marginal scores, but it would require further information from other social skills assessments to indicate whether they should receive training or not. As this example indicates that all these children were involved in training, their changes in social status and popularity can be seen across the training phases. All the children improved or maintained their sociometric rating, which shows that the training was effective to some degree. As previously mentioned, peer sociometric status may not change either during or immediately after training due to the time required for peers to recognize and respond to more positive social skills of previously unpopular peers.

is referred to Michelson and Wood (1982) for additional psychometric and normative data on CABS. Overall, the mean CABS equals 13 for fourth to sixth grade elementary school children with a standard deviation of approximately 7.

ASSESSMENT STEPS FOR THE CHILDREN'S ASSERTIVE BEHAVIOR SCALE (CABS)

1. Read the instructions on the first page of the child's test thoroughly. Make any modifications needed to transmit instructions effectively (have more examples included, comments, etc.).
2. Reproduce enough before- and after-test forms (Figure 15) and answer sheets (Figure 16) for all children.
3. Arrange the children in a suitable testing environment (nondistracting, quiet, adequate writing spaces, etc.) and pass out answer sheets, test forms, and sharpened pencils.
4. Read the instructions to the children and answer all immediate questions.
5. Be sure to determine whether any of the children cannot read the required material. If this is the case, it may be necessary to administer the test verbally during a private session.
6. Have the participants begin and then go from child to child and make sure that the answer sheet is being completed correctly. Instruct the children to answer

each question accurately and honestly and not just mark answers randomly. Collect *all* materials after testing.

7. Using the answer key (Figure 17), score each response on the answer sheet. Note that a high score means less assertiveness as each response is scored −2 for a very passive response, −1 for a partial passive response, 0 for an assertive response. Therefore a negative score would mean passive responses and a positive score aggressive responses.

8. Scoring of the self-report inventory ranges from simple to fairly complex, depending upon what specific information one wants to obtain. *Follow steps 6 through 10 provided for Sample D: Informant's Report of Youth's Behavior (CABS). Also examine the summary table (Figure 12) provided, as it demonstrates equivalent types of scoring and interpretation of results.*

9. *Please note that in general children's answers are more reliable and error free when children are allowed to answer the CABS questions directly instead of transfering their responses to answer sheets.*

You are going to answer some questions about what you do in various situations. There are no "right" or "wrong" answers. You are just to answer what you would really do. For example, a question might be:

"What do you do if someone does not listen to you when you are talking to him or her?"

You have to choose the answer which is like what you usually do. You would usually:
(a) Tell the person to listen.
(b) Keep on talking.
(c) Stop talking and ask the person to listen.
(d) Stop talking and walk away.
(e) Talk louder.

From these five answers, you decide which one is most like the one you would do if the "someone" in the question was (1) another youth or (2) an adult. Now circle the letter on the answer sheet for each question. After you have marked your answers for each question, go to the next one. If you cannot understand a word, question, or answer, raise your hand and you will be helped. Remember to answer honestly about how you would act. There is no time limit, but you should answer as quickly as possible.

DO NOT WRITE ON THE TEST. WRITE ON ANSWER SHEET ONLY

1. Someone says to you, "I think you are a very nice person."
   You would usually:
   (a) Say, "No, I'm not that nice."
   (b) Say, "Yes, I think I am the best!"
   (c) Say, "Thank you."
   (d) Say nothing and blush.
   (e) Say, "Thanks, I am really great."

2. Someone does something that you think is really great.
   You would usually:
   (a) Act like it wasn't that great and say, "That was all right."
   (b) Say, "That was all right, but I've seen better."
   (c) Say nothing.
   (d) Say, "I can do much better than that!"
   (e) Say, "That was really great!"

FIGURE 15. Children's Assertive Behavior Scale Instructions.

3. You are working on something you like and think is very good. Someone says "I don't like it!"
   You would usually:
   (a) Say, "You're a dummy!"
   (b) Say, "I think it's good."
   (c) Say, "You are right," although you don't really agree.
   (d) Say, "I think this is great; besides, what do you know!"
   (e) Feel hurt and say nothing.

4. You forget something you were suppose to bring and someone says, "You're so dumb! You'd forget your head if it wasn't screwed on!"
   You would usually:
   (a) Say, "I'm smarter than you any day; besides, what do you know!"
   (b) Say, "Yes, you're right, sometimes I do act dumb."
   (c) Say, "If anybody is dumb, it's you!"
   (d) Say, "Nobody's perfect. I'm not dumb just because I forgot something!"
   (e) Say nothing or ignore it.

5. Someone you were supposed to meet arrives 30 minutes late, which makes you upset. The person says nothing about why they are late.
   You would usually:
   (a) Say, "I'm upset that you kept me waiting like this."
   (b) Say, "I was wondering when you'd get here."
   (c) Say, "This is the last time I'll wait for you!"
   (d) Say nothing to the person.
   (e) Say, "You're a jerk! You're late!"

6. You need someone to do something for you.
   You would usually:
   (a) Not ask for anything to be done.
   (b) Say, "You gotta do this for me!"
   (c) Say, "Would you please do something for me?" and then explain what you want.
   (d) Give a small hint that you need something done.
   (e) Say, "I want you to do this for me."

7. You know that someone is feeling upset.
   You would usually:
   (a) Say, "You seem upset; can I help?"
   (b) Be with the person and not talk about his or her being upset.
   (c) Say, "What's wrong with you?"
   (d) Not say anything and leave the person alone.
   (e) Laugh and say, "You're just a big baby!"

8. You are feeling upset, and someone says, "You seem upset."
   You would usually:
   (a) Turn your head away or say nothing.
   (b) Say, "It's none of your business!"
   (c) Say, "Yes, I am upset, thank you for asking."
   (d) Say, "It's nothing."
   (e) Say, "I'm upset, leave me alone."

Continued

9. Someone blames you for a mistake made by another.
   You would usually:
   (a) Say, "You're crazy!"
   (b) Say, "That wasn't my fault; someone else made the mistake."
   (c) Say, "I don't think it was my fault."
   (d) Say, "Wasn't me, you don't know what you're talking about!"
   (e) Take the blame or say nothing.

10. Someone asks you to do something, but you don't know why it has to be done.
    You would usually:
    (a) Say, "This doesn't make any sense, I don't want to do it."
    (b) Do as you're asked and say nothing.
    (c) Say, "This is dumb; I'm not going to do it!"
    (d) Before doing it, say, "I don't understand why you want this done."
    (e) Say, "If that's what you want," and then do it.

11. Someone says to you they think that something you did was terrific.
    You would usually:
    (a) Say, "Yes, I usually do better than most."
    (b) Say, "No, that wasn't so hot."
    (c) Say, "That's right, because I'm the best."
    (d) Say, "Thank you."
    (e) Ignore it and say nothing.

12. Someone has been very nice to you.
    You would usually:
    (a) Say, "You have been really nice to me, thanks."
    (b) Act like the person weren't that nice and say, "Yea, thanks."
    (c) Say, "You have treated me all right, but I deserve even better."
    (d) Ignore it and say nothing.
    (e) Say, "You don't treat me good enough!"

13. You are talking very loudly with a friend and someone says, "Excuse me, but you are being too noisy."
    You would usually:
    (a) Stop talking immediately.
    (b) Say, "If you don't like it, get lost!" and keep on talking loudly.
    (c) Say, "I'm sorry, I'll talk quietly," and then talk in a quiet voice.
    (d) Say, "I'm sorry," and stop talking.
    (e) Say, "All right" and continue to talk loudly.

14. You are waiting in line and someone steps in front of you.
    You would usually:
    (a) Make quiet comments such as, "Some people have a lot of nerve," without actually saying anything directly to the person.
    (b) Say, "Get to the end of the line!"
    (c) Say nothing to the person.
    (d) Say in a loud voice, "Get out of this line, you creep!"
    (e) Say, "I was here first; please go to the end of the line."

Continued

15. Someone does something to you that you don't like and it makes you angry.
    You would usually:
    (a) Shout, "You're a creep, I hate you!"
    (b) Say, "I'm angry, I don't like what you did."
    (c) Act hurt about it but not say anything to the person.
    (d) Say, "I'm mad. I don't like you!"
    (e) Ignore it and not say anything to the person.

16. Someone has something that you want to use.
    You would usually:
    (a) Tell the person to give it to you.
    (b) Not ask to use it.
    (c) Take it from the person.
    (d) Tell the person you would like to use it and then ask to use it.
    (e) Make a comment about it but not ask to use it.

17. Someone asks if they can borrow something that belongs to you, but it is new and you don't
    want to let the person use it.
    You would usually:
    (a) Say, "No, I just got it and I don't want to lend it out; maybe some other time."
    (b) Say, "I really don't want to, but you can use it."
    (c) Say, "No, go get your own!"
    (d) Give it to the person even though you don't want to.
    (e) Say, "You're crazy!"

18. Some people are talking about a hobby you really like, and you want to join in and say
    something.
    You would usually:
    (a) Not say anything.
    (b) Interrupt and immediately start telling about how good you are at this hobby.
    (c) Move closer to the group and enter into the conversation when you have a chance.
    (d) Move closer and wait for the people to notice you.
    (e) Interrupt and immediately start talking about how much you like the hobby.

19. You are working on a hobby and someone asks, "What are you doing?"
    You would usually:
    (a) Say, "Oh, just something." or, "Oh, nothing."
    (b) Say, "Don't bother me. Can't you see I'm working?"
    (c) Keep on working and say nothing.
    (d) Say, "It's none of your business!"
    (e) Stop working and explain what you were doing.

20. You see someone trip and fall down.
    You would usually:
    (a) Laugh and say, "Why don't you watch where you're going?"
    (b) Say, "Are you all right? Is there anything I can do?"
    (c) Ask, "What happened?"
    (d) Say, "That's the breaks."
    (e) Do nothing and ignore it.

Continued

21. You bump your head on a shelf and it hurts. Someone says, "Are you all right?"
    You would usually:
    (a) Say, "I'm fine, leave me alone!"
    (b) Say nothing and ignore the person.
    (c) Say, "Why don't you mind your own business?"
    (d) Say, "No, I hurt my head, thanks for asking."
    (e) Say, "It's nothing, I'm OK."

22. You make a mistake and someone else is blamed for it.
    You would usually:
    (a) Say nothing.
    (b) Say, "It's their mistake!"
    (c) Say, "I made the mistake."
    (d) Say, "I don't think that person did it."
    (e) Say, "That's their tough luck!"

23. You feel insulted by something someone said to you.
    You would usually:
    (a) Walk away from the person without saying that you were upset.
    (b) Tell the person not to do it again.
    (c) Say nothing to the person, although you feel insulted.
    (d) Insult the person back and call him or her a name.
    (e) Tell the person you don't like what was said and tell the person not to do it again.

24. Someone often interrupts you when you're speaking.
    You would usually:
    (a) Say, "Excuse me, I would like to finish what I was saying."
    (b) Say, "This isn't fair; don't I get to talk?"
    (c) Interrupt the other person by starting to talk again.
    (d) Say nothing and let the other person continue to talk.
    (e) Say, "Shut up, I was talking!"

25. Someone asks you to do something that would keep you from doing what you really want to do.
    You would usually:
    (a) Say, "I did have other plans, but I'll do what you want."
    (b) Say, "No way! Find someone else."
    (c) Say, "OK, I'll do what you want."
    (d) Say, "Forget it, shove off!"
    (e) Say, "I've already made other plans; maybe next time."

26. You see someone you would like to meet.
    You would usually:
    (a) Yell at the person and tell them to come over to you.
    (b) Walk over to the person, introduce yourself, and start talking.
    (c) Walk over near the person and wait for him or her to talk to you.
    (d) Walk over to the person and start talking about great things you have done.
    (e) Not say anything to the person.

27. Someone you haven't met before stops and says hello to you.
    You would usually:
    (a) Say, "What do you want?"
    (b) Not say anything.
    (c) Say, "Don't bother me. Get lost!"
    (d) Say hello, introduce yourself, and ask who the person is.
    (e) Nod your head, say hi, and walk away.

Name:_____   Date:_____

                                                 Assessment:_____

What would you do if the "someone" in the questions was (1) another youth or (2) an adult?

Another Youth	An Adult (Optional)
1. a, b, c, d, e	1. a, b, c, d, e
2. a, b, c, d, e	2. a, b, c, d, e
3. a, b, c, d, e	3. a, b, c, d, e
4. a, b, c, d, e	4. a, b, c, d, e
5. a, b, c, d, e	5. a, b, c, d, e
6. a, b, c, d, e	6. a, b, c, d, e
7. a, b, c, d, e	7. a, b, c, d, e
8. a, b, c, d, e	8. a, b, c, d, e
9. a, b, c, d, e	9. a, b, c, d, e
10. a, b, c, d, e	10. a, b, c, d, e
11. a, b, c, d, e	11. a, b, c, d, e
12. a, b, c, d, e	12. a, b, c, d, e
13. a, b, c, d, e	13. a, b, c, d, e
14. a, b, c, d, e	14. a, b, c, d, e
15. a, b, c, d, e	15. a, b, c, d, e
16. a, b, c, d, e	16. a, b, c, d, e
17. a, b, c, d, e	17. a, b, c, d, e
18. a, b, c, d, e	18. a, b, c, d, e
19. a, b, c, d, e	19. a, b, c, d, e
20. a, b, c, d, e	20. a, b, c, d, e
21. a, b, c, d, e	21. a, b, c, d, e
22. a, b, c, d, e	22. a, b, c, d, e
23. a, b, c, d, e	23. a, b, c, d, e
24. a, b, c, d, e	24. a, b, c, d, e
25. a, b, c, d, e	25. a, b, c, d, e
26. a, b, c, d, e	26. a, b, c, d, e
27. a, b, c, d, e	27. a, b, c, d, e

COMMENTS:

FIGURE 16. Self-Report Inventory Answer Sheet (CABS).

Name:_____   Date:_____

                                                     Assessment:_____

How would the youth answer if the "someone" in the question was (1) another youth or (2) an adult.

	Another Youth						An Adult				
	a	b	c	d	e		a	b	c	d	e
1.	−2	2	0	−1	1	1.	−2	2	0	−1	1
2.	−1	1	−2	2	0	2.	−1	1	−2	2	0
3.	2	0	−2	1	−1	3.	2	0	−2	1	−1
4.	1	−2	2	0	−1	4.	1	−2	2	0	−1
5.	0	−1	1	−2	2	5.	0	−1	1	−2	2
6.	−2	2	0	−1	1	6.	−2	2	0	−1	1
7.	0	−1	1	−2	2	7.	0	−1	1	−2	2
8.	−2	2	0	−1	1	8.	−2	2	0	−1	1
9.	2	0	−1	1	−2	9.	2	0	−1	1	−2
10.	1	−2	2	0	−1	10.	1	−2	2	0	−1
11.	1	−2	2	0	−1	11.	1	−2	2	0	−1
12.	0	−1	1	−2	2	12.	0	−1	1	−2	2
13.	−2	2	0	−1	1	13.	−2	2	0	−1	1
14.	−1	1	−2	2	0	14.	−1	1	−2	2	0
15.	2	0	−1	1	−2	15.	2	0	−1	1	−2
16.	1	−2	2	0	−1	16.	1	−2	2	0	−1
17.	0	−1	1	−2	2	17.	0	−1	1	−2	2
18.	−2	2	0	−1	1	18.	−2	2	0	−1	1
19.	−1	1	−2	2	0	19.	−1	1	−2	2	0
20.	2	0	−1	1	−2	20.	2	0	−1	1	−2
21.	1	−2	2	0	−1	21.	1	−2	2	0	−1
2.	−2	2	0	−1	1	22.	−2	2	0	−1	1

FIGURE 17. Self-Report Inventory Scoring Key (CABS). See Figure 12 for an example of a summary sheet (in the informant's report sections) that can be used for the CABS.

23	−2	1	−1	2	0	23.	−2	1	−1	2	0
24.	0	−1	1	−2	2	24.	0	−1	1	−2	2
25.	−1	1	−2	2	0	25.	−1	1	−2	2	0
26.	2	0	−1	1	−2	26.	2	0	−1	1	−2
27.	1	−2	2	0	−1	27.	1	−2	2	0	−1

B

Social Skills Films for Children

This appendix provides an extensive compilation of films that are relevant to the training of children's social skills. Although we have no empirical data to support the effectiveness of these films, the use of supplemental audiovisual aids should prove beneficial in facilitating the acquisition of new social behavior. Research presented in the Introduction and in the sections on training methods supports the usefulness of providing modeling and films for children.

Films can provide a common basis for group discussion and can serve as an excellent "lead in" or illustration of a particular topic area. The films described below have been compiled after an exhaustive search through numerous film catalogues. Although not inclusive of all children's social skills films, every effort was made to identify films that might be potentially applicable to developing social competency in children.

Each film contains a brief description, a statement on its appropriateness for recommended age or grade levels, film length, film format (e.g., 16mm) black and white versus color, and information regarding the producer and/or distributor. Since these films have not been individually reviewed by the authors, we cannot endorse any particular production. However, we would be most interested in receiving feedback from individuals who use these films in regard to the film's quality, class reactions, and any related details.

AGGRESSION—ASSERTION

Personal violence is on the increase in a world that stockpiles frustrations. One Saturday morning, 10-year-old Joe becomes the victim of the handed down hostilities of his mother, father, and older brother. Finally, escaping the family battlefield to play with friends, Joe carries his angers with him—the chance to vent his feelings on his friends is one of multiple choices, and five filmed alternatives are presented. BU, –, 8, C, 1972.[1]

ANGEL AND BIG JOE

Angel is a 15-year-old Chicano whose family work as migrant laborers. While waiting for his father to call with news of work, Angel meets a telephone repairman and they become

[1] Line indicates code of distributor (see p. 243), estimate of grade level for which film is appropriate, length of film in minutes, whether film is in color(C) or in black and white(BW), and date of release. Dashes indicate that information is not available.

231

friends. They go into business together, and when Joe offers Angel an opportunity to get away from the hand-to-mouth existence of migrant workers, Angel has to make a difficult decision. Very dramatic. Children were reportedly absorbed in and moved by this film. LCA, primary–intermediate, 27, C, 1975.

ARE MANNERS IMPORTANT?

Presents the case of a boy who thinks "kids don't need manners," and shows how he loses his friends through inconsiderate acts. UOAF, primary, 11, BW, 1954.

BECAUSE IT'S FUN

Presents Bill, who thinks that winning is the only thing that really counts and can't understand why others enjoy themselves just playing for the fun of it. Explores the good feelings produced by skillfully engaging in physical activity. AITV, –, 15, C, –.

BEEP BEEP

A story about sharing. Children become involved as the action develops and the boys build a car from found objects. The car, and perhaps the friendship, is destroyed because the first boy can't share. The open ending leaves room for the children to resolve it in discussion. CHUR, primary, 12, C, 1975.

BEGINNING RESPONSIBILITY: BEING A GOOD SPORT

Familiar play situations at home and at school illustrate the meaning of good sportsmanship not only in games but in other types of competitive situations. Shows that good sportsmanship is more than just following rules—it is understanding one's own feelings and the feelings of others. Suggests ways in which friends can help one another be better sports. UOAF, primary, 10, C, 1969.

BEGINNING RESPONSIBILITY: BEING ON TIME

Jim, who has a habit of being late discovers that it isn't much fun when he misses a puppet show at the library. An examination of reasons for being late leads to suggestions for planning time and preparing for upcoming events, bringing more enjoyment for everyone. BU, –, 11, C, 1973.

BEGINNING RESPONSIBILITY: BOOKS AND THEIR CARE

Two children learn the important steps in the proper care of books. Shows children that books are to be appreciated and enjoyed. BU, –, 9, –, 1960.

BEGINNING RESPONSIBILITY: DOING THINGS FOR OURSELVES IN SCHOOL

Steve and his classmates illustrate ways they can do things for themselves. They enjoy attempting new tasks, are eager to learn from others and from their own mistakes, show ingenuity, and are willing to help others learn. UOAF, primary, 11, C, 1969.

BEGINNING RESPONSIBILITY: GETTING READY FOR SCHOOL

Contrasts the behavior of two boys to show the importance of an established routine for getting ready for school. Ricky stays up late, oversleeps in the morning, has to rush, forgets things, and is often late for school. But when he spends a night with his friend Pete, he sees how well his time and belongings can be organized to get ready for school. UOAF, primary, 11, C, 1969.

BEGINNING RESPONSIBILITY: LEARNING TO FOLLOW INSTRUCTIONS

When David can't seem to learn how to follow instructions, some of his toy animals magically come to life through animation to help him. A wonderful turtle, a very special owl, and three marvelous elephants remind David to pay attention all the way, understand or ask questions, and remember the order of the instructions. UOAF, primary, 11, C, 1968.

BEGINNING RESPONSIBILITY: LUNCHROOM MANNERS

Phil and the other children in Miss Brown's class are watching a puppet show, "Mr. Bungle Goes to Lunch." Although Mr. Bungle is funny, the children see that he is clumsy and impolite, and that it wouldn't be much fun to eat with someone like him. When Phil goes to lunch, he remembers to look neat, to go to the end of the line, to chew his food slowly, to leave his place at the table clean, and to show good manners in order to make lunch pleasant for everyone. UOAF, primary, 11, BW, 1960.

BEGINNING RESPONSIBILITY: TAKING CARE OF THINGS

Uses the unhappy experiences of Andy to illustrate how and why children should care for things at school and at home. Stresses the importance of having definite places to keep things, putting articles back where they belong, cleaning up after playtime, and storing and handling things properly to prevent accidents or damage. UOAF, primary, 10, BW, 1951.

BUT NAMES WILL NEVER HURT

Focuses on the feelings of an English-Canadian boy who, in sudden anger, calls a young French-Canadian boy a "dirty French frog" and then comes to realize how prejudice separates one person from another and affects the feelings of everyone involved. BU, –, 15, C, –.

BUT THEY MIGHT LAUGH

This film introduces Becky and her teacher, both of whom are afraid to go ice skating. They admit their fears to each other and then decide to go skating together. BU, –, 15, C, –.

COMMUNICATION FUNDAMENTALS: FIVE BASIC SKILLS

This film is designed to teach young children communication skills. A theater group demonstrates the five basic types of communication skills: reading, writing, speaking, listening, and nonverbal communication. SU, primary–6, 15, C, 1977.

COURTESY—A GOOD EGGSAMPLE

Eggs are the stars of this animated film showing the value of being kind, helpful, and courteous to others. UOWM, 1–3, 10, C, 1976.

DAD AND ME

A positive portrait of a young black boy and his family in New York City that concentrates on the father–son relationship. BFA, primary, 11, C, 1971.

DEVELOPING FRIENDSHIPS

While a group of friends waits for Joe at the railroad station, one boy reminisces about how Joe has taught him the value of friendship. He has learned that friendship is infectious and that he should develop an appreciation of people of varying personalities. BU, –, 10, –, 1950.

DONNA (LEARNING TO BE YOURSELF)

Introduces Donna, a blind girl, who has to learn to be herself as well as she can. Helps children understand how people come to accept the things that make them different from others. Show how the process of becoming a person is in many ways the same for everyone. BU, –, 15, C, 1973.

DR. SUESS: GREEN EGGS & HAM

Conveys the message that things might not always be as they appear. UOU, primary–9, 9, C, 1973.

DR. SUESS: THE FOX

Shows how absurd stubbornness and the inability to change can really be. UOU, primary–9, 6, C, 1973.

FEELINGS: DON'T STAY MAD

The neighborhood gang and their puppet friends Herky and Gooney all meet on a day when "mad feelings" seem to be inside everyone. Actually these feelings was born when Kevin's dad did not let him take his new kite to school. Kevin kicked Melissa's lunchbag down the block, and Melissa caught the "mad feelings" and passed them on to Gooney, who then fought with Herky. Lou, the older boy, helps them discover ways to "get the mad out." As a result of talking and role playing, they gain insight into what caused their anger . . . and also learn that pent-up anger can make a person very unhappy. BU, primary–intermediate, 15, C, 1973.

FRIENDS

A sensitive portrayal of children's games and relationships. This is the story of two girls who are good friends and what happens to their friendship when a third girl becomes involved. The film is unusual in its level of realism and in the fact that the protagonists are female and have some depth of character. Fine for discussions and role playing. CHUR, primary–intermediate, 18, C, 1972.

FRIENDS OF THE ELEPHANT GOSHKO

Goshko is a circus elephant with a bad case of sneezes who runs away from a mean ringmaster. A group of children protect him and nurse him to health. A basic cooperation plot that young children reportedly enjoy. MAC, primary, 10, C, 1968.

GET USED TO ME

The theme of the film is accepting each other. A young girl who is ridiculed and ostracized at school feels that her peers are being cruel to her because of the way her father earns a living—he is the local garbage man. PP, –, 16, C, –.

GREEDY HANK'S BIG POCKETS

Hank wears a smock that has a big pocket which he fills with toys, since he's so greedy. However, his pocket becomes so full that he gets stuck in a doorway. A little girl helps him, but all the toys fall out and Hank wishes he hadn't been so greedy. AIU, Kindergarten–3, 8, C, 1970.

GROUP CONFORMITY/REJECTION: HOW'S YOUR NEW FRIEND?

Discusses an individual's responsibility to a group and the forces that work to hold a group together or pull it apart. Examines personal versus group values. UOU, 10–12, 12, C, 1975.

GUIDANCE FOR THE '70S: SELF-ESTEEM

How do you see yourself? Do you have a good image of your abilities? What is self-image? How does a person build self-esteem? Young people at a seminar form images in clay, representing their self-images; they then discuss and evaluate the figures. Through their discussion, we learn that it's all right to think well of ourselves; it's important to build good feelings about ourselves because self-esteem is a basic quality of an effective human being. BU, –, 16, C, 1972.

Hey! What about Us?

Fresh insight into sex-role stereotyping in physical activities in schools, including physical education classes, playground games, and boisterous behavior in the classroom. For purposes of comparison, begins with four situations in which sex-role stereotyping is relatively absent, then depicts a wide range of incidents in which stereotyping often occurs. Consider the exclusion of girls from sports, the reinforcement of the hero ethic in boys, differential teacher treatment of girls and boys on the playground, exclusion of boys from dance, and differential physical interaction of teachers with girls and boys. The first four situations challenge the usual conceptions of "masculinity" and "femininity" by showing children engaged in activities "typical" of the opposite sex: a girl displays competence in football and a boy excels in dance. Most events occur in elementary school settings. UOC, –, 15, C, 1974.

Hopscotch

A boy who wants to make friends but tries too hard is the theme of this film. His inappropriate attempts to join another boy and girl playing hopscotch involve all manner of showing off; when he finally gives up playing roles, he is accepted. This film is reportedly unusually and imaginatively animated. Children watched with rapt attention. The film is quite good and the action is riotous. The film may be too sophisticated for very young children. CHUR, –, 12, C, –.

Huckleberry Finn: What Does Huckleberry Finn Say?

Clifton Fadiman discusses the intellectual content of the novel. He points out that it can be viewed as an adventure story, as a picture of the world, and as a drama or moral conflict. Scenes include some of the more complex relationships in the novel. UOC, –, 27, C, 1965.

I Am How I Feel

Children express their feelings. Gives suggestions about how to feel better about yourself. CHUR, –, 14, C, 1975.

I Am How I Look

Explores how children see themselves. Emphasizes the importance of differences in developing a self-concept. CHUR, –, 13, C, 1975.

I Dare You

A new girl in town, Clarissa, must carry out a potentially dangerous dare to belong to a neighborhood gang. KU, –, 15, C, 1972.

I Feel Loving

Helps children understand the meaning of love. KU, –, 15, C, 1973.

I Is for Important

Focuses on sex-role stereotyping in social interactions and emotional expression. Includes sequences depicting sex-role biases displayed by teachers in their disciplinary actions and task assignments, resistance by children to role reversal in kindergarten play, anxiety felt by boys over appearing to be "sissies" before their peers, frustration experienced by boys who attempt to assume a nurturing role or express emotions such as sorrow or tenderness, and indoctrination of girls with commercial definitions of beauty. Pupils range from kindergarten through eighth grade. See also *Hey! What about Us?* and *Anything They Want to Be.* UOC, –, 12, C, –.

In My Memory

Presents Linda, who is bewildered and upset when her grandmother dies. The film shows how she tries to understand what death means to her own life and how to accept the event as a natural part of the human condition. AITV, –, 15, C, 1973.

Jack and the Beanstalk

Old English tale depicting the fact that excessive greed can get one into trouble. SU, primary–elementary, 9, C, 1977.

Katy

When Katy's brother goes to camp, she takes over his newspaper route despite harassment by the man in charge and boys on other routes. The film deals with questions about sex roles and equality. Some boys viewed the film as silly, while girls liked it. BFA, primary–intermediate, 17, C, 1974.

Let's Be Clean and Neat

Throughout the day, Bobby, Jane, and their parents demonstrate how cleanliness and neatness contribute to family life, social acceptance, good health, and a feeling of well-being. Shows the children washing, selecting clothing for the next day, and preparing for bed. UOAF, kindergarten–primary–intermediate, 11, C, 1957.

Let's Be Good Citizens at Home

A typical day with the Lewis family shows the need for sharing, taking turns, being cheerful, saving, and making home a better place generally. UOAF, kindergarten–primary, 8, BW, 1953.

Let's Be Good Citizens at Play

Stories about a group of children playing show the value of cheerfulness, sportsmanship, cooperation, and generosity in getting along with others. UOAF, kindergarten–primary, 8, BW, 1953.

Let's Be Good Citizens at School

Shows importance of sharing, cheerfulness, sportsmanship, kindliness and tidiness in relations between children in school. UOAF, kindergarten–primary, 10, BW, 1953.

Let's Be Good Citizens at the Library

The need for a book on soap-box cars leads two boys to the public library, where they learn the reasons for good care of books and buildings and respect for common rights. Benefits of reading are stressed. UOAF, kindergarten–primary, 10, BW, 1954.

Let's Be Good Citizens in Our Neighborhood

How children can show pride in their neighborhood by thoughtfulness, avoiding property destruction, keeping yards neat, and respecting their neighbors is pointed out in a typical day with Jack and Susan. UOAF, kindergarten–primary, 10, BW, 1952.

Let's Be Good Citizens in Our Town

From a parade to a picnic in the park, Jack and Susan learn of the duties of citizens toward their community and the benefits accrued. The reasons for laws and rules are stressed. UOAF, kindergarten–primary, 10, BW, 1954.

Let's Be Good Citizens When Visiting

Jack and Susan vacation on a farm and teach us a guest's responsibilities. They learn that being thoughtful, cooperative, and careful helps one adjust to new situations and environments. UOAF, kindergarten–primary, 10, BW, 1953.

Let's Have Respect

Four situation-type episodes involving respect for rights and property allow viewers to find their own answers to the problem. UOAF, primary–intermediate, 10, C, 1969.

Let's Share with Others

Sharing is demonstrated to be a desirable and essential discipline of democratic living. Illustrates when to share and when not to share. UOAF, kindergarten–primary, 11, C, 1950.

Schools and Rules: Rules to Visit a Zoo By

Shows the importance of making rules and following them (AC2453). McGraw, –, 10, C, 1967.

SELF-IDENTITY/SEX-ROLE SERIES (PP)[2]

I Only Want You to Be Happy (BC3108)	*Getting Closer* (BC3073)
By Whose Rules? (BC3089)	*My Friend* (BC3083)
Changes (BC3086)	*No Trespassing* (BC3081)
The Clique (BC3087)	*Pressure Makes Perfect* (BC3088)
Different Folks (BC3092)	*Trying Times* (BC3072)
Double Trouble (BC3090)	*Two Sons* (BC3091)
Down and Back (BC3093)	*What's Wrong with Jonathan?* (BC3080)
Family Matters (BC3071)	*Who Wins?* (BC3082)

SIU MEI WONG—WHO SHALL I BE?

Siu Mei is an 11-year-old Chinese girl who lives with her family in Los Angeles. Her father insists she attend Chinese classes after public school each day. When she finally works up the courage to confront him with her desire to take ballet lessons instead, he makes a wise decision. The film has minimal Chinese dialogue with English subtitles; this limits the film's use to older children. Excellent for examining life goals. LCA, primary–intermediate, 18, C, 1970.

SOCIAL ACCEPTABILITY

Shows the importance of social acceptance in the personality development of adolescents. Presents the case study of Mary, a shy girl, who is rejected by others of her group. KU, –, –, BW, 1948.

SOCIAL DEVELOPMENT

Offers an analysis of social behavior at different age levels and the reasons underlying the changes in behavior patterns as the child develops. McGraw, –, 16, BW, 1950.

SOCIAL RESPONSIBILITY—"IT'S MY HOBBY"

A high school boy discovers that his best friend is dealing drugs. The film is designed to initiate discussion on social responsibility through the presentation of an "interlocutor" at the end of the film. McGraw, 7–12, 11, C, 1974.

SWIMMY

This animated film, based on the book by Leo Lionni, is about a school of little fish who learn to defend themselves against the big fish. Swimmy devises a plan to outsmart the brawnier fish: brine versus brains. The musical background and optical effects are sufficiently aquatic. The simple, straightforward story works with all ages, and the film is enhanced by a subtle "strength in unity" message. CONN, –, 6, C, –.

---

[2] Films under this heading list only catalogue number. No other information available.

THE AMAZING COSMIC AWARENESS OF DUFFY MOON

Shows how Duffy Moon, picked on by the other boys in his class for being a "shrimp," develops talents and powers that enable him to meet unexpected challenges. TL, –, 32, C, –.

THE BIG LIGHTHOUSE AND THE LITTLE STEAMSHIP

A traditional story film, in which the narrator relates what we are seeing. This is the story of a conflict between a callow young steamship and a lighthouse whose feelings of self-importance almost lead to disaster. The children are fascinated by objects with human qualities, and they reportedly understood the underlying messages of cooperation and the axiom "You're never too old to learn." The narration is easy to understand and children reportedly were engrossed by the story. CORON, –, 8, C, –.

THE CASE OF THE ELEVATOR DUCK

A film by Joan Silver based on the book by Polly Berrien Berends. An 11-year-old black detective takes on the case of a homeless duck. Gilbert solves the case despite the fact that his housing project has a "no pets" rule and his mother, who is afraid of eviction, gives him an impossible time limit. Kids empathized with Gilbert's situation and said the film was very realistic. They enjoyed his casual humor and the clever way he solved his problems. This film may be too dependent on narration for most children under six, but older viewers asked to see it again. LCA, primary–intermediate, 17, C, 1974.

THE FABLE OF HE AND SHE

The droll creatures of an imaginary island divide their work by specializing in what we recognize as sex-stereotyped job roles. A natural disaster brings about some changes, which remain in effect once the crisis has passed. This is a whimsical and humorous fable with a clear story line and excellent animation. Young and middle groups reportedly enjoyed the film and were sad to see it end. LCA, primary–intermediate, 11, C, 1974.

THE FOOLISH FROG

Pete Seeger sings and tells this tale from "way down south in the yankety yank" where a foolish frog puffed himself up with pride and got the whole countryside singing about it. Infectious banjo picking and whistling, along with the colorful patchwork-look animation, turn this folk song into an exciting film. A book by Pete and Charles Seeger was adapted from the film. WW, primary–intermediate, 9, C, 1971.

THE FOX AND THE ROOSTER

This fable from Aesop illustrates the moral that even a clever scheme can be outsmarted when good friends help each other. Enacted completely by farm and forest animals. AIU, kindergarten–6, 11, BW, 1951.

THE FROG PRINCE

This is the story of a stubborn princess who doesn't want to keep her promise. After her father, the king, compels her to be true to her word, she discovers that doing the right thing can have its own reward. AIU, kindergarten–3, 7, C, 1969.

THE HIDEOUT

Two young children are building a secret fort in the woods and need wood planks to complete it. A neighbor has some he intends to use for shelves. When another child wishes to join the fort, his contribution is the neighbor's two shelving planks. The young girl says they should be returned, the boy thinks it is all right to keep them. Designed to promote discussions in primary grades on ethics, stealing, and honesty. CHUR, –, 16, C, 1974.

THE HUNTER

A young Ozarks boy gets a BB gun for his birthday. He plays with it for awhile—pretending and fantasizing about shooting—but later on he shoots a bird and discovers the consequences of using a gun, none of which were part of his fantasies. According to other users, the film handles a difficult subject without being heavy-handed and produces some great discussions, particularly among children who have actually had contact with guns. ACI, primary–intermediate, 10, C, 1971.

THE HUNTSMAN

There is some dialogue but the film is mostly nonverbal. A young boy hunts out lost balls on a golf course and sells them until two bullies take over. He spends a lot of time fantasizing about getting even and finally gets his chance, but finds revenge isn't as satisfying as he thought it would be. Children reportedly enjoy the film, which stimulates much discussions about getting even. LCA, primary–intermediate, 17, C, 1972.

THE SNEETCHES

In this film about prejudice, there are two kinds of Sneetches: those without stars on their bellies and those with. The Star-Belly Sneetches feel superior to the Plain-Belly Sneetches. A clever salesman changes the existing social order by selling stars to the Plain-Belly Sneetches, after which he convinces the original Star-Bellies to remove their stars by using a special machine. BFA, primary–intermediate, 13, C, 1973.

THE THEFT

A boy in his early teens becomes involved with an older boy in a burglary. But following the incident, the younger boy realizes what a terrible mistake he made. He begins anew by getting a job in a fast-food restaurant. This film may be useful in facilitating group discussion concerning peer pressure. LITTL, 5–9, –, C, 1976.

To Tell or Not to Tell

A high school girl, seeing a classmate cheating on an important scholarship test, debates with her sister whether she should have reported it. Pros and cons are presented impartially to allow the viewing students to discuss the question and draw their own conclusions. BU, –, 7, C, 1967.

Values: Being Friends

The meaning of friendship between three boys is depicted in this film. UOWM, 4–6, 9, C, 1969.

Values: Cooperation

Three boys are shown having fun playing together and cooperating. Cooperation, whether at school, work, or play, is stressed. UOWM, 1–6, 11, C, 1969.

Values: Telling the Truth

An example of telling the truth is graphically illustrated when three boys throw a rock through a window and only one of them tells the truth about it. This film is a good prompt for discussion about housing. UOWM, 1–6, 10, C, 1969.

Warty the Toad

A beautifully photographed fable about vanity, with an unusual twist. Warty the toad is proud of being ugly, but he learns that there is more to life than how one looks. Warty's animal neighbors help him learn about social conscience and save him from becoming a snake's dinner. Recommended ages are five to eight. CORON, 1–6, 13, C, 1973.

What Is a Friend?

Fat Albert and the Cosby kids teach the values of being honest and fair with others to get the same kind of treatment in return (starring Bill Cosby). UOWM, 1–9, 13, C, 1976.

What's Right

Four open-ended interpersonal episodes concerning moral decisions are presented to allow viewers to form their own judgements. UOAF, primary–intermediate, 10, C, 1969.

Who Do You Think Should Belong to the Club?

A group of children are presented with another child who displays negative interpersonal behavior. The film shows values of human relations, achievement, cooperation, and ethics. BU, 1–12, 17, C, 1977.

Why We Need Each Other: The Animals' Picnic Day

One group of animals is enjoying a picnic when another group tries to join them, but the latecomers are ridiculed so much that they leave. However, when the valley is threatened with destruction, all the animals cooperate and work together to save it, teaching the original picnic group a valuable lesson. A moralizing story; however, the point is well made. Young children reportedly enjoyed the film. LCA, primary, 10, C, 1973.

Woof, Woof

A large dog who bullies others meets a cat who is not afraid to stand up and fight. The film's message has to do with brotherhood, tolerance, and the generation gap. This Czechoslovakian fable is done with animated line drawings. C/McG, –, 10, C, –.

Yes, I Can

Presents both the benefits and limits of independent action and the need for thorough preparation. Introduces nine-year-old David, who insists that he is ready to go out on his own to an overnight summer camp. AITV, –, 15, C, –.

Key to Distributors

ACI Films (ACI)[3]
35 West 45th Street
New York, NY 10036
(212) 582-1918

American Educational Films (AEF)
132 Lasky Drive
Beverly Hills, CA 90212
(213) 278-4996

Aims Instructional Media Services (AIMS)
626 Justin Avenue
Glendale, A 91201
(213) 240-9300

Agency for Instructional TV (AITV)
Box A
Bloomington, IN 47402

Allegheny Intermediate Unit (AIU)
5-B 1 Allegheny Square
Pittsburgh, PA 15212

A-V Explorations (AVEX)
2000 Eggert Road
Amherst, NY 14226
(716) 833-2706

Barr Films (BARR)
3490 East Foothill Blvd.
P.O. Box 5667
Pasadena, CA 91107
(213) 793-6153

Benchmark Films (BENCH)
145 Scarborough Road
Briarcliff Manor, NY 10510
(914) 762-3838

BFA Educational Media (BFA)
2211 Michigan Avenue
Santa Monica, CA 90404
(213) 829-2901

Stephen Bosustow Productions (BOSU)

---

[3] To locate a specific film contact Educational Film Library Association, 43 West 61st Street, New York, New York 10023, (212) 246-4533.

1649 11TH STREET
SANTA MONICA, CA 90904
(213) 394-0218

BOSTON UNIVERSITY (BU)
ABRAHAM KRASKER MEMORIAL FILM
LIBRARY
765 COMMONWEALTH AVENUE
BOSTON, MA 02215

BILLY BUDD FILMS (BUDD)
235 EAST 57TH STREET
NEW YORK, NY 10022
(212) 755-3968

CENTRON EDUCATIONAL FILMS (CENTR)
1621 WEST 9TH STREET
LAWRENCE, KS 66044
(913) 843-0400

CREATIVE FILM SOCIETY (CFS)
7237 CANBY AVENUE
RESEDA, CA 91335
(213) 881-3887

CHURCHILL FILMS (CHUR)
662 NORTH ROBERTSON BLVD.
LOS ANGELES, CA 90069
(213) 657-5110

CONTEMPORARY/MCGRAW-HILL FILMS
(C/MCG)
1221 AVENUE OF THE AMERICAS
NEW YORK, NY 10020
(609) 448-1700

CONNECTICUT FILMS (CONN)
6 COBBLE HILL ROAD
WESTPORT, CT 06880
(203) 227-2960

CORONET INSTRUCTIONAL MEDIA
(CORON)
65 EAST SOUTH WATER STREET
CHICAGO, IL 60601
(312) 332-7676

TOM DAVENPORT FILMS (DAVEN)
PEARLSTONE DELAPLANE, VA 22025
(703) 592-3701

WALT DISNEY EDUCATIONAL MEDIA
(DISNE)
800 SONORA
GLENDALE, CA 91201
(213) 240-9160

DOUBLEDAY MULTIMEDIA (DOUBL)
NO LONGER IN BUSINESS

ENCYCLOPAEDIA BRITANNICA EDUCATION
CORP. (EB)
425 N. MICHIGAN AVENUE
CHICAGO, IL 60611
(312) 321-6800

FILMS, INC. (FI)
1144 WILMETTE AVENUE
WILMETTE, IL 60091
(312) 256-4730

FILM IMAGES (FIM)
17 WEST 60TH STREET
NEW YORK, NY 10003
(212) 279-6653

FOLKLORE PUPPETS FILMS (FOL)
657 AVENUE C
BAYONNE, NJ 07002
(201) 339-3617

GROVE PRESS FILMS (GP)
53 E. 11 STREET
NEW YORK, NY 10003
(212) 677-2400

INTERNATIONAL FILM BUREAU (IFB)
332 SOUTH MICHIGAN AVENUE
CHICAGO, IL 60604
(312) 427-4545

INTERNATIONAL FILM FOUNDATION (IFF)
475 FIFTH AVENUE
NEW YORK, NY 10017
(212) 685-4998

IMAGE RESOURCES (IR)
267 WEST 25TH STREET
NEW YORK, NY 10001
(212) 675-5330

KENT STATE UNIVERSITY—A-V SERVICES
(KU)
330 LIBRARY BUILDING
KENT, OH 44242

LEARNING CORPORATION OF AMERICA
(LCA)
711 FIFTH AVENUE
NEW YORK, NY 10022
(212) 751-4400

LITTLE RED FILMHOUSE (LITTL)
119 SOUTH KILKEA DR.
LOS ANGELES, CA 90048
(213) 655-6726

LSB PRODUCTIONS (LSB)
1310 MONACO DRIVE
PACIFIC PALISADES, CA 90272
(213) 454-1676

MACMILLAN FILMS (MAC)
34 MACQUESTIN PARKWAY, SOUTH
MOUNT VERNON, NY 10550
(914) 664-5051

MCGRAW-HILL FILMS (MCGRAW)
1221 AVENUE OF THE AMERICAS
NEW YORK, NY 10020
(212) 997-1221

MENTAL HEALTH MATERIALS CENTER
(MHMC)
419 PARK AVENUE SOUTH
NEW YORK, NY 10016
(212) 889-5760

ARTHUR MOKIN PRODUCTIONS (MOKIN)
17 WEST 60TH STREET
NEW YORK, NY 10023
(212) 757-4868

NATIONAL FILM BOARD OF CANADA
(NFBC)
1251 AVENUE OF THE AMERICAS
NEW YORK, NY 10020
(212) 586-2400

PARAMOUNT/OXFORD FILMS (PARA)
5451 MARATHON STREET

HOLLYWOOD, CA 90038
(213) 463-0100

PERENNIAL EDUCATION, INC. (PER)
1825 WILLOW ROAD
NORTHFIELD, IL 60093
(312) 446-4153

PERSPECTIVE FILMS (PERS)
369 WEST ERIE STREET
CHICAGO, IL 60610
(312) 332-7676

PHOENIX FILMS (PHOEN)
470 PARK AVENUE, SOUTH
NEW YORK, NY 10016
(212) 684-5910

PAULIST PRODUCTIONS (PP)
17575 PACIFIC COAST HIGHWAY
BOX 1057
PACIFIC PALISADES, CA 90272

PYRAMID FILMS (PYR)
BOX 1048
SANTA MONICA, CA 90406
(213) 828-7577

REMBRANDT FILMS (REM)
267 WEST 25TH STREET
NEW YORK, NY 10001
(212) 675-5330

SIM PRODUCTIONS (SIM)
WESTON, CT 06990
(203) 226-3355

STERLING EDUCATIONAL FILMS (STER)
241 EAST 34TH STREET
NEW YORK, NY 10016
(212) 682-6300

EDUCATIONAL RESOURCE CENTER
SYRACUSE UNIVERSITY—SCHOOL OF
EDUCATION (SU)
150 MARSHALL STREET
SYRACUSE, NY 13210

SYRACUSE UNIVERSITY FILM RENTAL
(SUFR)

1455 E. CALVIN STREET
SYRACUSE, NY 13210

TEXTURE FILMS (TEX)
1600 BROADWAY
NEW YORK, NY 10019
(212) 586-6960

THREE PRONG TELEVISION PRODUCTIONS
(3 PRONG)
SUITE 1208
100 NORTH LA SALLE STREET
CHICAGO, IL 60602
(312) 368-1088

TIMELIFE (TL)
100 EISENHOWER DRIVE
PARAMUS, CA 07652

REFERENCE LIBRARY
TIME-LIFE BOOKS, INC. (TLBI)
777 DUKE STREET
ALEXANDRIA, VA 22314

UNIVERSAL EDUCATION & VISUAL ARTS
(UED)
221 PARK AVENUE SOUTH
NEW YORK, NY 10003
(212) 677-5658

SCHEDULING OFFICE
UNIVERSITY OF ARIZONA FILMS (UOAF)
BUREAU OF AUDIOVISUAL SERVICES
UNIVERSITY OF ARIZONA
TUCSON, AZ 85721

EXTENSION MEDIA CENTER
UNIVERSITY OF CALIFORNIA (UOC)
2223 FULTON STREET
BERKELEY, CA 94720

INSTRUCTIONAL MEDIA CENTER
UNIVERSITY OF UTAH (UOU)
207 MILTON BENNION HALL
SALT LAKE CITY, UT 84112

AUDIOVISUAL CENTER FILM LIBRARY
UNIVERSITY OF WISCONSIN AT LACROSSE
(UOWL)
1705 STATE STREET
LACROSSE, WI 54601

BUREAU OF AUDIO VISUAL INSTRUCTION
LIBRARY
UNIVERSITY OF WISCONSIN AT MADISON
(UOWM)
1327 UNIVERSITY AVENUE
BOX 2093
MADISON, WI 53701

WALT DISNEY EDUCATIONAL MATERIALS
CORP. (WD)
800 SONORA AVENUE
GLENDALE, CA 91201
(213) 240-9160

WOMBAT PRODUCTIONS (WOMBA)
77 TARRYTOWN ROAD
WHITE PLAINS, NY 10607
(914) 428-6220

U.S. CONN LIBRARY
WAYNE STATE COLLEGE (WSC)
200 E. 10 STREET
WAYNE, NE 68787

WESTON WOODS PRODUCTIONS (WW)
WESTON WOODS, CT 06880
(203) 226-3355

XEROX FILMS (XEROX)
1200 HIGH RIDGE ROAD
STAMFORD, CT 06905
(203) 329-0951

YELLOW BALL WORKSHOP (YBW)
62 TARBELL AVENUE
LEXINGTON, MA 02173
(617) 862-4283

YOUNG DIRECTORS' CENTER (YDC)
267 WEST 25TH STREET
NEW YORK, NY 10001
(212) 675-5330

References

Alba, E., & Alvarez, C. M. *Learned helplessness: Its implication to education.* Paper presented at the Association for Advancement of Behavior Therapy Convention, Atlanta, Georgia, November 1977.

Alberti, R., Emmons, M., Fodor, I., Galassi, J., Galassi, M., Jakubowski, P., & Wolfe, J. *Ethical principles and guidelines for assertiveness training leaders and groups.* Paper presented at the meeting of the Association for Advancement of Behavior Therapy, New York, November 1976.

Alberti, R. E., & Emmons, M. L. *Your perfect right.* San Luis Obispo, Calif.: Impact Publishers, 1970.

Allen, G. J., Chinsky, J. M., Larsen, S. W., Lockman, J. E., & Selinger, H. V. *Community psychology and the schools.* Hillsdale, N.J.: Erlbaum, 1976.

Allen, K. E., Hart, B., Buell, J. S., Harris, F. R., & Wolf, M. M. Effects of social reinforcement on isolate behavior of a nursery school child. *Child Development,* 1964, *35,* 511–518.

Anastasi, A. *Psychological testing.* New York: MacMillan, 1982.

Asher, S. R., & Parke, R. D. Influence of sampling and comparison processes on the development of communication effectiveness. *Journal of Educational Psychology,* 1975, *67,* 64–75.

Asher, S. R., Singleton, L. C., Tinsely, B. R., & Hymel, S. The reliability of a rating scale sociometric method with preschool children. *Developmental Psychology,* 1979, *15,* 443–444.

Baer, D. M., & Wolf, M. M. Recent examples of behavior modification in preschool settings. In C. Neuringer & J. L. Michael (Eds.), *Behavior modification in clinical psychology.* New York: Appleton-Century-Crofts, 1970.

Baer, D. M., Wolf, M. M., & Risley, T. R. Some current dimensions of applied behavior analysis. *Journal of Applied Behavior Analysis,* 1968, *1,* 91–97.

Bandura, A. *Principles of behavior modification.* New York: Holt, Rinehart, & Winston, 1969.

Bandura, A. *Aggression: A social learning analysis.* Englewood Cliffs, N.J.: Prentice-Hall, 1973.

Bandura, A., & Walters, R. H. *Social learning and personality development.* New York: Holt, Rinehart & Winston, 1963.

Barclay, J. R. Interest patterns associated with measures of social desirability. *Personnel and Guidance Journal,* 1966, *45,* 56–60.

Beck, A. T., Weissman, A., Lester, D., & Trexler, L. The measurement of pessimism: The Hopelessness Scale. *Journal of Consulting Clinical Psychology,* 1974, *42,* 861–865.

Beck, S., Forehand, R., Wells, K. C., & Quante, A. *Social skills training with children: An examination of generalization from anologue to natural settings.* Unpublished manuscript, University of Georgia, 1978.

Beilin, H. Teachers' and clinicians' attitudes toward the behavioral problems of children: A reappraisal. *Child Development,* 1959, *30,* 9–25.

Bellack, A. S. Behavioral assessment of social skills. In A. S. Bellack & M. Hersen (Eds.), *Research and practice in social skills training.* New York: Plenum Press, 1979.

Bellack, A. S., & Hersen, M. (Eds.), *Research and practice in social skills training.* New York: Plenum Press, 1979.

Bellack, A. S., Hersen, M., & Turner, S. M. Role-play tests for assessing social skills: Are they valid? *Behavior Therapy*, 1978, 9, 448–461.

Bellack, A., Hersen, M., & Lamparski, D. Role-play tests for assessing social skills. Are they valid? Are they useful? *Journal of Consulting and Clinical Psychology*, 1979, 47, 335–342.

Bornstein, M. R., Bellack, A. S., & Hersen, M. Social-skills training for unassertive children: A multiple-baseline analysis. *Journal of Applied Behavior Analysis*, 1977, 10, 183–195.

Bornstein, M., Bellack, A. S., & Hersen, M. Social skills training for highly aggressive children in an inpatient psychiatric setting. *Behavior Modification*, 1980, 4, 173–186.

Brown, D. Factors affecting social acceptance of high school students. *School Review*, 1954, 62, 151–155.

Bryan, T. S. An observational analysis of classroom behaviors of children with learning disabilities. *Journal of Learning Disabilities*, 1974, 7, 34–43.

Buell, J., Stoddard, P., Harris, F. R., & Baer, D. M. Collateral social development accompanying reinforcement of outdoor play in a preschool child. *Journal of Applied Behavior Analysis*, 1968, 1, 167–173.

Camp, B. W., Blom, G. E., Herbert, F., & van Doorninck, W. J. "Think aloud": A program for developing self-control in young aggressive boys. *Journal of Abnormal Child Psychology*, 1977, 5, 157–169.

Cartledge, G., & Milburn, J. F. The case for teaching social skills in the classroom: A review. *Review of Educational Research*, 1978, 1, 133–156.

Chance, J. E. *Internal control of reinforcements and the school learning process.* Paper presented at the meeting of the Society for Research in Child Development, Minneapolis, Minnesota, 1965.

Charlesworth, R., & Hartrup, W. W. Positive social reinforcement in the nursery school peer groups. *Child Development*, 1967, 38, 993–1002.

Chittenden, G. F. An experimental study in measuring and modifying assertive behavior in young children. *Monograph of the Society for Research in Child Development*, 1942, 7, 1–87.

Clarfield, S. P. The development of a teacher referral form for identifying early school maladaptation. *American Journal of Community Psychology*, 1974, 2, 199–210.

Clark, H. B., Caldwell, C. P., & Christian, W. P. Classroom training of conversational skills and remote programming for the practice of these skills in another setting. *Child Behavior Therapy*, 1980, 1, 139–160.

Cohen, A. S., & de Van Tassell, E. A. A comparison of partial and complete paired comparisons in sociometric measurement of preschool groups. *Applied Psychological Measurement*, 1978, 2, 31–40.

Coleman, J. S., Campbell, E. Q., Hobson, C. J., McPartland, J., Wood, A. M., Weinfeld, F. D., & York, R. L. *Equality of educational opportunity.* Washington, D.C.: U.S. Government Printing Office, 1966.

Combs, M. L., & Slaby, D. A. Social skills training with children. In B. B. Lahey & A. E. Kazdin (Eds.), *Advances in clinical child psychology* (Vol. 1). New York: Plenum Press, 1977.

Cone, J. D. The relevance of reliability and validity for behavioral assessment. *Behavior Therapy*, 1977, 8, 411–426.

Cone, J., & Foster, S. L. Naturalistic observation methods. In P. C. Kendall & J. N. Butcher (Eds.), *Handbook of research methods in clinical psychology.* New York: Wiley, 1982.

Cone, J. D., & Hawkins, R. P. (Eds.). *Behavioral assessment: New directions in clinical psychology.* New York: Brunner/Mazel, 1977.

Conger, J. C., & Keane, S. P. Social skills intervention in the treatment of isolated or withdrawn children. *Psychological Bulletin*, 1981, 90, 478–495.

Cooke, T. P., & Apolloni, T. Developing positive social-emotional behaviors: A study of training and generalization effects. *Journal of Applied Behavior Analysis*, 1976, 9, 65–78.

Cowen, E. L. Social and community interventions. In P. Mussen & M. Rosenzweig (Eds.), *Annual review of psychology* (Vol. 24). Palo, Alto, Calif.: Annual Reviews, Inc., 1973.

Cowen, E. L., Dorr, D., Clarfield, S., Kreling, B., McWilliams, S. A., Pokracki, F., Pratt, D. M., Terrell, D., & Wilson, A. The AML: A quick-screening device for early identification of school maladaptation. *Journal of Community Psychology*, 1973, 1, 12–35.

Cowen, E. L., Pederson, A., Babigian, H., Izzo, L. D., & Trost, M. A. Long-term follow-up of early detected vulnerable children. *Journal of Consulting and Clinical Psychology*, 1973, *41*, 438–446.

Crandall, V. C., Katkovsky, W., & Crandall, V. J. Children's beliefs in their own control of reinforcements in intellectual-academic achievement situations. *Child Development*, 1965, *36*, 91–109.

D'Amico, W. *Revised Rathus Assertiveness Scale for Children, Grades 3–8*. Marblehead, Mass.: Educational Counseling and Consulting Services, 1976.

Deluty, R. H. Children's Action Tendency Scale: A self-report measure of aggressiveness, assertiveness, and submissiveness in children. *Journal of Consulting and Clinical Psychology*, 1979, *47*, 1061–1071.

Dorman, L. Assertive behavior and cognitive performance in preschool children. *The Journal of Genetic Psychology*, 1973, *123*, 155–162.

Dorworth, T. R. Learned helplessness and RET. *Rational Living*, 1973, *8*, 27–30.

Drabman, R., Spitalnik, R., & Spitalnik, K. Sociometric and disruptive behavior as a function of four types of token reinforcement programs. *Journal of Applied Behavior Analysis*, 1974, *7*, 93–101.

Dunnington, M. J. Behavioral differences of sociometric status groups in a nursery school. *Child Development*, 1957, *28*, 103–111.

Durlak, J. A., & Mannarino, A. P. The social skills development program: Description of a school-based, preventively-oriented mental health program for young children. *Journal of Clinical Child Psychology*, 1977, *6*, 48–52.

Dweck, C. S. the role of expectations and attributions in the alleviation of learned helplessness in a problem solving situation (Doctoral dissertation, Yale University, 1972). *Dissertation Abstracts International*, 1972, *29*, 536.

Dweck, C. S., & Reppucci, N. D. Learned helplessness and reinforcement responsibility in children. *Journal of Personality and Social Psychology*, 1973, *25*, 109–116.

Eisler, R. M. Behavioral assessment of social skills. In M. Hersen & A. S. Bellack (Eds.), *Behavioral assessment: A practical handbook*. New York: Pergamon Press, 1976.

Eisler, R. M., Hersen, M., & Agras, W. S. Videotape: A method for the controlled observation of non verbal interpersonal behavior. *Behavior Therapy*, 1974, *3*, 420–425.

Eisler, R. M., Hersen, M., Miller, P. M., & Blanchard, E. B. Situational determinants of assertive behaviors. *Journal of Consulting and Clinical Psychology*, 1975, *43*, 330–340.

Ellis, A. (Ed.), *Growth through reason*. Palo Alto, Calif.: Science and Behavior Books, 1971.

Ellis, A., & Grieger, R. *RET handbook of rational-emotive therapy*. New York: Springer, 1977.

Emmelkamp, P. M. G. The behavioral study of clinical phobias. In M. Hersen, R. M. Eisler, & P. M. Miller (Eds.), *Progress in behavior modification* (Vol. 8). New York: Academic Press, 1979.

Evers, W., & Schwarz, J. Modifying social withdrawal in preschoolers: The effects of filmed modeling and teacher praise. *Journal of Abnormal Child Psychology*, 1973, *1*, 248–256.

Feldhusen, J. F., Thurston, J. R., & Benning, J. J. Longitudinal analyses of classroom behavior and school achievement. *Journal of Experimental Education*, 1970, *38*, 4–10.

Feldhusen, J. F., Thurston, J. R., & Benning, J. J. A longitudinal study of delinquency and other aspects of children's behavior. *International Journal of Criminology and Penology*, 1973, *1*, 341–351.

Foster, S. L., & Ritchey, W. L. Issues in the assessment of social competence in children. *Journal of Applied Behavior Analysis*, 1979, *12*, 625–638.

Foster, S. L., & Ritchey, W. L. *A comparison of accepted, rejected, and ignored older elementary school children*. Unpublished manuscript, West Virginia University, 1982.

Frey, W. Generalization between areas of assertiveness: Assertiveness and depression. *Doctoral Dissertation Abstracts International*, 1976.

Gesten, E. L. A health resources inventory: The development of a measure of the personal and social competence of primary grade children. *Journal of Consulting and Clinical Psychology*, 1976, *44*, 775–786.

Gerwitz, H. B., & Gerwitz, J. L. Caretaking settings, background events and child-rearing environments: Some preliminary trends. In B. M. Foss (Ed.), *Determinants of infant behavior* (Vol. 4). London: Methuen, 1969.

Goldfried, M. R., & D'Zurilla, R. J. A behavioral analytic model for assessing competence. In C. D. Spielberger (Ed.), *Current topics in clinical and community psychology* (Vol. 1). New York: Academic Press, 1969.

Gottman, J. M. Toward a definition of social isolation in children. *Child Development*, 1977, *48*, 513–517.

Gottman, J., Gonso, J., & Rasmussen, B. Social interaction, social competence and friendship in children. *Child Development*, 1975, *46*, 709–718.

Graubard, P., Rosenberg, H., & Mlller, M. B. Student applications of behavior modification to teachers and environments or ecological approaches to social deviancy. In E. Ramp & B. Hopkins (Eds.), *A new direction for education: Behavior analysis.* Lawrence: University of Kansas, 1971.

Greenwood, C. R., Walker, H. M., Todd, N. M., & Hops, H. *Preschool teachers' assessments of social interaction: Predictive success and normative data* (Report No. 26). Eugene: University of Oregon Press, 1976.

Greenwood, C. R., Walker, H. M., & Hops, H. Some issues in social interaction/withdrawal assessment. *Exceptional Children*, 1977, *43*, 490–499.

Greenwood, C. R., Walker, H. M., Todd, N. M., & Hops, H. *Normative and descriptive analysis of preschool free play social interactions* (Report No. 29). Eugene: University of Oregon Press, 1977.

Greenwood, C. R., Walker, H. M., Todd, N. M., & Hops, H. *Description of withdrawn children's behavior in preschool settings* (Report No. 40). Eugene: University of Oregon Press, 1978.

Greenwood, C. R., Walker, H. M., Todd, N. M., & Hops, H. *Cost effective prediction and screening variables for preschool social withdrawal* (Report No. 39). Eugene: University of Oregon Press, 1979.

Groundland, H., & Anderson, C. Personality characteristics of socially accepted, socially neglected and socially rejected junior high school pupils. In J. Seidman (Ed.), *Educating for mental health.* New York: Cromwell, 1963.

Guinourd, D. E., & Rychlak, J. F. Personality correlates of sociometric popularity in elementary school children. *Personnel and Guidance Journal*, 1962, *40*, 438–442.

Harper, G. F. *Relationship of specific behaviors to the academic achievement and social competence of kindergarten, first and second grade children.* Unpublished doctoral dissertation, Kent State University, 1976.

Hartup, W. W. Peer interaction and social organization. In P. H. Mussen (Ed.), *Carmichael's manual of child psychology* (Vol. 2). New York: Wiley, 1970.

Hartup, W. W., Glazer, J. A., & Charlesworth, R. Peer reinforcement and sociometric status. *Child Development*, 1967, *38*, 1017–1024.

Helton, G. B., & Oakland, T. D. Teachers' attitudinal responses to differing characteristics of elementary school children. *Journal of Educational Psychology*, 1977, *69*, 251–265.

Henriques, M. *Measures of social skills. Head Start test collection.* Princeton, N.J.: Educational Testing Service, 1977.

Hersen, M., & Bellack, A. S. (Eds.), *Behavioral assessment: A practical handbook.* New York: Pergamon Press, 1976.

Hersen, M., & Bellack, A. S. Assessment of social skills. In A. R. Ciminero, K. S. Calhoun, & H. E. Adams (Eds.), *Handbook of behavioral assessment.* New York: Wiley, 1977.

Hersen, M., Michelson, L., & Bellack, A. S. (Eds.), *Issues in psychotherapy research.* New York: Plenum Press, in press.

Hiroto, D. S. Locus of control and learned helplessness. *Journal of Experimental Psychology*, 1974, *102*, 187–193.

Hops, H., & Greenwood, C. R. Assessment of children's social skllls. In E. J. Mash & L. G. Terdal (Eds.), *Behavioral assessment of childhood disorders.* New York: Guilford Press, 1980.

Hops, H., Fleischman, D. H., Guild, J. J., Paine, S. C., Wahler, H. M., & Greenwood, C. R. *PEERS (Program for socially withdrawn children).* Eugene: University of Oregon Press, 1978.

Hops, H., Walker, H. N., & Greenwood, C. R. PEERS: A program for remediating social withdrawal in the school setting: Aspects of a research and development process. In L. A. Hamerlynck

(Ed.), *The history and future of the developmentally disabled: Problematic and methodological issues*. New York: Brunner/Mazel, 1979.

Houston, B. K. Control over stress, locus of control, and response to stress. *Journal of Personality and Social Psychology*, 1971, *21*, 249–255.

Hymel, S., & Asher, S. R. *Assessment and training of isolated children's social skills*. Paper presented at the Biennial Meeting of the Society for Research in Child Development, New Orleans, Louisiana, 1977.

Hynes, K., Feldman, J. F., & Widlak, F. W. *A comparison of peer rating and sociometric nomination data*. Paper presented at the Annual Meeting of the National Council on Measurement in Education, Washington, D.C., 1975.

Israel, A. C., & O'Leary, K. D. Developing correspondence between children's words and deeds. *Child Development*, 1973, *44*, 575–581.

Izard, C. E. *The face of emotion*. New York: Appleton-Century-Crofts, 1971.

Jewett, J. F., & Clark, H. B. Teaching pre-schoolers to use appropriate dinner-time conversation: An analysis of generalization from school to home. *Behavior Therapy*, 1979, *10*, 589–605.

Johnson, S. M., & Bolstad, O. D. Methodological issues in naturalistic observation: Some problems and solutions for field research. In L. A. Hamerlynck, L. C. Handy, & E. J. Mash (Eds.), *Behavior change: Methodology, concepts, and practice*. Champaign, Ill.: Research Press, 1973.

Jones, R. R., & Cobb, J. A. *Validity of behavioral scores derived from teachers' ratings vs. naturalistic observations*. Paper presented at the Annual Meeting of the Western Psychological Association, Anaheim, California, 1973.

Kagan, J., & Moss, H. A. *Birth to maturity: A study in psychological development*. New York: Wiley, 1962.

Kazdin, A. E. Artifact, bias, and complexity of assessment: The ABC's of reliability. *Journal of Applied Behavior Analysis*, 1977, *10*, 141–150.

Kazdin, A. E. *Behavior modification in applied settings* (2nd edition). Homewood, Ill.: Dorsey, 1980.

Kazdin, A. E., & Polster, R. Intermittent token reinforcement and response maintenance in extinction. *Behavior Therapy*, 1973, *4*, 386–391.

Keller, M., & Carlson, P. The use of symbolic modeling to promote social skills in preschool children with low levels of social responsiveness. *Child Development*, 1974, *45*, 912–919.

Kendall, P. C., & Hollon, S. D. (Eds.), *Cognitive-behavioral interventions: Theory, research, and procedures*. New York: Academic Press, 1979.

Kendall, P. C., & Hollon, S. D. (Eds.). *Assessment strategies for cognitive-behavioral interventions*. New York: Academic Press, 1981.

Kent, R. N., & Foster, S. L. Direct observational procedures: Methodological issues in applied settings. In A. R. Ciminero, K. S. Calhoun, & H. E. Adams (Eds.), *Handbook of behavioral assessment*. New York: Wiley, 1979.

Kent, R. N., Kanowitz, J., O'Leary, K. D., & Cheiken, M. Observer reliability as a function of circumstances of assessment. *Journal of Applied Behavior Analysis*, 1977, *10*, 317–324.

Kim, Y., Anderson, H. E., & Bashaw, W. L. Social maturity achievement and basic ability. *Educational and Psychological Measurement*, 1968, *28*, 535–543.

Kirby, F. D., & Toler, H. C. Modification of preschool isolate behavior: A case study. *Journal of Applied Behavior Analysis*, 1970, *3*, 309–314.

Klien, S. S. Student influence on teacher behavior. *American Educational Research Journal*, 1971, *8*, 402–421.

Kohn, M. *Social competence, symptoms and underachievement in childhood: A longitudinal perspective*. New York: Holt, Rinehart & Winston, 1977.

Kohn, M., & Rosman, B. Relationship of pre-school social-emotional functioning to later intellectual achievement. *Developmental Psychology*, 1972, *11*, 445–452. (a)

Kohn, M., & Rosman, B. A social competence scale and symptom checklist for the preschool child: Factor dimensions, their cross-instrument generality, and longitudinal persistence. *Developmental Psychology*, 1972, *6*, 430–444.(b)

Ladd, G. W. *Social skills and peer acceptance: Effects of a social learning method for training verbal social skills.* Paper presented at the Biennial Meeting of the Society of Research in Child Development, San Francisco, 1979.

Lange, A. J., & Jakubowski, P. *Responsible assertive behavior.* Champaign, Ill.: Research Press, 1976.

Laughlin, F. *The peer status of sixth and seventh grade children.* New York: Bureau of Publications, Teachers College, Columbia University, 1954.

Lazarus, A. A. Behavior therapy in groups. In G. M. Gazda (Ed.), *Basic approaches to group psychotherapy and group counseling.* Springfield, Ill.: Charles C Thomas, 1968.

Lazarus, A. A. *Behavior therapy and beyond.* New York: McGraw-Hill, 1971.

Lazarus, A. A. On assertive behavior: A brief note. *Behavior Therapy,* 1973, *4,* 697–699.

Lazarus, A. A. *Multimodal behavior therapy.* New York: Springer, 1976.

Lesbock, M. S., & Salzberg, C. L. *The use of role-playing techniques in the development of generalized adaptive social behavior with emotionally disturbed beahvior disordered adolescents.* Paper presented at the Annual Meeting of the Association for Advancement of Behavior Therapy Convention, Chicago, November 1978.

Lewinsohn, P. M. The behavioral study and treatment of depression. In M. Hersen, R. M. Eisler, & P. M. Miller (Eds.), *Progress in behavior modification* (Vol. 1). New York: Academic Press, 1975.

Libet, J. M., & Lewinsohn, P. M. Concept of social skill with special references to the behavior of depressed persons. *Journal of Consulting and Clinical Psychology,* 1973, *40,* 304–312.

Mannarino, A. P., Michelson, L., Beck, S., & Figueroa, J. Treatment and research in a child psychiatric clinic: Implementation and evaluation issues. *Journal of Clinical Child Psychology,* 1982, *11,* 50–55.

Mannarino, A. P., Michelson, L., Marchione, K., & Martin, P. *Relative and combined efficacy of behavioral social skills training and interpersonal problem-solving for elementary schoolchildren.* Manuscript submitted for publication, 1982.

Marchione, K., Michelson, L., & Mannarino, A. *Behavioral, cognitive, and combined treatments for socially maladjusted school children.* Unpublished manuscript, University of Pittsburgh, 1983.

Marshall, R. J., & McCandless, B. R. A study in prediction of social behavior of preschool children. *Child Development,* 1957, *28,* 149–159.

Mash, E. J., & McElwee, J. D. Situational effects on observer accuracy: Behavioral predictability, prior experience, and complexity of coding catagories. *Child Development,* 1974, *43,* 367–377.

McCandless, B. R., & Marshall, H. R. Sex differences in social acceptance and participation of preschool children. *Child Development,* 1957, *28,* 421–425.

McFall, R. M., & Marston, A. R. An experimental investigation of behavior rehearsal in assertiveness training. *Journal of Abnormal Psychology,* 1970, *76,* 295–303.

McFall, R. M., & Twentyman, C. T. Four experiments on the relative contributions of rehearsal, modeling, and coaching to assertion training. *Journal of Abnormal Psychology,* 1973, *81,* 100–218.

McGhee, P. E., & Crandall, V. C. Beliefs in internal-external control of reinforcements and academic performance. *Child Development,* 1968, *39,* 91–102.

McPhail, G. W. Developing adolescent assertiveness. In R. E. Alberti (Ed.), *Assertiveness.* San Luis Obispo, Calif.: Impact, 1977.

Meichenbaum, D. *Cognitive-behavior modification: An integrative approach.* New York: Plenum Press, 1977.

Meighan, M., & Birr, K. *The infant and its peers.* Unpublished manuscript, University of Kansas Medical Center, Kansas City, Kansas, 1979.

Meyer, W., & Thompson, G. Sex differences in the distribution of teacher approval and disapproval among sixth-grade children. *Journal of Educational Psychology,* 1956, *47,* 385–396.

Michelson, L. Behavioral approaches to prevention. In L. Michelson, M. Hersen, & S. M. Turner (Eds.), *Future perspectives in behavior therapy.* New York: Plenum Press, 1981.

Michelson, L., & DiLorenzo, T. M. Behavioral assessment of peer interaction and social functioning in institutional and structured settings. *Journal of Clinical Psychology,* 1981, *87,* 499–504.

Michelson, L., & Mannarino, A. T. Social skills training with children: Research findings and clinical issues. In P. S. Strain, J. M. Guralnick, & H. Walker (Eds.), *Children's social behavior: Development, assessment, and modification.* New York: Academic Press, in press.

Michelson, L., & Wood, R. A group assertive training program for elementary school children. *Child Behavior Therapy*, 1980, 2, 1–9. (a)

Michelson, L., & Wood, R. Social skills assessment and training with children and adolescents. In M. Hersen, R. M. Eisler, & P. Miller (Eds.), *Progress in behavior modification* (Vol. 9). New York: Academic Press, 1980. (b)

Michelson, L., & Wood, R. Development and psychometric properties of the Children's Assertive Behavior Scale. *Journal of Behavioral Assessment*, 1982, 4, 3–14.

Michelson, L., Wood, R., & Flynn, J. *Development and evaluation of an assertive training program for elementary school children.* Paper presented at the Annual Meeting of the Association for Advancement of Behavior Therapy, Chicago, 1978.

Michelson, L., Foster, S., & Ritchey, W. Behavioral assessment of children's social skills. In B. B. Lahey & A. E. Kazdin (Eds.), *Advances in clinical child psychology:* (Vol. 3). New York: Plenum Press, 1981.

Michelson, L., Hersen, M., & Turner, S. M. (Eds.). *Future perspectives in behavior therapy.* New York: Plenum Press, 1981.

Michelson, L., Andrasik, F., Vucelic, J., & Coleman, D. Temporal stability and internal reliability of measures of children's social skills. *Psychological Reports*, 1981, 48, 678.

Michelson, L., DiLorenzo, T., Calpin, J., & Ollendick, T. Situational determinants of the BAT-C. *Behavior Therapy*, 1982, 13, 724–734.

Michelson, L., Mannarino, A. P., Marchione, K., Stern, M., Figueroa, J., & Beck, S. A comparative outcome study of behavioral social skills training, cognitive problem solving, and Rogerian treatments for child psychiatric outpatients: Process, outcome, and generalization effects. *Behaviour Research and Therapy*, in press.

Miller, L. C. School Behavior Checklist: An inventory of deviant behavior for elementary school children. *Journal of Consulting and Clinical Psychology*, 1972, 38, 134–144.

Moore, S. Correlates of peer acceptance in nursery school children. In W. Hartup & W. Smothergill (Eds.), *The young child: Review of research* (Vol. 2). Washington, D.C.: National Association for the Education of Young Children, 1967.

Morris, H. H. Aggressive behavior disorders in children: A follow-up study. *American Journal of Psychiatry*, 1956, 112, 991–997.

Muma, J. R. Peer evaluation and academic performance. *Personnel and Guidance Journal*, 1965, 44, 405–409.

Muma, J. R. Peer evaluation and academic achievement in performance classes. *Personnel and Guidance Journal*, 1968, 46, 580–585.

Myers, C. E., Atwell, A. A., & Orbet, R. E. Prediction of fifth grade achievement from kindergarten test and rating data. *Educational and Psychological Measurement*, 1968, 28, 457–463.

Nay, R. W. Analogue measures. In A. R. Ciminero, K. S. Calhoun, & H. E. Adams (Eds.), *Handbook of behavior assessment.* New York: Wiley, 1977.

Noble, C. G., & Nolan, J. D. Effect of student verbal behavior on classroom teacher behavior. *Journal of Educational Psychology*, 1974, 68, 342–346.

Nowicki, S., & Roundtree, J. Correlates of locus of control in a secondary school population. *Developmental Psychology*, 1971, 4, 477–478.

Nowicki, S., & Strickland, B. R. *A locus of control scale for children.* Paper presented at the Annual Meeting of the American Psychological Association, Washington, D.C., 1971.

Nowicki, S., & Strickland, B. R. A locus of control scale for children. *Journal of Consulting and Clinical Psychology*, 1973, 40, 148–154.

O'Connor, R. D. Modification of social withdrawal through symbolic modeling. *Journal of Applied Behavior Analysis*, 1969, 2, 15–22.

O'Connor, R. D. The relative efficacy of modeling, shaping and the combined procedures for the modification of social withdrawal. *Journal of Abnormal Psychology,* 1972, *79,* 327–334.

Oden, S., & Asher, D. R. Coaching children in social skills for friendship making. *Child Development,* 1977, *48,* 495–506.

O'Leary, K. D., & Kent, R. Behavior modification for social action: Research tactics and problems. In L. A. Hamerlynck, L. C. Handy, & E. J. Mash (Eds.), *Behavior change: Methodology, concepts and practice.* Champaign, Ill.: Reserach Press, 1973.

Ollendick, T. H., & Hersen, M. Social skills training for juvenile delinquents. *Behaviour Research and Therapy,* 1980, *17,* 547–554.

Palmer, P. *Liking myself, and the mouse, the monster, and me.* San Luis Obispo, Calif.: Impact, 1977.

Patterson, G. R. An empirical approach to the classification of disturbed children. *Journal of Clinical Psychology,* 1964, *20,* 326–337.

Patterson, G. R. *Families: Applications of social learning to family life.* Champaign, Ill.: Research Press, 1971.

Patterson, G. R., Reid, J. G., Jones, R. R., & Congber, R. E. *A social learning approach to family intervention* (Vol. 1). Eugene, Oreg.: Castaglia, 1975.

Payne, P. A., Halpin, G. W., Ellett, C. D., & Dale, J. B. General personality correlates of creative personality in academically and artistically gifted youth. *Journal of Special Education,* 1975, *9,* 105–108.

Pekarik, E. G., Prinz, R. J., Liebert, D. E., Weintraub, S., & Neale, J. M The Pupil Evaluation Inventory: A sociometric technique for assessing children's social behavior. *Journal of Abnormal Child Psychology,* 1976, *4,* 83–97.

Percell, L. P., Berwick, P. T. & Beigel, A. The effects of assertive training on self-concept and anxiety, *Archives of General Psychiatry,* 1974, *31,* 502–504.

Pinkston, E. M., Reese, N. M., Le Blanc, J. M., & Baer, D. M. Independent control or a preschool child's aggression and peer interaction by contingent teacher attention. *Journal of Applied Behavior Analysis,* 1972, *6,* 115–124.

Porterfield, D. V., & Schlichting, G. F. Peer status and reading achievement. *Journal of Educational Research,* 1961, *54,* 291–297.

Prociuk, T. J., Breen, L. J., & Lussier, R. J. Hopelessness, internal-external locus of control, and depression. *Journal of Clinical Psychology,* 1976, *32,* 299–300.

Quay, H. Patterns of aggression, withdrawal and immaturity. In H. Quay & J. Werry (Eds.), *Psychopathological disorders of childhood.* New York: Wiley, 1972.

Quay, H. C., & Peterson, D. R. *Manual for the behavior problem checklist.* Unpublished manuscript, University of Miami, 1967.

Rachman, S., & Hodgson, R. *Obsessions and compulsions.* Englewood Cliffs, N.J.: Prentice-Hall, 1980.

Rathus, S. A. A 30-item schedule for assessing assertive behavior. *Behavior Therapy,* 1973, *4,* 398–406.

Reardon, R. C., Hersen, M., Bellack, A. S., & Foley, J. M. Measuring social skill in grade school boys. *Journal of Behavioral Assessment,* 1979, *1,* 87–105.

Rehm, L. P., & Marston, A. R. Reduction of social anxiety through modification of self-reinforcement: An instigation therapy technique. *Journal of Consulting and Clinical Psychology,* 1968, *32,* 565–574.

Reid, J. B. (Ed.), *A social learning approach to family intervention* (Vol. 2). *Observation in home settings.* Eugene, Oreg.: Castaglia, 1973.

Reimanis, G. School performance, intelligence, and locus of reinforcement control scales. *Psychology in the Schools,* 1973, *10,* 207–211.

Rie, E. D., & Friedman, D. P. *A survey of behavior rating scales for children.* Columbus, Ohio: Office of Program Evaluation and Research, Division of Mental Health and Mental Retardation, 1978.

Rinn, R. C., & Markle, A. Modification of social skill deficits in children. In A. S. Bellack & M. Hersen (Eds.), *Research and practice in social skills training.* New York: Plenum Press, 1979.

Rinn, R. C., Mahia, G., Markle, A., Barnhart, D., Owen, D. L., & Supernick, J. *Analogue assessment of social skills deficits in children.* Unpublished manuscript, Huntsville, Alabama, 1978.

Risley, T., & Hart, B. Developing correspondence between the nonverbal and verbal behavior of preschool children. *Journal of Applied Behavior Analysis*, 1976, *9*, 335–354.

Robbins, L. N. *Deviant children grown up*. Baltimore: Williams & Wilkins, 1966.

Rodgers-Warren, A., & Baer, D. M. Correspondence between saying and doing: Teaching children to share and praise. *Journal of Applied Behavior Analysis*, 1976, *9*, 335–354.

Roff, M. Children social interactions and young adult bad conduct. *Journal of Abnormal Social Psychology*, 1961, *63*, 333–337.

Roff, J. E., & Hasazi, J. E. Identification of preschool children at risk and some guidelines for primary intervention. In G. W. Albee & J. M. Joffe (Eds.), *Primary prevention of psychopathology* (Vol. 1). Hanover, N.H.: University Press of New England, 1977.

Roff, M., Sells, B., & Golden, M. M. *Social adjustment and personality development in children*. Minneapolis: University of Minnesota Press, 1972.

Romanczyk, R. G., Kent, R. N., Diament, C., & O'Leary, K. D. Measuring the reliability of observational data: A reactive process. *Journal of Applied Behavior Analysis*, 1973, *6*, 175–186.

Rosenthal, T. L., & Bandura, A. Psychological modeling: Theory and practice. In S. L. Garfield & A. E. Bergin (Eds.), *Handbook of psychotherapy and behavior change: An empirical analysis* (2nd edition). New York: Wiley, 1978.

Ross, A. O., Lacey, H. M., & Parton, D. A. The development of a behavior checklist for boys. *Child Development*, 1965, *36*, 1013–1027.

Ross, D. M., Ross, S. A., & Evans, T. A. The modification of extreme social withdrawal by modeling with guided participation. *Journal of Behavior Therapy and Experimental Psychiatry*, 1971, *2*, 273–279.

Rotter, J. B. Generalized expectancies for internal versus external control of reinforcement. *Psychological Monograph*, 1966, 80, 1–28.

Rotter, J. B., & Mulry, R. C. Internal versus external control of reinforcement and decision time. *Journal of Personality and Social Psychology*, 1965, *2*, 598–604.

Salter, A. *Conditioned reflex therapy*. New York: Farrar, Straus, & Giroux, 1949.

Schindler, P. The psychogenesis of alcoholism. *Quarterly Journal of the Study of Alcoholism*, 1941, *2*, 277–292.

Seligman, M. E. *Helplessness*. San Francisco, Calif.: W. J. Freeman, 1975.

Seligman, M. E., & Groves, D. Non-transient learned-helplessness. *Psychonomic Science*, 1969, *19*, 191–192.

Seligman, M. E. & Maier, S. F. Failure to escape traumatic shock. *Journal of Experimental Psychology*, 1976, *74*, 1–9.

Seligman, M. E., Maier, S. F., & Solomon, R. L. Unpredictable and uncontrollable aversive events. In F. R. Brush (Ed.), *Aversive conditioning and learning*. New York: Academic Press, 1969.

Shure, M. B., & Spivack, G. *A mental health program for kindergarten children: A cognitive approach to solving interpersonal problems*. Philadelphia: Department of Mental Health Sciences, Hahnemann Community Mental Health/Mental Retardation Center, 1974. (a)

Shure, M. B., & Spivack, G. *Preschool Interpersonal Problem Solving (PIPS) Test: Manual*. Philadelphia: Department of Mental Health Sciences, Hahnemann Community Mental Health/Mental Retardation Center, 1974. (b)

Spivack, G., & Shure, M. B. *Social adjustment of young children: A cognitive approach to solving real life problems*. San Francisco: Jossey-Bass, 1974.

Spivack, G., & Shure, M. B. The cognition of social adjustment: Interpersonal cognitive problem solving thinking. In B. B. Lahey & A. E. Kazdin (Eds.), *Advances in clinical child psychology* (Vol 5). New York: Plenum Press, 1982.

Spivack, G., Platt, J. J., & Shure, M. *The problem-solving approach to adjustment*. San Francisco: Jossey-Bass, 1976.

Stengel, E. *Suicide and attempted suicide*. Middlesex, England: Penguin, 1971.

Stephens, T. M. *Social skills in the classroom*. Columbus, Ohio: Cedar Press, 1978.

Stewart, N. Teacher's concepts of "behavior problems." In *Growing points in education research*. Washington, D.C.: American Educational Research Association, 1949.

Stokes, T. F., & Baer, D. M. An implicit technology of generalization. *Journal of Applied Behavior Analysis*, 1977, *10*, 349–367.

Strain, P. S. An experimental analysis of peer social initiations on the behavior of withdrawn preschool children: Some training and generalization effects. *Journal of Abnormal Child Psychology*, 1977, *5*, 445–455.

Strain, P. S., & Fox, J. J. Peers as behavior change agents for withdrawn classmates. In B. B. Lahey & A. E. Kazdin (Eds.), *Advances in clinical child psychology* (Vol. 4). New York: Plenum Press, 1981.

Strain, P. S., Shores, R. E., & Kerr, M. M. An experimental analysis of "spillover" effects on the social interaction of behaviorally handicapped preschool children. *Journal of Applied Behavior Analysis*, 1976, *9*, 31–40.

Strain, P. S., Shores, R. E., & Timm, M. A. Effects of peer social initiations on the behavior of withdrawn preschool children. *Journal of Applied Behavior Analysis*, 1977, *10*, 289–298.

Strain, P. S., & Timm, M. A. An experimental analysis of social interaction between a behaviorally disordered preschool child and her classroom peers. *Journal of Applied Behavior Analysis*, 1974, *7*, 583–590.

Sugai, D. P. *The implementation and evaluation of a social skills training program for preadolescents: A preventive approach*. Paper presented at the Annual Meeting of the Association for Advancement of Behavior Therapy, Chicago, November 1978.

The Ohio State University Research Foundation. *Adaptive behavior scale development*. Columbus: Ohio State University Press, 1979.

Thornton, J. W., & Jacobs, P. D. Learned helplessness in human subjects. *Journal of Experimental Psychology*, 1972, *87*, 367–372.

Trower, P. M. Fundamentals of interpersonal behavior: A social-psychological perspective. In A. S. Bellack & M. Hersen (Eds.), *Research and practice in social skills training*. New York: Plenum Press, 1979.

Trower, P., Bryant, B., & Argyle, M. *Social skills and mental health*. Pittsburgh, Pa.: University of Pittsburgh Press, 1978.

Ullmann, C. A. Teachers, peers and tests as predictors of adjustment. *Journal of Educational Psychology*, 1957, *48*, 257–267.

Urbain, E. S., & Kendall, P. C. Review of social-cognitive problem-solving interventions with children. *Psychological Bulletin*, 1980, *88*, 109–143.

Vaal, J. J., & McCullagh, J. The Rathus Assertiveness Schedule: Reliability at the junior high school level. *Behavior Therapy*, 1975, *6*, 566–567.

Van Hasselt, V. B., Hersen, M., Bellack, A. S., & Whitehill, M. B. Social skill assessment and training for children: An evaluative review. *Behaviour Research and Therapy*, 1979, *17*, 413–438.

Wahler, R. G. Some structural aspects of deviant child behavior. *Journal of Applied Behavior Analysis*, 1975, *8*, 27–42.

Waldrop, M. F., & Halverson, C. F. Intensive and extensive peer behaviors. Longitudinal and cross sectional analyses. *Child Development*, 1975, *46*, 19–26.

Walker, H. M. *Walker Problem Behavior Identification Checklist*. Los Angeles, Calif.: Western Psychological Services, 1970.

Walker, H. M., Greenwood, C. R., Hops, H., & Todd, N M. Differential effects of reinforcing topographic components of social interaction: Analysis and direct replication. *Behavior Modification*, 1979, *3*, 291–321.

Walls, R. T., Werner, T. J., Bacon, A., & Zane, T. Behavior checklists. In J. D. Cone & R. P. Hawkins (Eds.), *Behavioral assessment: New directions in clinical psychology*. New York: Bruner-Mazel, 1977.

Winder, C., & Rau, C. Parental attitudes associated with social deviance in preadolescent boys. *Journal of Abnormal Social Psychology*, 1962, *69*, 418–424.

Wolf, M. M. Social validity: The case for subjective measurement or how applied behavior analysis is finding its heart. *Journal of Applied Behavior Analysis*, 1978, *11*, 203–214.

Wolpe, J. Neurotic depression: Experimental analog, clinical syndromes and treatment. *American Journal of Psychotherapy*, 1971, *25*, 362–368.

Wolpe, J. *The practice of behavior therapy*. New York: Pergamon, 1973.

Wood, R., Michelson, L., & Flynn, J. *Assessment of assertive behavior in elementary school children*. Paper presented at the Annual Meeting of the Association for Advancement of Behavior Therapy, Chicago, November 1978.

Zax, M., Cowen, E. L., Izzo, L. D., & Trost, M. A. Identifying emotional disturbance in the school setting. *American Journal of Orthopsychiatry*, 1964, *34*, 447–454.

Zax, M., Cowen, E. L., Rappaport, J., Berch, D., & Laird, J. Follow-up study of children identified early as emotionally disturbed. *Journal of Consulting Psychology*, 1968, *32*, 369–373.

Zold, A. C., & Speer, D. C. Follow-up study of child guidance clinic patients by means of the Behavior Problem Checklist. *Journal of Clinical Psychology*, 1971, *27*, 519–525.

Author Index

Subject Index

268